MW00856855

My Life Beyond the 1320

DON PRUDHOMME
WITH ELANA SCHERR

DON *The* **Snake** S PRUDHOMME

CarTech®

CarTech®, Inc.
838 Lake Street South
Forest Lake, MN 55025
Phone: 651-277-1200 or 800-551-4754
Fax: 651-277-1203
www.cartechbooks.com

Edit by Wes Eisenschenk
Layout by Monica Seiberlich

ISBN 978-1-61325-518-6
Item No. CT662

Library of Congress Cataloging-in-Publication Data Available

Written, edited, and designed in the U.S.A.
Printed in China
10 9 8 7 6 5 4 3 2

CarTech books may be purchased at a discounted rate in bulk for resale, events, corporate gifts, or educational purposes. Special editions may also be created to specification. For details, contact Special Sales at 838 Lake Street S., Forest Lake, MN 55025 or by email at sales@cartechbooks.com.

Frontispiece image: Courtesy Leslie Lovette and Teresa Long

Title page image: Courtesy Firebird Raceway/New Family Archives

Cover Image: Courtesy National Hot Rod Association/NHRA National Dragster

Bottom image on page 185: Courtesy Barrett-Jackson

PUBLISHER'S NOTE:
In reporting history, the images required to tell the tale will vary greatly in quality, especially by modern photographic standards. While some images in this volume are not up to those digital standards, we have included them, as we feel they are an important element in telling the story.

DISTRIBUTION BY:

Europe
PGUK
63 Hatton Garden
London EC1N 8LE, England
Phone: 020 7061 1980 • Fax: 020 7242 3725
www.pguk.co.uk

Australia
Renniks Publications Ltd.
3/37-39 Green Street
Banksmeadow, NSW 2109, Australia
Phone: 2 9695 7055 • Fax: 2 9695 7355
www.renniks.com

Canada
Login Canada
300 Saulteaux Crescent
Winnipeg, MB, R3J 3T2 Canada
Phone: 800 665 1148 • Fax: 800 665 0103
www.lb.ca

Table of Contents

ACKNOWLEDGMENTS 6

FOREWORD by Rusty Wallace 8

PREFACE 9

CHAPTER 1: The Starting Line 10

CHAPTER 2: The Lure of Speed 16

CHAPTER 3: The 1960s 32

CHAPTER 4: The 1970s 87

CHAPTER 5: The 1980s 133

CHAPTER 6: The 1990s 159

CHAPTER 7: The 2000s 174

ACKNOWLEDGMENTS

Don Prudhomme

There's been this story that I've been wanting to tell, but I've been so busy racing my whole life that it never came up in all the interviews and other books that I've been a part of. It was always in the background. It's my story, the part behind the racing. It's also the story of anyone who came up in the world with the deck stacked against them. If you're reading this hoping for a book of numbers, of this race and that race and how many wins and what the timing was set at for which record, this is not that book. Go read Don Garlits's book. He's good with the numbers.

This is a book about what it took to get to the races and through the races. There were a lot of wins, and I'm proud of that, but it wasn't an easy thing to do. Even writing this book was hard. There were so many memories, and some of them hurt to think about even today, more than half a century later. I felt like it was worth getting it all down though in case it helps someone down the road. I felt like I was making mistakes along the way, but when I look back at it, I see a lot more friends than enemies. So that's where I need to start with my acknowledgments.

I want to start with everyone who ever stepped into my pits and lent us a hand in the early days. There are so many people who helped me, guys who really didn't get any credit for it: the spectators who helped me pack my parachute and the folks who pushed the car around or handed me a wrench at the right time or just stopped by with a beer or a hot dog. I didn't often have time to recognize them in the moment, but I want to thank them now.

I also need to thank every parent who bought their kid a Hot Wheels set and every kid who played with one. We couldn't have done this without you.

Not only do the kids who collected the toy cars deserve thanks, but also the full-scale collectors who keep the original race cars safe and display them so that the public can see how it used to be done. Bruce Canepa, Bruce Meyer, Rick Hendrick, I really appreciate you keeping the history alive.

There are names you'll read in this book, but they need to be thanked here too: Roland Leong (still my best buddy), Waterbed Fred, Rusty Wallace, Chip Ganassi, Ed Pink, Tom Prock, Pat Galvin, Bob Brandt, Larry Bowers, Donnie Couch (who will motherf—— me to the moon if I leave him out), and all the guys and gals in the car clubs and cacklefests who still get together and keep these sto-ries going and occasionally invite me to lunch.

Then there are the guys who aren't here anymore but will always be important to me: Ralph Whitworth, Tom McCourry, Dick Landy, Keith Black, Raymond Beadle, Billy Bones, Bill Carter, Dale Armstrong, Bill Doner, Bill Simpson, and of course, Tom McEwen. I miss Tom every day. I almost didn't want to do the book because he wasn't around to fill in the other half of the story. We were that close; it's incomplete without him. Since we started the book a year and a half ago, I've lost people. I'll pick up my phone to call someone, and their name's there but they're not. I tried to include as many of their stories in the book as possible so that you can know them like I did.

Big thanks to all the folks I've met since retirement, who've kept me busy and entertained: Ron Pratt, Tony Stewart, Walker Evans, Parnelli Jones, Jeff Gordon, Ray Evernham, all the NASCAR, IndyCar, off-road, and motorcycling folks who have made me feel so at home in their racing and rallies.

It isn't even possible for me to thank my wife, Lynn, and daughter, Donna, as much as they deserve. They put up with me, they make me laugh, and they have always made me look good. I could not have done it without their support. Same goes for my sisters Joyce, Judy, and Jeanette, and all the Louisiana family who welcomed us into our Creole heritage.

A million thank yous to the photographers who helped with the images for this book, with an extra nod to Phil Burgess, David Kennedy, and Lewis Bloom from the NHRA. Thank you to CarTech for thinking my story was worth a book, and thank you to Elana Scherr for helping me get it down on paper. I'm going to leave people out, it's just impossible to name everyone, so please, if you were a part of this, know that I know it and am grateful to you.

My hope is that this book reaches someone who thinks they can't go after their dream because of their ethnicity, a learning disability, or financial limitations, and I hope they see that I was able to do it, and they can too. I always think of Dan Gurney telling me, "If you want to do it bad enough kid, you'll find a way." I have a big picture of Dan Gurney hanging up in my office. Every day when I look at that it reminds me, "You'll find a way."

Elana Scherr

When Don Prudhomme looks at himself, I think he still sees the gawky kid in Tommy Ivo's photos, standing apart from the crowd, looking at a dragster with desire visible even in grainy black and white. He said it over and over during our interviews for this book, that he never felt like he had "made it." Failure was always just one race away, waiting.

It's hard to imagine that for anyone who saw him in action, as a driver or a team owner. He was, and still is, a titan of cool, towering over mere mortals with a focused green gaze and a cobra's deadly menace. That he could ever doubt his success seems impossible. Here's a man who won 49 NHRA event races and 389 out of 589 rounds of competition overall, and that isn't counting match races, IHRA, or AHRA. He was the first Funny Car over 250 mph and the first Funny Car to run in the 5s. He's a guy who had beers with Clint Eastwood and trades Christmas cards with Mario Andretti. If I tried to write him as a character in a movie, they'd tell me to dial it back a little on the "cool guy thing."

The thing is, he really is that cool. Even when he does something dopey, it's cooler than the rest of us when we're trying to be hip. I remember talking to him at a car show soon after we did our first *Hot Rod* magazine story together, around 2012. "Oh, man, I did something so dumb," he said. "I busted the front windshield out of my truck trying to get a fly out of the cab." Ok, so far, so good, that sounds pretty regular-guy. "How did you break the window chasing a fly?" I asked. "Oh, well, I was shooing at him and I knocked my ring into the window and it shattered." Ah, his ring. His 1978 NHRA Championship ring. One of four. Don Prudhomme can't even do something dumb without being cool.

I think it was around the same time that he told me about his trip to Louisiana with his sisters and discovering his African American background. He won't let me forget that I reacted by saying, "How did you not know?" which led to a lesson in passing, and in the power that parents have in molding their children's self-image. "You should tell this story," I told him, and he said that when he was ready, he'd let me know. In 2018, he touched briefly on it in a feature we did together for *Hagerty* magazine, and later that year, he asked me if I'd help him with this book.

What followed was 17 months of interviews. We worked in his shop, in his living room, at Pomona, Bakersfield, and Indy, and toward the end of the caption process, over FaceTime, as we were all stuck at home due to coronavirus restrictions in early 2020. I'd heard horror stories about the process of working on a biography with someone, but every second of our time together has been a delight. I'd make him repeat things and ask him questions so personal that I expected him to throw something at me, but he was always honest, always thoughtful, and in a move that surprised me, grateful. "I think you saved me some money on therapy, girl," he'd joke when we were deep in the difficult sections. I wish you could see him, hunched over a table spread with faded photographs and newspaper clippings, pointing out technical details on the cars or telling me stories about the people in the background. The best moments were when he'd describe a run, rolling his r's to make engine sounds and raising his hands to mime out tire smoke and header flames. His eyes would get bright, and then he'd squint and lean forward over an imaginary steering wheel, taking us both down a dragstrip in his mind. Then he'd laugh and feed snacks to one of his many dogs and say, "Okay girl, what next?"

It wasn't just the two of us. Lynn and Donna were there too, scanning photos, and helping us with dates and names and bringing us sandwiches so that we wouldn't starve to death during the process. Everything that is correct in this book is because of Lynn. Everything that is wrong is all mine. So, my first thank yous go to the Prudhommes for trusting me to tell the story. Thank you also to everyone who did supporting interviews for the book. Each of you deserves a book of your own! I also have to thank the NHRA crew for access to races and archives. In particular, a world's worth of gratitude to Brian Lohnes, who dutifully laughed or gasped appropriately at all the transcript outtakes I sent him along the way and was the first person to read the draft. He said it didn't suck; so if it does, blame him. Thank you to David Freiburger for giving me my first writing job at *Hot Rod* magazine. Thank you to Brett, Abby, Phil, Aaron, Derek, and Laura for believing that I could do this even while I was sure I could not, and thank you to my husband, Tom, for buying me a ramp truck that led to us meeting Don Prudhomme.

FOREWORD

If someone said to me, "Who's Don Prudhomme?" I'd say, "Well, Don Prudhomme is one of the finest drag racers in the world. He's known by everybody on the planet and if you don't know that, you ought to feel bad." But then I'd want them to meet him, and I'd say, "You're going to see a tall guy, a tall, good-looking dude who can really carry himself. When he opens his mouth and starts talking to you, you're going to immediately like him. He has this comforting way about him that makes everyone feel wonderful."

When Don called me to do the foreword for his book, I was honored. He is one of my best friends, and he was my partner with Miller Brewing Company back in the day when I was driving the Miller Lite car in NASCAR and he had the Miller Lite dragster with Larry Dixon. I knew Don before that though. We first met through the legendary drag racer, Raymond Beadle. I drove for Beadle's NASCAR team, and won a championship with him, and that's where I first met Don. I knew who he was back then, even though I wasn't a drag racer. I would say that everybody knew who Don "the Snake" Prudhomme was. He was *that* popular at the time and still is that popular.

When he walks into a room, boy, they all stand up at attention. He can make a room smile. He can turn a room on. When he's at dinner with somebody, he's the center of conversation. Everyone looks him straight in the eye and wants to ask him all about racing and cars. He'll answer everything and then maybe turn it and ask them some questions. He doesn't dominate the spotlight; he wants to share it. He's like, "Man, let's hear about you. Tell me about your dog, man. Tell me about your new car you just bought. Tell me about your family."

One thing you might not know about Prudhomme is that he's a massive information sponge. He is constantly asking questions and always wanting to educate himself. You can pretty well guarantee that every question that Don asks you, he knows the answer to, but he wants to hear your story and maybe get a different look at it. He might already know the answer, but he wants to know for damn sure that he's got it right. Because of that, he's really knowledgeable. He also has integrity and the respect of a lot of important people.

When you hang out with Don Prudhomme or go places with him, he legitimizes everything you do because everyone knows what he's capable of. They know that he's a guy who knows what the hell he's talking about. He's been up and down, up and down, up and down, and he was out, and he always makes a good move and comes out back on top. I'm glad I was able to be a part of that when I introduced him to Miller, and I'm glad we've been able to hang out away from the track as well. Don isn't just a racer, he knows how to put his swimming trunks on and jump in a pool with a Miller Lite in his hand and enjoy himself.

When he retired, I said, "What are you going to do?" And he said, "Oh, man. I'm going out with my buddies on a boat. I'm going here. I'm going there." He's going all over the place. I think that Don right now is living some of the most exciting times of his life, and he deserves it too. With all those races he's won and everything he's done and how well he represented his sport, he's able now to kick back and have a good time.

Don has it all. He has the knowledge, the championships, the swagger, and the likeability. I've talked to many people who met him and said afterward, "Man, I wish I was like him." I hear that all the time. "I wish I was as cool as Don Prudhomme." They just idolize him. Actually, I have to say that I do too.

— Rusty Wallace
1989 NASCAR Cup Series Champion,
1984 Rookie of the Year,
and 55-time Cup Series Race Winner

PREFACE

Most people root for the underdog. Not me. I like champions. I like people who start with nothing and become winners, and I like to see them keep winning. I know what it takes to get there, and how hard it is to stay there.

I wanted to start out this story with a great first line. Something like Charles Barkley's "I may be wrong, but I doubt it," or "As a matter of fact, I am Parnelli Jones," but it seems like all the best first lines are taken. For once, I'm late on the lights.

1 THE STARTING LINE

Donald Ray Prudhomme was born on April 6, 1941, to Ida and Newman Prudhomme. It's pretty wild to look at yourself as a baby and think, "Kid, you had no idea where you'd end up."

My earliest memories are probably pretty average for a kid in the late 1940s. I was born April 6, 1941, in downtown Los Angeles, and grew up in the San Fernando Valley just over the mountains from Santa Monica, California.

My parents were Ida and Newman, but he went by Tex. I was one of five kids. My older brother, Monette, came first by about a year and half, and we were followed by Judy, Joyce, and Jeanette. There was a lost baby between me and Judy, but that wasn't something I really knew as a kid. I would have been about five when he was born, and he only lived a few hours. They didn't even name him. He's buried as "Baby Boy Prudhomme."

My dad worked in automotive body shops. I don't recall my mom ever having a job outside the house. I guess five kids and a house and livestock was enough work.

Monette, Judy, Joyce, my mom, and me. Those were our little pet calves. I thought they were pets anyhow, and I named mine Don the Bull. I was pretty crushed when we came home from the movies one evening and Don the Bull became Don the Dinner.

I don't have great memories of my dad. Certainly, he wouldn't find them flattering. Picture a receding hairline, a big-time pug nose, and a face that was always red and patchy from alcohol. Of course, he thought he was a good-looking guy. He would take pictures and pose with his hat on, and I used to think, "God, I hope I don't look like him!"

My mom, on the other hand, was a very pretty woman. All the relatives and older people back along the Cane River in Louisiana just raved about how beautiful my mom was, when I finally met them.

"My family was from the Creole part of Louisiana, but that wasn't something we talked about when I was little."

Identity

My family was from the Creole part of Louisiana, but that wasn't something we talked about when I was little. I didn't understand why until long after my folks had passed, when I finally did DNA testing with my sisters. That's when I found out about my Creole heritage and my African-American roots. It would have been nice to know that I was Black back when I was a kid, and I went home crying because some other kid used a nasty slur and I couldn't understand why it was directed at me. My mom would always respond by getting mad at me; she never acknowledged the Black side of our family, and it caused a lot of confusion and insecurity in us kids. Nowadays, it's much more common to see mixed families, and people can be proud of having a complex heritage, but back then it wasn't talked about, and my parents chose to present themselves as White.

You might be picturing me and thinking, "Well, how did he not know?" Hopefully the answer to that is in the family photos. Some of us were dark-haired and some of us blonde, and where we grew up there weren't a lot of other Black kids to compare myself to. It was very difficult trying to make sense of my darker skin and curly hair and everything else when my own

There were car people in our family going way back. That's my mom's father (my grandfather). My brother Monette was named after him. Monette's full name was Vincent Monette Prudhomme, but no one could call him Vincent; he hated that. These photos are from an album my sister made for my daughter Donna.

Columbus Monette

COLUMBUS MONETTE
DEC. 10, 1872

"It was like a secret, something they were afraid of."

family would lie to me. If they'd just told me the truth and said, "Here, sit down. Let me tell you exactly who you are," I would have liked that a lot better.

But it didn't happen that way. Maybe they were just trying to protect me from the prejudice they faced in the South. I'm sure they were. They gave up a lot to leave their own families in Louisiana and move to California. I wonder if that's what made them unhappy or if they would have been that way no matter where or how they lived. I can't ask them because they both passed on and took their secrets with them. I only know any of this because my sister Jeanette started looking into our family history after our mother died in 2008.

Growing up, I didn't get to meet many of my relatives from the South. My folks would go back and visit sometimes, but they never talked about them. Joyce remembers a time when my dad's parents came to visit, and she overheard a neighbor asking my mom who the Black folks were who were at our house. Well, that really upset my mom, and my grandparents didn't visit again. That's what it was like, a secret, something they were afraid of. It would come up again and again in our lives in these small ways, just overheard

I don't have any early photos of my father. This is around 1969 with Lynn, my brother Monette, me, and my dad.

I was a cute kid. Did I look like I was going to become a drag racer?

whispers. When we finally learned more as adults, it's like so many small pieces fell into place. That's why I'm starting the story with it here, so that you will know what we did not. Maybe that way it will all make more sense to you than it did to us.

There were other family members out in California. The lighter ones I guess you'd say. My dad's brothers were in the auto body business too. They lived up in Bakersfield. I remember my dad's brother Leonard would come visit with my cousins. I always thought Uncle Leonard and my mom should have been married instead. They would laugh and joke, and I liked Leonard a whole lot. I don't remember any loving moments between my parents. That was not how I thought a married couple should be; you should have a true partner and friendship. I had to learn about those things when I got married because I didn't see that growing up.

Big Brother

My sisters were babies at this time. Jeanette wasn't even born yet, so it was mostly me and Monette. Monette looked like he'd be in one of those *Our Gang* comedies, like one of the rough kids, you know? He was really strong. He was real tough. He used to beat me up a lot. He'd get me in a headlock, choke me. Either he was extra tough or I was a little wimpy—I'm not sure. Actually, I am sure: he was tough. I was about 2 years younger than him and that's a big age gap when you're little, so we weren't buddies.

At the same time, he was also my protector. He'd beat me up, but he wouldn't let anyone else beat me up. I looked up to him, but mostly I was scared of him. I didn't ever know if he was going to want to play or be in a bad mood and want to pummel me.

Later, when we were teenagers, I'd be with a friend going to a party, we'd walk into the house, and they'd be like, "The cops were just here, your brother just left, and he beat the s—— out of some guy." So, we'd turn around and go to a different party.

TV had just come about, or at least it had just trickled down to the homes of regular people. The first kid in the neighborhood to get a TV was a guy named Howard Cartier, who lived next door. The family would let us all come over to watch. Western movies like *Hopalong Cassidy* were a big deal to us

Monette and I are just out of toddler-hood and entering the navy.

Monette and I were about 4 or 5 years old in this photo. He has his arm around me, but it was probably about to become a headlock.

I'm all dressed up for first communion. Even back then, I didn't like anything about dressing up and going to church. I was scared that the nuns would give me a hard time about tuition.

kids. We eventually got a little black-and-white TV, and we were glued to that. We had these Hopalong Cassidy cap guns. We were probably about 4 or 5, and we'd run through the neighborhood, hiding behind trees and being very much into it. The noise and the smoke, and the *Snap! Bam! Bam!* of the caps.

Back then, my family seemed pretty normal. I think we were probably poor, but at that age you don't know what poor is. Everyone was pretty much the same. We owned a house on Densmore Street in Van Nuys, which back then was quite a ways out of town, so there were only a few houses on our street. It was a ranch-style house, and I know my dad was pretty proud of it because we had some land and some chickens. We weren't wealthy by any means, but we weren't poor-poor. We always had food.

The San Fernando Valley was fabulous at that time, at least to a kid who liked cars and sunshine. It was farmland mainly with lots of orange groves. It was just like those pictures you see of the 1950s. Drive-ins and cruising and the drugstore where you'd get a 10-cent Coke.

We were all pretty easy to please back then. When Butler Brothers (the big department store across from the dealership where my dad worked) got an elevator, we used to go there and ride it up and down. That was a thrill. We didn't know any place other than the Valley.

After the cap guns, we got BB guns. We would have gunfights and shoot at each other. One day, Monette got shot in the eye, and it really messed him up. That ended the BB guns, and I'm sad to say, that sort of ends my happy family memories too. It was brutal after that, as my folks ran into problems with alcohol and with money. I wish I had a lot of good things to say about my childhood, but I don't. I'd like to say, "Oh, my dad used to take me camping, and we went fishing and hiking and played baseball," or things like that, but none of that s—— happened. I was on my own, which was okay, because I didn't know any differently. I didn't know then, but looking back I'm always envious of these guys who had those relationships with their parents—so close and everything. When things are rough as a kid, you spend a lot of time trying to wash out those bad memories, and therefore the good memories (if there are any) get thrown out with the bad.

School Blues

When school started, that was a nightmare for me. I was going to Catholic school, and I hated it. I can still picture the sisters, the nuns, just standing over me with their hands in their sleeves, and I knew there was a ruler in there. My family was Catholic, Southern Catholic, so they were religious, but in a messed-up way. They would make you go to church, but then they would fight and scream and "motherf——" each other at home. It made me question a lot of it, and that didn't make me real popular in a religious school.

It didn't help that I had a real hard time with reading. Now they would know it was dyslexia, and they could have helped me learn, but back then they just figured I wasn't the sharpest knife in the drawer, and they treated me accordingly.

School was pretty awful from the earliest memory of it, but there was one thing I remember from it that I think really changed me. While it was terrible at the time, I am grateful for the lesson. At the Catholic school, you had to pay tuition. The sisters would hand you a little envelope and say, "Give this to your parents. They have not paid the tuition yet and you're not going to get your books until you pay your tuition." I had to go home and ask my dad for money.

"I can't get my books until we pay the tuition." And my dad would be half s—— -faced or something on the couch.

"Tell them we haven't got the money. Goddamn it! I don't have the money now."

Then I'd have to go back and say, "We don't have it. We need more time." It was humiliating. I hated it, and it always pissed me off about the sisters. How could they put a little kid in that position and make him go deal with it? I don't know how ever I got books, but somehow or another I would get hand-me-down books. The books didn't do me any good anyhow since I couldn't read. So that memory stuck and stings, but I really think that it also shaped my life when I got older.

I'd end up having that experience with my parents many times from about age 7 on up. Their behavior (in particular with money) made me know that I wanted to do the opposite in my own life. I think that drove me to succeed. Looking back, it's easy to say now that I'm grateful, but it was hard times then.

That's sort of it for the really early stuff. I'm not one of those people who can remember their first moment out of the womb or anything. Those days were just being a kid, playing outside, struggling with reading and the nuns, and staying out of the way of my dad. I liked feeding the chickens in the yard and watching Westerns. I wasn't anyone you would have picked out of the crowd and said, "That one is going to make something of himself."

"I wasn't anyone you would have picked out of the crowd and said, 'That one is going to make something of himself.'"

MEMORIES FROM JOYCE PRUDHOMME

Don is a little embarrassed about complaining when he talks about our childhood, but he's not exaggerating. It was rough. I hated it. We all did. Our household sucked. Our parents were crazy.

When Judy and I were in grade school, we'd be walking home and making bets if Mom was drunk on the couch. And the minute that Dad came home from work, he was hitting it, and it was Friday Night at the Fights every night of the week. I mean, it was just always crappy. Donnie and Monette were out of the house already, or just about. By that time, Donnie had met Ivo, and he was always over there working on his car in the garage. He was in car clubs. He was well in his teens, and Monette had just gotten married.

The night that Donnie left to go marry Lynn, we were at the house and we were chasing after him and he turned to us and said, "Girls, I've got to go." And he never looked back. We said, "Don't forget us!" He said, "No, no, no. I won't, but I'm never coming back." There were some years where it got real bad, and we'd pick up the phone and say, "Come help us." First, Judy and I lived with Monette, and then I went and lived with Donnie and Lynn. Poor Jeannette was still at home.

When we went to live with Don and Lynn, I had a beautiful room but couldn't sleep at night because nobody was fighting. I loved Lynn. She taught me how to clean a house right, put on mascara, and be a grown-up. She would take my girlfriends and me dancing, but Don never knew about it until about 2 years ago because he wouldn't have wanted us to go. She'd take me to Hollywood Boulevard, we'd go to Pandora's Box, and she'd say, "You be on this corner at 11:30, and if you're not here when I get here, it'll never happen again. And we're not going to tell your brother." She was like a big sister.

Our mom didn't sober up until Monette died. That was her breaking point, and she stopped drinking but my dad didn't. My dad never did. She didn't leave my dad until, I think, 1978. We never really talked about it until Don's 70th surprise birthday party. Jeannette came from Maine, I came from Missouri, and Judy came from Texas. He saw us, his face lit up, and you could see the tears coming down his cheeks. He couldn't believe we came. In the speech that he gave that night, he said out of all he sacrificed for his career, his relationship with the three of us was the thing he was most sorry about. We've always tried to reassure him that we get it. We're so proud of him. He was just a little guy from Van Nuys, and he did it all himself with no money. He and Lynn. You put the two of them together, and they were magic.

2

THE LURE OF SPEED

My first memory of a cool car (because it's about time that we get to cars) was a 1932 Ford that my cousin Harold had. Harold was my mom's nephew, and they lived east of us, out in Gardena. They would come to the Valley to go street racing, and that's my first memory of a hot rod. They would park in the garage, and I can clearly picture myself just sitting there looking at it. It was amazing.

Harold was about five years older than me, at least, or more. So, I must have been maybe 10 or 12. It was in the early 1950s. He was pretty young, but he had these amazing cars. Oh my God, I was blown away. It was primer; in today's world, I guess you'd call it a rat rod. It was the first time that I laid eyes on something like that: a street car with this big engine in it. There were hot rods in the 1940s of course. But Harold's was the first time I was ever connected with one. Harold and his friends came and stayed at our house. They'd go racing, and I wanted to go so bad and hang out with them, but I was just too young. They weren't going to take me, get the f—— out of here.

Since Harold wouldn't take me out, my first taste of speed wasn't in a car at all; it was on roller skates. I was maybe 10 years old, and we used to go to a place in Van Nuys called the Rainbow Roller Rink, and on skates I was pretty

The first cool car I remember was a roadster that my cousin Harold brought by the house. He had many hot rods, including this 1932 coupe.

Harold was older than me, so he never took me along back in his street-racing days, but later when I was painting cars, he would come by and have me work on his rides. I painted a lot of friends' cars.

damn good. They used to have this boys-only time out on the rink, and we would race. Things were divided up like that then. Nobody figured the girls would want to race. We'd line up across and take off and go around corners, and I'd race around there, and I would win. You'd get a little ticket if you won, and then you'd go up to the counter and get a Coke. That was the first thing I ever won: a free Coke.

That speed thing really got to me. That was about the time when we'd see hot rods on the street with big wheels in the back and little ones in the front. They would dump the front of it and raise the back. They called it "raked." I figured I'd try it on my skates. I put big wheels on the back and little wheels in the front, and oh man, that was cool. I loved skating and I loved racing, and I had long legs and I could outpace a lot of the guys. It was a good feeling to finally be good at something, but more importantly, I met Tom McCourry there, and it's wild how one friend can change your life.

"I met Tom McCourry there, and it's wild how one friend can change your life."

Tom McCourry

I feel sort of embarrassed describing my childhood, really running myself down. I wasn't a cool kid: definitely shy and a little lonely. McCourry was my first real friend, and we stayed friends from the moment we met. He was a year older than me, stocky and fairly tall. He was like my brother. Well, not like my actual brother, not like Monette (intimidating and unpredictable) but like what I thought a brother should be. I was closer to McCourry than I was to Monette—by far.

McCourry and I were instant pals because he wasn't quite old enough to run with guys like my brother. Or maybe he wasn't tough enough to run with that crowd, but he was just tough enough where we could run together. We hung out every day. Somehow, some way, we would see each other every day. I'd go over to his house or he'd come to my house, especially when he got a car and his driver's license. We'd be out all night, trying to drag race somebody and losing. We'd get our asses kicked all the time. We'd talk about girls. Girls and cars. Maybe cars even more than the girls; it was such an exciting time for cars. We'd go down to the Chevrolet dealership and see the new Corvette when it first came out in 1953, the 1954 and the '55 Chevys, just anything. We had the hood up on every car that we came across. Everybody was into the engines, looking at them. Just wow.

I didn't get a car of my own right away, but McCourry had a 1936 Ford. It was powder blue with primer spots on it. We'd wash it, shine that old paint up, even polish the primer, and then head to Bob's Big Boy. The burger place was the cruise spot where all the kids would check each other out. There was one in every town it seemed. We'd go to the Van Nuys Bob's, but there was the Burbank Bob's and other local hangouts, and every one had its car clubs and sort of its own personality. We were pretty young, and I hate to say it but, we were kind of punks. McCourry's car wasn't fast or really very cool, but having a car at all was just the best.

The First Drag Races

I don't have many memories of my dad taking me anywhere, but I do remember being with him the first time I went to the drag races. We went to San Fernando Raceway when I was around 13 or 14. I have no idea why he would have gone. He wasn't a race fan or even really a car guy. He worked

My dad is in the red, and my uncle Leonard is in the gray. I always got along better with Leonard than I did with my father. This is from Donna's album.

Great Uncle Leonard & Granda (Newman)

Your Grandpa

I apologize Donna — I could not find a photo of the other two brothers, Joseph Leonard (known to all as José or Wade) and James. Actually, we weren't around them much as kids (trust me, that was a good thing!) Uncle Leonard was our favorite guy!! i¨

"McCourry's car wasn't fast or really very cool, but having a car at all was just the best."

on cars, so he always had a project in the yard, but it wasn't because he was building something for the love of it. It was a way to make money. He'd work on something, fix body damage, and sell it. So maybe he had a customer or someone he was meeting at the track, and I ended up going with him.

San Fernando was about 20 miles from our place in Van Nuys, which was pretty close. The track was almost in a little valley. You could park your car up on the bank and then get out and sit on these telephone poles that lined the edge and watch them race below you. I was just overwhelmed by it all.

There was this guy by the name of Dick Harriman. He had, I think, a 1950 Olds, with a B&M automatic transmission, which was a big deal. The Olds didn't have a front bumper, it just had the mouth of the grille and the front end was raised up. The time slip booth (where you'd get your results) was right by where we were sitting, and he'd come up to get his ticket and rev it up, *vroom, vroom.* That was the greatest thing I had ever seen, that trick transmission and that car sitting there and him getting on the gas and the whole car going *vruuup* and scooting out. Once I saw that, I thought, "Oh my God, I

Tom McCourry was my first real friend, and we were friends from the day we met to the day he passed away. He was more than a friend; he was a brother.

gotta do that. Somehow, some way, I gotta do that." I didn't have any means to do it. But I never forgot it, and once McCourry got his car, we'd go to any drag strip that was running. There were a lot of them back then. We didn't race then, at least not on the track. We'd just go to watch, and then we'd go to Bob's to look at girls and try to street race.

Pressure Pump

The girls weren't very interested in us, so we'd just hang out and talk about how we could make McCourry's car go faster. I wanted to get some gears for the transmission, just to have a reason to work on it. We didn't know anything about being mechanics, and it wasn't like today where you call up Jegs or Summit or some big automotive parts house and get anything you want. Back then, they didn't have many speed shops, and what there was, we couldn't afford anyhow. There was this place on Victory Boulevard in Van Nuys called the Chrome House, but we couldn't do much more than look in the windows.

One thing that McCourry bought for the car that we thought was going to be the hot ticket was a pressure pump for the fuel tank. The old race cars, they'd pump them up, put pressure in the gas tank to push the gas through faster. We didn't really know much about it. We just knew that these hot rod guys had them because we'd seen them on some modded cars.

By that time, we were going to the drag strip, walking around looking at stuff in the pits. We'd see a dragster guy come up to the starting line. He'd be pumping his pressure up in his fuel tank so that when he hit the accelerator, it'd spurt gas, and off he'd go. McCourry said, "I'm going to get one of those pumps. We'll put it in the car."

So, we cut out the dash and put the pump in the car. We took a copper line and ran it right to the gas tank. We didn't have a clue that that's not the way you're supposed to do it. First off, McCourry's car had a big gas tank in it. The dragsters had little racing tanks. You'd have to pump a lot to pressurize a stock gas tank, but that wasn't even the worst of it. See, it was vented. We didn't have enough sense to realize that any pressure we put in went right out the vent.

So, us dummies, we get in a race. We're going down Sepulveda Boulevard. McCourry is floored, and he'd say, "Pump it." He's winding it out and I was over there pumping the s—— out of it, pumping, pumping it like a son of a bitch. He says, "Pump it harder!" and I say, "I'm pumping as hard as I can." It wasn't going any faster. Well, it took quite a while before we really realized that that's not the way you're supposed to do it. Eventually, someone probably said, "Hey, guys, this isn't how it works." But just the thought of doing it, pumping it, made me feel like I was really participating. It was fun even though it was a total failure.

McCourry and I were inseparable. It wasn't even, "Where are we going Friday night?" We wouldn't even have to ask what we were going to do, we just went and did it. His family ran a motel over on Sepulveda Boulevard, so he'd get some spending money working there. We'd use it to buy gas or car parts at the junkyard, and then we'd work on his car in the carport, mainly polishing it and cleaning it.

Neither one of us really knew how to work on the engine that much, just enough where we could adjust the carburetor, tune it, and get the idle where we wanted it. We'd leave the choke sort of half pulled out so that it would sound like the car had a cam: *Bubba-da, bubba-da.* Sounds cool, right? We didn't have a cam. S—— like that was the best we could do with no money and no real skills. When you were cruising, having the windows rolled down at a certain height when you drove through the parking lot, that was important. Having it actually be fast? Not so much. Not yet.

Lost in Transmission

I don't remember where we'd get our ideas back then. *Hot Rod* magazine was over our heads. I think we'd just see other cars at the drive-in or the junkyards. Everything was used. We didn't have any money. Maybe McCourry had a little money, but I had none.

One time, the transmission expired in his car. We couldn't buy a new one, so we scoped out the local junkyard, spotted a 3-speed, and crawled under the fence that night to steal it. The problem was that we were miles away from the garage, and we had to walk the distance carrying this transmission, ducking behind bushes every time we saw headlights, so sure we were about to be arrested. We finally get the thing back and we open it up and the f——ing thing is broken in exactly the same way as the one we started with. That's when I learned that crime doesn't pay. I needed to make some money.

Odd Jobs

It probably won't surprise you to hear that my parents weren't the sort who gave us an allowance. If I asked for money, like "I want to go the

"Back then, they didn't have many speed shops, and what there was, we couldn't afford anyhow."

movies," I'd be mowing lawns. When Tom McCourry and I started hanging out, we would look for jobs together. I remember this one guy, an old German guy with a thick accent, had a chicken ranch, and we'd feed chickens and pick up the eggs. We were kids, so we'd screw around a lot (throw the feed or just be messy), and he used to say, "Don't feed the sparrows!" We were sloppy, the grain would be on the ground, and the wild birds would be ready to eat it before the chickens could get to it. "Don't feed the sparrows!"

We had another job mowing lawns. That guy, the lawn guy, had an old 1937 LaSalle with the lawnmowers strapped to the side of it and on the front and back to carry them. He would drop us off on a corner, and then we'd mow the lawns, run back, strap the machines back on the bumper, and he'd head to the next job. He'd drive down Van Nuys Boulevard, and we would be so embarrassed. We'd be like "No, don't take the main street!" We didn't want anybody to see us in his car with s—— all strapped on the hood. I used to hide in the back seat going down the road. We were trying to be cool, and we were so uncool, you couldn't believe it.

So Long, School Days

Now, I already mentioned that I wasn't doing so well in school. The reading was just really hard for me; it didn't make sense. I didn't have any place to turn to because my parents weren't very helpful. You know, in the movies where the mother or the father takes the kid to school and they sit down and they try to work out problems? None of that happened to me. In real life, you

MEMORIES FROM JUDY PRUDHOMME MAXWELL

Whatever Donnie says about our childhood, he's not blowing it out of proportion. It was hard (our parents were less than parents because of being alcoholics and all that jazz), but we somehow all got through it. We helped each other. I don't recall there ever being a discussion about it, but we were always close and watched out for each other. I have a lot of respect for both of my brothers—Monette and Donnie—they went through so much and came out to be really great men.

We were all in the San Fernando Valley and you'd hear Don's name on the radio, "Prudhomme! Garlits! San Fernando Raceway! Irwindale!" and that was when I realized he was a pretty big deal. People at school would come over and say, "Oh man, the Snake, he's your brother," and they'd be all excited about it. Guys would want to date me just so they could meet my brother. None of us ended up dating any of the drag racing guys. Mostly they were older, but also, Donnie and Monette would have told anyone who was interested that they better leave his sisters alone!

Monette and Donnie were a lot older, but they were always there for us. Even once Don was busy with sponsors and stuff, we always knew that if we needed him

we could call him. He was there, and Lynn too for that matter, both of them. Lynn's the best. We all looked up to her. She is a special woman to live that life and never complain. She was always right behind him, whatever Don needed, she took care of it. She took care of him.

It's funny, I never worried about something happening to Donnie on track. I don't know why, but he always seemed to have it so together and know what he was going for that it seemed impossible that anything could go wrong for him. Even to this day, he's ageless or something; he's so strong. He's got that personality and that drive in him, that he just keeps on going. He started with something he loved and just made a wonderful career out of it. And when he retired, we all went together to Louisiana to learn about our family, and that was really interesting and special for all of us. If he'd still been working, I don't think it would've ever happened because he was always too busy to stop for anything personal; he had too many things he had to fulfill for everybody. He never did anything but race. When he did retire, I said, "Good, now you can get out there and do things that you never could do before." And he is.

have to fend for yourself. I knew I had to read, eventually, and I did, eventually. Not in the way they were teaching me, but more by memory.

When I was still in school, I didn't have any help and it was embarrassing. I hated it, and I decided pretty early, "Man, if it's gonna be like this, I've reached my full potential." Outside school, I didn't feel like such an idiot. I was good with my hands, and I could fix things. If I had a little lawn mower engine or something, I could take it apart and put it back together, and it might even run after that.

I was surrounded by people who made money working on cars. My dad did and my uncle did. While I was still in school, I used to go by Ray Brooks, where my dad worked. Ray Brooks was a Chrysler/Plymouth dealer on Van Nuys Boulevard and a hotbed of car action. I would go there after school, and they would put me to work for a few hours each afternoon. This was when I was 12 or 13. I couldn't wait to get out of school so that I could go over there and sand cars, and I started making a little bit of money.

When I started working on cars, I realized I was pretty good at it—especially a little later, when I started painting. I had finally found something I was good at that I could make a living doing, which was the complete opposite of what was happening in school. When you meet people at a shop or you're working on someone's car, they don't ask you, "Hey, how's your reading doing today?" They just don't care about that. As long as you can read enough to know what it says on the label of a paint can, that's all that matters. Nobody in the shop is going to say, "Oh, well your vowels are wrong." It was just cut and dried. Either you're good or you're not. So, I left school behind.

McCourry was done with school too. We both dropped out about the same time. He didn't drop out because of dyslexic problems or anything like that, he dropped out because he was just done with it. He wanted to work and build cars. We just didn't see any reason to stay in school.

All Cars, All the Time

Once I was out of school, I was just all about cars. I was working at the dealership. I got the job because my dad was there doing the bodywork, but I didn't do any bodywork. I was mainly a painter's helper. I sanded cars and taped them up for the painters. That might have been the best time for me and my dad in terms of relationship. I wouldn't say we were super close, but I think he was proud that I was working and doing a good job. He just wasn't a particularly emotional guy, so it's hard for me to say what he thought.

Driver's Test

When I was about 15, I got my first car. It was a 1948 Mercury. A four-door, not two-door. It was a 3-speed manual, column-shifted, "Three on the Tree." I didn't have a license yet, but I still drove it. I think I called it my car, but it was really my mom's car. She's the one who taught me how to drive. She was a good teacher, and I took to it like a duck to water. I mean, apparently.

It wasn't my first time behind the wheel of a car. Before the Mercury, I'd done plenty of driving with McCourry in a dirt lot behind his dad's motel. He used to buy these old junkers that he would spot on his paper route. He could get them for $10 or $15, and he must have had four or five of them parked in the back. We used to go over there and drive around and race each other.

> *"When I started working on cars, I realized I was pretty good at it—especially a little later, when I started painting."*

This is the first car that was really mine: a 1955 Buick. When I got it, I painted it silver and cobalt blue, and then later I redid it in candy apple red. I got a lot of attention for that car.

We'd have the time of our lives out there just drifting in the dirt, banging fenders, and spinning each other out.

By the time my mom got me in the Mercury, I was an ace already, and I wasn't worried about passing the DMV test, at least, not the driving test. I was worried about the written, because I really couldn't read. I'm embarrassed about this next bit, but I figure it's long enough ago that they can't take my license away now. I cheated on my driver's test. Tom knew I had a problem, so he came in the room to help me. He already had his license, but back in those days there were no computers, and nobody was really watching over the room. I could ask him a question quietly, and he could give me the answer. I'm sorry I had to do it, but I wasn't going to get a license without his help. I think I ended up being an okay driver all the same.

Once I had my license and my mom's car, I was something. I was working multiple jobs. I was painting cars during the day and working at night on the line for General Motors. Technically, you had to be 18 to work there, but McCourry was there, and I told them that I was 18 (even though I was 16) so that I could work there too. There was a big Van Nuys plant, and I was making a ton of money. Imagine it! Two jobs. I was making more money than I ever dreamed I would. I was kicking in at home and helping my mom if she was short, and I saved some too. That's how I ended up buying my own car.

"Wow, Look at That"

I saved up enough money to put a down payment on a 1955 Buick. It was a couple years old, but it was really nice. I painted it myself: cobalt blue with a silver-blue top. I got that idea from the new Chevrolet Impala, which had dark blue on the bottom and a lighter top. I painted my Buick like that, lowered it down, and when I'd go to Bob's people were like, "Woooow." It was the first time I had something where people responded like that. "Wow, look at that." Having something that caused some attention, f—— yeah, I liked it.

McCourry and I used to polish that car for hours. Because the Buick was so nice, we got invited to join the local car club, the Chancellors. They were all about having club meetings, and they all had matching jackets and would go to Bob's Big Boy and cruise around. They'd have the meetings at one of the club members' houses—I think they'd alternate. Funny thing is, I don't even know what the f—— we talked about, besides where we were having the meeting, but it was pretty cool to be a part of this group and to have something of a reputation. I was one of the youngest guys, but I had a cool car and I knew how to paint, so I was popular. Guys were asking, "Hey, can you paint my car?" and I was getting known as a pretty good painter. Not as a racer.

By then, my dad started his own paint and body place. It was called Van Nuys Auto Body. He partnered with a guy who was an insurance adjuster, and they got a space on Oxnard Street and opened up a body shop. I was one of the painters. At that shop, I could work all night long painting a buddy's car or whatever I wanted to work on. My dad was my boss, and as long as I did the job during the day, he didn't care what I did at night. I got a reputation for good work and I liked that notoriety. "Hey, you're Don Prudhomme, and you're going to paint my car." That was kind of cool.

Cruising Didn't Cut It

Being in the Chancellors club was a good deal for me. I was still a young guy, and to be able to have a car like the Buick and be in the Chancellors was pretty cool. I kind of got known in town because I'd go to Bob's and it'd be like, "Whoa, look at that." It was pretty smooth. It was a nice car. There was nothing under the hood. It was just a cruiser. I wasn't into performance yet.

I entered a car show at Devonshire Downs, and I won a trophy. That was the first award that I ever won. I didn't win any in school, so it was kind of a big deal to get that trophy. I forget what place I got. Maybe I got the trophy just for being there. Whatever it was, it made me feel good. I was starting to get some recognition.

I was pretty happy with McCourry and just cruising in the Chancellors. Although, even then, I don't know, it seemed like there might be something better out there. The president of the Chancellors was a guy named Leon Clutterham. What a name. He's one of the reasons I didn't want to be involved. He used to drive down Van Nuys Boulevard. He had I think a 1953 or 1955 Ford pickup and he'd sit sideways in it with his arm out the window. He was this big guy and it just looked, well, not how he imagined he looked. I wanted to throw up every time I saw him driving that car. Nobody drives a car like that but Leon Clutterham. That's enough to make you quit the club right there. They were nice guys, but it wasn't really that fulfilling. Every night, "Okay. What are you going to do? Cruise up and down the street?" Okay.

You've Got to Meet Ivo

Now, back when I was still going to the roller rink, I met this dude, Skip Torgeson. He really stood out. You always notice the cool guys. Either guys

"I got a reputation for good work and I liked that notoriety. 'Hey, you're Don Prudhomme, and you're going to paint my car.'"

are cool or not cool, and Skip was cool. He had cool dripping off of him. He had the hair, the duck tail. He always had a sharp car. He could skate like the wind. He had good-looking girls hanging around him. It didn't hurt that he was a Hollywood actor.

At that time, there were a fair number of young actors in the area because the studios were just a town over in Burbank and Studio City. So, one day we're at Bob's and Skip says, "Hey, you've got to meet this guy Tom Ivo. He's got a 1955 Buick just like yours, and I know he'd love to meet you and see your car. He's in the Road Kings of Burbank, and I'm in the club too."

I didn't know that Skip was in a club. He said, "How about going to a meeting?" McCourry and I went to one Road Kings meeting and that was it for the Chancellors. I met the Road Kings and oh my God, they had a dragster. I ended up selling my 1955 Buick.

If Skip Torgerson hadn't introduced me to Tommy Ivo and the Road Kings, I probably would have made my career painting cars instead of driving them. It still would have been a good life, maybe even a less-stressful one, but I'm glad things went the way they did.

"You Look Good in There"

The cruising thing didn't do it for me. There was something that I wanted more than just cruising, and when I met the Road Kings, I found it. There was

There it is, the dragster that changed everything. That's me in the Road Kings club dragster at San Fernando with Rod Peppmuller in the push car.

this little guy there, Tommy Ivo. Now I already knew of Ivo, everyone knew of him because he was on TV, and he had the most bitchin' cars.

Ivo and I, for some reason, we took to each other. I think because I had that 1955 Buick and he had a 1955 Buick. We had that in common. He also had this little T-roadster with the half-moon window. That was a really cool car. That wasn't just a cool car for a kid in the Valley. That was a cool car universally across hot rodding. That was an important car. When I met him, the engine was out of it and it was in the garage sitting in the corner. I was just drooling over that car, but he had taken the engine out to put it in a little dragster. He was totally a drag racer and all the guys in the club were the same way. All they talked about was drag racing. I said, "God, I like this."

They said I could be in the club, but to do that, I had to be initiated. I was pretty easily embarrassed back then. I didn't have a great sense of humor, especially if I was the butt of the joke, but man, I wanted to be in this club so bad that it didn't matter what they dreamed up. I was willing to do anything if it got me near that dragster.

Road Kings

The night that I was initiated, it was me and a guy named Bob Muravez, who later became another great friend. They sent us through the Van Nuys Bob's Big Boy's parking lot, where the Chancellors hung out. The Chancellors

MEMORIES FROM TOMMY IVO

Don was building a roadster with a Buick motor in it when my friend Skip introduced us. Later, Skip told me, "That guy's one heck of a painter, you ought to maybe consider having him paint your cars for you." Ended up that I helped Don put the Buick motor together, he painted my car for me, and we got to be pretty good friends. He's cool now, but he was just another kid into cars when we met—not a big shot.

He had this terrible laugh, the worst horsey laugh you've ever heard in your life. Something would strike him funny and he'd start laughing, and everybody in the room would end up laughing because he'd go *Haw Haw Haw* and just lose it. Even today he'll *haw* just a little bit when something really strikes him funny, but he's managed to contain it. We were all just having a good time back then, playing jokes on each other and working in the garage all night long.

The way the tour started is that some of the tracks back East all got together and said, "We've heard about all of these racers and seen them in magazines. Why don't we hire some of these guys to come back here and race at our track?" So, they got 10 guys together and they called up out here and said, "We can offer you a three-month tour running once a week all over the United States." Most of the guys they talked to had families or day jobs, and they couldn't just take off for the summer. That's why I was the first one to go back because I didn't have a movie shooting, so I had nothing but time.

Once we set that up, other tracks heard about it and they'd call and say, "You're going to be in the area here for Sunday. Can you come to our track on Saturday night?" We ran everything from airport landing strips to dirt tracks. I think Don told you the story of the dirt track in the rain. He wanted to drive the car. Well, he drove it. When we got back to the trailer, I looked in the seat, and there was just a big mountain of dirt with two little eyes.

Don only ever talks about the racing, but we went to amusement parks, did tourist things, and went to the movies. One time we went up to Minnesota and the local guys took us out waterskiing in March. The water's a little cold about then. He went on the skis, and I tried to dump him. I could not get him to fall. Finally, I just shut off the engine and with one hand over the other he pulled himself along on the ski rope until he got to the back of the boat and jumped in. He won that one.

You probably don't know this, but Don's kind of a soft center. One time we went to a movie in Denver. A Disney movie, *Pollyanna* I think. Hayley Mills played a little girl in a wheelchair. Well, when it was over and the lights came up, I turned around, and tears were just running down his face.

Don talks about his ethnicity in this book, and he's right that we didn't think about it much back then in California. However, when we went through the South, they still had the segregated drinking fountains and movie theaters, and we may not have thought much about it but some of the Southerners did. At that last race, we won and Prudhomme laid a solid kiss on the trophy girl. As we were packing up, the track manager came over to me and said, "When you leave the track tonight, why don't you drive down the road a bit before you stop." I guess there were some people who took a little bit of an offense to that. We were on our way home anyway. We climbed in that Cadillac and drove straight back to Los Angeles. Years later, I talked to some guy who said he saw us in Montgomery, Alabama. He said, "We were just floored that you came in here with a Black guy as crew." I didn't think about it back then because he was just my best buddy. It didn't occur to me that anyone would care one way or another.

When we came home, I said, "If they like two motors, they're going to love four." So that's where the idea came from for the four-engine car. We tested that car in the street around the corner from my house, over where Forest Lawn Drive is now. We called it the River Road before the freeway went in, and it had a good straightaway down in front of the cemetery there. I was in the push car, and we fired it up. Don stepped on it, and the thing took off. I saw a car coming the other way, and I looked at the driver and you should have seen the look on his face when this ball of smoke was racing at him in the lane on the other side of the road. After that, we went out to San Fernando and ran it. Prudhomme was the guinea pig on the thing, and I used to always make jokes that I let him test pilot it before I'd ride in it myself.

The plan was that maybe he'd take it on tour, but the problem was that he was a big man with the ladies, so he'd work at the body shop and then he'd go to the roller rink and he didn't really want to come over to my place and pound on the car. He kept sending McCourry over here to help me polish it and load it. And McCourry always came over with his helmet in a helmet bag. I couldn't understand why he was doing that, but he slowly convinced me that Prudhomme was a deadbeat and he should drive the car. So, I was the first one to ever fire Prudhomme. His heart wasn't in the car. That wasn't what he lived. At that point, he was pretty sweet on Lynn, and she might have told him to choose between her and another tour.

When we started out, we were just in it for the fun of it. When we started to get some money, it changed the whole thing. By the time it got to championships and

sponsors, if you ran well, you were going to break parts. You had to be pretty serious, and Don, he was always more serious than I was. He was 19 or so, and I was 24 going on 16. Eventually, I moved on to other adventures, and he was all in on the racing, running multiple cars, and all that stuff. I envy the success that he's had and the money that he has, but I wouldn't trade him lives. We both got a good run out of the deal, I think. Had the privilege of living long enough to grow old too. That's kind of nice, isn't it?

were all there, and I had to go in there with a baby bottle around my neck, wearing nothing but a diaper and carrying a rickshaw with Muravez riding in the back of it. I think he had to wear a dress.

I can't believe I did it. I can't believe I'd do something like that, but I didn't care at the time. It was like going to the dentist and getting a root canal. You knew it was going to be over with soon and you just had to bear it. It was so worth it. I found a family in those people. I found a family in the Road Kings—camaraderie and stuff that I hadn't had in the past with anyone else. The Chancellors were nice guys, but they didn't have what the Road Kings had.

The Road Kings are still together. They're still going, that's how tight that group was. It changed my life completely being in the Road Kings. Ivo was part of that. We got along great. Some others included Ed Janke and Kenny Safford. We'd hang out at Bob's in Burbank and for sure go to a drag strip on the weekend, whether it was Lions or Colton Drag Strip or wherever was running.

The Dragster

As for the Chancellors, they didn't take it well, but that passed. It wasn't a big earthshaking deal. They were just interested in different things, and what I was interested in was that Road Kings' club dragster.

There were other guys in the club who had their own door cars that they'd race, but for the most part they were a dragster club. Ivo had his own dragster, and there was the club dragster that everyone shared. It looks like a little thing now, but it was a pretty modern build at the time. It had what they call a trapeze roll cage in it, just like the roll cage that Ivo had in his first single-engine dragster. It had a little Hemi in it; I don't think it was a 392 because it was smaller than that. Maybe it was a DeSoto; it was an early Hemi engine. I didn't really care about engines then. That came later. It had a clutch and a little gearbox in it. I think it was a LaSalle gearbox, again, it was the same type that Ivo had in his single-engine car, a 2-speed.

A guy named Rod Peppmuller built it and kept it at his house, but other guys would drive it. They'd take turns. Pretty much if you worked on it, you could take a turn driving it. I don't remember there being a huge line of guys wanting to drive it. It was just a gas dragster, but all the same, it was pretty scary to jump into something like that. It wasn't like a door car. For some reason, it didn't bother me at all, not even a little bit. I just jumped in it and ran it right down through the quarter mile.

"I was willing to do anything if it got me near that dragster."

"When Ivo asked me if I wanted to on a tour . . . it ended up being some of the best education I could ever have asked for."

The first time I drove it was at San Fernando Raceway. That was before the Christmas tree lights, when they'd start you off with an arm drop or a flag start. They did have timers at the end so you'd get a proper time slip. I took to it like a duck to water. I shouldn't say it like that because it sounds arrogant, but from watching Ivo and watching other cars run at the track, it just seemed like I knew what to do. I didn't need anyone to tell me how to stage it or not stage it or anything. I just jumped in and did it.

The guys would push it down alongside the track startup to make a loop. You'd turn around, and they'd push you back, and then when it was running, you'd just get lined up and approach the starting line. You'd have to be able to read the starter. You'd go up and watch him start other cars, and you'd get to know how he did it. Every starter was different. Sometimes guys would turn their head back and forth before they'd drop their arms, and you'd be ready to pop the clutch.

The cars would spray gas out of the carburetor, and it would get on your goggles. That was all normal. There would always be a little bit of oil leaking out of it that would get on your goggles or your face mask. Made you feel tough. It's funny that I don't remember all the details of running that car because it really changed my life. One thing that I do remember is that Tommy Ivo came over when I was sitting in the car, and he said, "You look good in there," or something like that. It was a compliment, and I hadn't had a whole lot of compliments before that, so I always remembered him saying it.

I drove that car on and off for pretty much the whole summer. Rod Peppmuller and I raced it together. I believe Rod owned the engine in the car, and the Road Kings helped support the car with a rebuilt chassis and wheels, tires, and the rest of the stuff. I don't know all the particulars of that. I would be surprised if there was more than $1,500, maybe $2,000, in the whole thing.

At the same time, I was starting to help Ivo run his car, not driving it, but painting for him, cleaning up parts, and driving to the different races around town with him. We had so many drag strips you could go to: San Fernando, Lions, and Colton. A lot of times, guys would race Saturday night at Lions and then race San Fernando on Sunday. Drag racing was starting to be something. The *Drag News* paper would come out, and you'd hear about people such as Ivo, Chris Karamesines, and Don Garlits.

Ivo was in there all the time, and he was on the cover of *Hot Rod* magazine a lot. He was a real stickler for detail, and his cars were always bitchin', so they shot him for *Hot Rod*. He worked too. It wasn't like he was some prima donna. He worked putting the engines together, wrenching on the cars, and designing all the multi-engine setups. He built a twin-engine dragster, and I bought his single-engine dragster, so I was helping him, racing my own car, and painting cars.

It didn't seem like it could get any better. I felt like I was on top, which was great because there wasn't anything great happening back at the family house. My dad just couldn't control his drinking; he lost the shop, he lost the house, and then we were just moving from place to place, skipping out on rent. My folks were fighting all the time, and I just tried to stay out of there as much as I could. When Ivo asked me if I wanted to go on a tour with him, it seemed like a good idea to me, since I wasn't in school and didn't have a full-time job. Ended up being some of the best education I could ever have asked for.

LOVING LYNN

Going on the road with Ivo changed everything, but he wasn't the only important person in those days. My wife, Lynn, played a big part in my whole racing career, and we have to go back a few years to get to the start of her story. We've been married for 56 years now, but I met her in junior high school in seventh grade art class. If we hadn't met or she hadn't liked me and stuck by me, this would be a very different story.

Now, this wasn't a "That's the girl I'm going to marry" kind of first-sight thing. Marriage! That wasn't even on the radar, but I can still remember the first time that I saw her. It was art class, which is one of the few subjects in school that I was any good at. I walked into class, turned to my left, and there was this little blonde standing over by the bench, washing her brushes out. She was cute. She was *wow* cute. I don't know what gave me the confidence to ask such a pretty girl out. I was shy back then, especially around girls. I never thought I could get anybody like her. Have you seen the movie *She's Out of my League*? It was that kind of mismatch.

Dating back then, it wasn't super serious. When you went on a date you'd go to the drive-in or to Bob's Big Boy, and that was a date. The girls and the cars, they were pretty much separate. I really didn't have many girlfriends. Lynn was pretty much it. It was her and the cars. We'd go to the movies and the skating rink. She had her own world too. She had her girlfriends, they used to go to parties, sometimes we'd meet up there, and other times I'd go racing and she'd do her own thing.

On the surface, we were sort of an odd couple. There I was, struggling with school, everyone fighting at home, and she was a good student, an only child. There was no reason it should have worked for us, but I think we understood each other on a very deep level. We were both in families that weren't happy. Hers wasn't as dramatic as mine, but her folks didn't want to help her go to college, and they didn't really care what she did as long as she stayed out of their way. We both came from households where we weren't expected or encouraged to do anything big with ourselves or our lives. I think we saw in each other, I don't know what exactly. Ambition? Optimism? Some kind of hope that there was something better than the way we were brought up. Somehow, she believed that I could be

I still wonder how I had the courage to ask Lynn out. She really was the prettiest girl I'd ever seen and still is.

more, that she could be more, and that we could be more together. We just needed each other.

She's the one who finally taught me how to read and write. I feel like I went through school after we got married because she'd teach me. I'd go home and ask, "What is this word in this contract? How do you pronounce it?" Things like that, and she was always right there for me.

It sounds very romantic (and it turned out to be), but when we first met, we were just kids. Nobody was going steady; nothing was serious. We'd fight and break up and get back together. When Ivo asked me to go on the road, all I cared about was going to the races. I knew I was gonna lose Lynn, but I was willing to take that chance. I hate to say it. I had been wanting to race so bad that I wanted it more than anything else. I had nothing to offer her if I stayed, so I left.

3

THE 1960s

Working on Ivo's twin-engine car. He designed that whole dragster, and we built it on the floor of Kent Fuller's shop. (Photo Courtesy Tommy Ivo Collection)

Push it down the track and turn around at the end. Then head back toward the starting line. The guy you're racing is right next to you and he's pushing down too at the same time. Let the clutch out and build oil pressure in the engine and hit the switch. Pow! The engine goes Rrrrrr, it starts running, dut, dut, dut, dut, dut, and you go up to the starting line, make a big U-turn, and set up to stage. Rev the engine and raise the RPM, watching the starter.

It's a flag starter, and you gotta read him, when is he going to twitch? Pop the clutch, the front end comes up, tire smoke comes off the tires, flames coming up on the side, and oil spattering your goggles. You're about halfway down the course before it clears and you can see who you're racing. That's a front-engine dragster. That's drag racing in the 1960s.

Tommy Boy

When I hit the road with Ivo in the summer of 1960, that was pretty much the first big trip I'd ever taken. I'd been back to Louisiana with my mom maybe once when I was really young, but all I remember about that trip was the back of the car. Once I started racing, I'd go up to Bakersfield and Half Moon Bay for a few races, but I hadn't really seen the country. This was a real new experience, and it was a commitment. It wasn't like I could change my mind and fly home. Heck, I couldn't even call home. That was expensive! If we did need to check in or find a place to stay, we had to find a payphone at a truck stop. I don't even remember calling home during that trip. We didn't have that kind of relationship, my parents and me. I was on my own. Me and Ivo.

I better tell you a little bit about Ivo. Down the road, our relationship wasn't the best, but at the time, we really liked each other, and we had a lot of fun together. We were a goofy pair—me tall, slouchy, and not very social and him just a tiny guy with a huge smile and no fear at all about talking to people and performing. He was smart, he worked hard, and his cars were really something.

Ivo had this Cadillac. The Cadillac was an amazing car. It was a pretty new car, and to ride around the country in that, we were living large. That was what we used to tow the twin-engine dragster on a trailer (they called them lollipop trailers—it was just a handle to attach to the tow car and then two wheels).

Ivo's mom went with us for the first part. She was going up to visit her sister in Denver, which was our first stop. I shouldn't say this, but the main

In front of my folks' place, getting ready to hit the road with Ivo. The car's all loaded up and we won't be back for months. (Photo Courtesy Tommy Ivo Collection)

Below Top: Ivo liked to take the scenic route, which sometimes led to moments like this, blocked in by a giant flock of sheep. I bet the sheep had never seen anything like our rig. (Photo Courtesy Tommy Ivo Collection)

Bottom: Our first stop on the tour was Continental Divide Raceway in Colorado. Everywhere we went, people just swarmed the car, and who can blame them? It was quite the scene: a twin-engine dragster with a parachute, pulled behind a Cadillac. (Photo Courtesy Tommy Ivo Collection)

thing I remember from leaving town is that she kept farting the whole time. She was in the back, just farting; Ivo would look at me, and we'd start laughing. We were kids. We stayed with his aunt when we got up there. Those first tours, we'd stay with friends and family when we could.

On the Road in 1960

We took the Continental Divide. There was some highway up there. I don't even know which one, but it was not where you're supposed to go during the winter, especially towing a dragster. You were supposed to go around, but he wanted to go over, and it was snowed in, but Ivo had special luck. He did risky things and had a blast.

We were driving his white 1957 Caddy with a twin-engine car on the back on an open trailer. Kent Fuller built the chassis. He had a shop in the back of Tony Nancy's shop, and we would work back there. Tony was a big-deal upholsterer as well as a racer, and he made some covers for the engines and

Below Top: Ivo liked to take the scenic route, which sometimes led to moments like this, blocked in by a giant flock of sheep. I bet the sheep had never seen anything like our rig. (Photo Courtesy Tommy Ivo Collection)

Bottom: Our first stop on the tour was Continental Divide Raceway in Colorado. Everywhere we went, people just swarmed the car, and who can blame them? It was quite the scene: a twin-engine dragster with a parachute, pulled behind a Cadillac. (Photo Courtesy Tommy Ivo Collection)

the cockpit of the car. The rest of it was out in the elements. I'd never even driven in snow before, but Ivo, he liked any kind of adventure.

We'd take turns driving the rig. I learned a lot being with him. I learned about weight distribution on the trailer—how to balance the trailer so that you didn't lose the damn thing going down the road. Traveling with him put me through school. All that helped when I went on tour by myself a few years later. He was so much more experienced, he had already been racing, and he knew how to make an entrance—just look at the cars he drove!

We had taken the engine out of my dragster (I had bought the single-engine chassis from Ivo when he built the twin-engine car), and we put it on the front of the trailer for a spare, and man, having a spare engine, that was something else.

I was excited about the trip. I was seeing the world for the first time. It was a totally new adventure, and the most exciting part to me was going to a drag strip that I hadn't seen before! A new track was more thrilling to me than the mountains, the scenery, or the night life. Ivo would enjoy the scenery and the drive. The only thing that I enjoyed was when we got to the racetrack. I didn't care about all the rest of it. He was into going to New York, going to the city, going to plays or amusement parks. I wasn't into that s—— at all. I was just . . . I call it s——, but I just wasn't into it. All I wanted to do was race.

It's not like I had money or time for night life. No, the exciting part was seeing the new tracks. The closest I ever got to seeing other racetracks before was opening up *Drag News* and seeing something about Denver Drag Strip or Continental Divide Raceway. Other people go to Europe and they want to see Paris or Rome, but I got all excited to see Union Grove and York U.S. 30.

Ivo would get us booked in to do a run, race the locals, or even just show up and let people look at the car. We were a big deal because the dragster had two engines and a parachute on it. A twin-engine car with a parachute had people going, "Whoo," "Whoa," before you even got it off the trailer. I was even impressed, and I had helped build it!

We'd run down these tracks, and at some of the tracks the people couldn't believe that we were real—these two guys from California. You're racing in Georgia or some little drag strip, and it was an event. We used to pack the

"A new track was more thrilling to me than the mountains, the scenery, or the night life."

On tour with Ivo. We're both wearing Iskenderian Cams T-shirts. Isky was the first guy to think of branding T-shirts, and he gave Ivo a bunch for us to wear on tour. (Photo Courtesy Tommy Ivo Collection)

house. A lot of people came to the track. We didn't have enough sense to sell T-shirts or anything. I'm surprised that Ivo didn't think of it. Ed Iskenderian was the first guy to be smart about that kind of marketing.

Dirty South

One stop I do remember was a dirt track in the South. It was a big, banked oval. I never cared where we raced, let's just go race it. We pulled into this track and I said, "God, this is kind of funny, a bunch of stock cars or something here, and we're the only drag car." Ivo had set it up to do an exhibition right there on the oval.

We pulled off the trailer, and he started it up, spun the tires in the dirt, and opened the parachute. Everyone loved it, and just then it started raining. I mean the skies opened up, and it just poured down. Ivo put me in the dragster and pushed me back to the pit area. The mud was caked on the wheels, it was sliding, mud was flinging all over me, and he was laughing. He thought it was the greatest thing in the world that I was all covered with mud and s——. Nowadays I'd be furious, but back then I wasn't pissed at all. I was just totally excited to be able to sit in the car and drive, even if it was just to take it back to the pits. We were both laughing, and it must have been hilarious to see—mud all over and us slipping and falling while we tried to load up the car.

In general, the drag racers were really open and supportive. They were glad we were there; they wanted to see the car and meet Ivo. People would take us in, we'd tell them about our car, and they'd show us theirs. It was a great way to learn about how to build these things and what makes them fast and beautiful.

When we went up to Minnesota, there was a car up there called the *Big Wheel*, and I fell in love with it. It was a blown front-engine dragster. We raced those guys, and they had a speed shop called the Big Wheel, a big tire shop. We kept Ivo's car there, and those guys were so nice even though we were racing each other. It really helped me later on because when I started driving and doing pretty well, guys said, "I remember you. You used to be with Ivo. You were that guy pushing him in the truck and working on the car." I'd say, "Yeah, that's me. That was me."

Earlier in this story, I talked about being Black but not Black. During the time that Ivo and I were traveling in the South, it was still a segregated place. I saw the bathrooms and the water fountains, and it gave me an uneasy feeling. We would joke about it, he would kind of rib me about that, and I didn't love it, but I also didn't think it really applied, right? My mom told me that it wasn't true, so what did I care what jokes Ivo told? I didn't like the South, but it never even occurred to me that any of it applied to me personally. I didn't think about which bathroom to use, nothing like that, and nobody ever said anything to me about it. The closest we came to a fight had nothing to do with me, it was all Ivo.

I don't actually remember if this happened on the road or if it was at a local race, but I was standing with Ivo and the dragster, and this guy came over and put his foot on Ivo's front tire. We had to move the car, so Ivo said, "Do you mind moving your foot?" And the guy says, "Make me." It was some deal like that, and I thought, "Oh s———. It's gonna happen here." There were a few people gathering around. And Ivo, little Ivo, goes over there and picks the guy's foot up and moves it off the tire. I thought, "F———, this guy's gonna kill Ivo." This guy's a big guy. But the guy must have thought, "Well, if this little kid had enough nerve to do that then maybe I better not f——— with him." And we went about our business. Ivo didn't back down. He was a skinny little s———, but he didn't ever back down, and I respected that about him.

Too Much Time Together

Ivo and I were two guys who left Los Angeles as the best of friends and came back not the best of friends because we were together all the time. After a while, too much time together can wear on you. I found that Ivo had such weird habits from all his time in the film industry. We'd get a room, and he'd be up all night and sleep all day. So, we'd be in this hot attic or this motel room with the windows all blacked out, and he'd be up until early morning and then sleep until 2 p.m. Then, he'd get up and do that whole cycle again. It was just the way he lived. And I had to adjust to that.

I'm sure it happens to a lot of people that you leave for somewhere as the best of friends and you come back almost like enemies. You just don't get along. It wasn't any one thing, it was just too much time together. It got to the point where I couldn't stand the way he'd pour salt on his food.

One thing that started the unraveling of our friendship was that I didn't know he was getting paid. Yeah. So funny. I didn't even dream about getting paid. We were at a drag strip in York, Pennsylvania, I think. The night was over, we were packing up everything, and the track operator came over. On the hood of his car, he had some cash. He was counting this money out to Ivo, I looked at it, and Ivo turned to me with the money and did this little laugh he does, *Heh-heh-heh*. If you've met him, you know that grin he's got. I had been paying my own way to go, and I ran out of money real quick and had to borrow from him. And that kind of started us on a downhill slide because I thought, "Hey, you should pay for my . . ."

But I say that now in hindsight. At the time, I would have paid him just

"It got to the point where I couldn't stand the way he'd pour salt on his food."

When I hit the road with Ivo, I was most excited about seeing all the drag strips that I'd been reading about in Drag News. *This was our second stop at Great Lakes Dragaway in Wisconsin. (Photo Courtesy Tommy Ivo Collection)*

When I first bought Ivo's single-engine car, I painted it white and raced it with the Buick engine before swapping in the Zeuschel 392 Hemi.

I drove Ivo's four-engine car a few times. Here we were testing it without any panels on it. It was a neat construction, but by the time it was done, the 392 Chrysler single-engine cars were so fast that a big, heavy, multi-engine car really wasn't competitive. (Photo Courtesy Tommy Ivo Collection)

I was working out of my dad's body shop at night, painting cars for other racers and hot rodders. This is the bodywork for the Ivo four-engine dragster. (Photo Courtesy Tommy Ivo Collection)

to be part of it. Imagine if you were in a band, you got a chance to play with the Rolling Stones, and you complained about not getting paid. I'd have paid him, or if we both had been doing it for free, that wouldn't have bothered me. However, I didn't know he was getting paid, I had to borrow money from him, and then I owed him money when I got home. It caused some hard feelings down the road. There are a few things we still disagree about to this day.

Cool Like Elvis: The Greek

I don't want you to think it was all bad—it was amazing. The highlight of the trip for me was when we went to Chicago and I got to meet the Greek, Chris Karamesines. I had not met him before, but I'd seen him in the magazines, and he was just so cool. The Greek. He had this bitchin' mustache, and the car looked great. I can still picture him doing a burnout, the f——ing smoke blowing out in front of the engine and you could see his hands in

I don't have any photos of when I first met the Greek, Chris Karamesines. This one is from later in the 1960s, but you can see how cool he is. Look at that handsome bastard sitting there. Any wonder that I was impressed by him?

there driving the thing. I thought that was the ultimate. When I got to meet him, he didn't disappoint. I was impressed. He and his wife took a liking to me, kind of took me under their wing. Later, he'd really help me learn some of the technical engine stuff that I didn't know at the time.

Karamesines invited us over to his house because they were having a party. I'm going, "Oh my God, I get to go to Chris Karamesines's house. Wow! Wow!" I was just blown away. We went over there, and here I'm this quiet-as-hell, skinny-as-hell, shy guy, and here's the Greek with a big mustache and big personality. The party was in his basement, and it was all so Chicago. I thought it was a pretty big deal to be in Chicago! I can still remember that he had a tommy gun sitting on the bar—a real one!

One of the things that I learned on that trip was how making friends (or learning how to be social at least) was crucial to making it through a tour like that. It wasn't like today where the racers fly to meet up with the trucks and everyone has cell phones and credit cards. We needed a network of places where we could stop, stay the night, and maybe work on the car if something needed to be repaired. The Greek was always so good about that. He'd say, "Yeah, yeah, come use my shop. Hang out."

I wanted to be like the Greek, not like Ivo. Karamesines had this blown fuel engine and he was cool like Elvis. Staying with him, that was like staying at Graceland or something. The biggest f——ing thing in the world. And to become friends with him at an early age was more than I ever thought. When I came back there a few years later with my own car and started driving it and winning races, he started asking me questions like, "How did you do this or that?" and it made me feel like I made it.

Winning Lynn Back

When I came back from being on the road with Ivo, I didn't know what I was going to do. I was walking around with my hands in my pockets. Being on the road was the best education I could have ever received for racing. But at the same time, I came back broke, and there wasn't anything waiting for me, not even my girl. Lynn found a new boyfriend, and the worst part of it was that his name was Don too.

When I got back to town, I saw one of Lynn's girlfriends and she told me the news. It really crushed me. I realized how much I liked her after only thinking about racing all summer. When I finally saw her again, I could tell she that liked me too, but it was still a few years of on-again, off-again.

It wasn't until 1963 that I finally got smart. I still might have let her get away if it wasn't for our friend Linda. We were at a bar, up on the balcony. I think Lynn was dancing; she wasn't nearby. Linda turns to me and says, "Why don't you two get married?" And I went, "Married?" I couldn't even take care of myself, let alone get married. But for some reason it really stuck in my mind, like, "Married? God, that would be amazing if that could happen because we could grow together." And so I asked her to marry me.

She made me ask her dad, and man, he didn't like me much, but he didn't have much to say. He didn't really have a choice because I think she was ready to run away anyhow. We would've taken off and eloped if they'd have said no. I didn't have to ask my parents anything. They didn't even come to our wedding. We got married in Vegas, just the two of us, her parents, my brother and his wife, McCourry, and Lynn's friend Doreen—who by the way, was my first crush and introduced me to Lynn. I think I ended up

"I came back broke, and there wasn't anything waiting for me, not even my girl."

Lynn and I were married in February 1963 in Las Vegas, Nevada. My brother and his wife, McCourry, Lynn's parents, and a few other people came, but my folks stayed home. It was a relief, really. I can only imagine what my dad would have been like in Vegas.

making a lot of good decisions over the years, but marrying Lynn, that was the best one ever. Best thing that ever happened to me. But that was a little later. First, I had some races to win.

The Zeuschel, Fuller, and Prudhomme Car: 1961–1962

At the same time as I was trying to win Lynn back from the other Don, I was also getting back to racing in my own car, the dragster that I bought from Ivo. We'd put the Buick back in after the tour, and he introduced me to Dave Zeuschel, who had a Chrysler motor—a 392. We put Zeuschel's engine in the

THE MONGOOSE WHEN HE WAS JUST MCEWEN

I met Mongoose back in those early days, and I can remember like it was yesterday. I was with Ivo, and he had his twin-engine Buick dragster. Ivo, being a showman, used to use his gorgeous T-bucket to push the dragster down the drag strip to start it or get it up to the line. We were at Lions Drag Strip, and I was sitting in it, and I didn't know anyone. I wasn't a guy who would come up to a group of strangers and be all, "Hey, Joe, how you doing?" I'd mind my own business. So, I was in the T, and this blond kid stepped in the way, had his white pants on, curly hair, and he asked if he could ride with me up to the line. Well, I was thinking I need to be professional, so I said, "No, you have to ask Ivo." Mongoose always held that against me, that I wouldn't let

him ride with me in the car–not a real great beginning to our friendship! I'm not exactly sure what happened after that except that he was at Lions Drag Strip every week and he'd come by Keith Black's, but that was later. He must have won me over or at least forgiven me–he really was such a nice guy.

When I got my own dragster, I wanted to beat him in the worst way, and he knew it. He got a kick out of making me mad. He'd screw me around at the starting line. He knew the starter at Lions, and when the lights would go down, he beat me more often than I liked. I would get mad as a son of a bitch at him, but he would just laugh, and I couldn't stay mad at him. I loved him. We were inseparable for years.

That's the dragster I got from Ivo after we put the Zeuschel motor in it and modified the bodywork to fit around the big Chrysler.

car, and it just hauled ass. It was very good, but it broke. The car wasn't really built for that kind of engine. It was a little short-wheelbase car, and putting the Chrysler in it was like putting a Corvette engine in a Volkswagen. So, Kent Fuller built this long-wheelbase dragster that was designed around the engine, and we called it the Zeuschel, Fuller, and Prudhomme dragster.

That was a state-of-the-art car. There weren't any dragsters out there better than that Fuller car. That car kind of put Fuller on the map as far as building the top dragster chassis, but it was a short-lived thing for me. Running a nitro Hemi was not like running the Buick engine. We couldn't race it every week. We just didn't have the money to do it. It was expensive to put gas in the truck and buy nitro and parts for the engine. With the Buick, I just ran up and down the track, put gas in it every so often, and off I went again. But nitro was a whole different ball game.

No Fear

What's amazing (at least to me) is that I had absolutely no fear of racing at all: get in, strap in, put my helmet on, fire it up, and *whoop-whoop, grrrrr* . . . pop the clutch and it would pop the front end up a little bit, then you nail it, put your foot in it, and the thing starts smoking the tires and goes right down through there . . . It was just natural for me.

Everybody would get all excited, and I'd say, "Yeah, it's bitchin'," but it never felt like I was over my head. I never felt like I was going to kill myself. It felt exciting, not dangerous. Maybe that's crazy because it was dangerous. Guys were getting killed every week at different drag strips. But for whatever reason, in that Zeuschel car, I felt in control of something, maybe for the first time in my life. Whatever it was, I was hooked, and we were good.

Smoking the Smokers

When 1962 came around, we went up to the Smokers race. The Smokers was a car club up in Bakersfield, and it put on this big race: The Fuel and Gas Championship. Well, we won. We won Bakersfield.

That race was the biggest thing in drag racing, and here's why: First, this

was during the nitro ban, when the NHRA had banned nitromethane as a fuel. Their races weren't drawing the same crowds as some of the club races where they were still running nitro. None of us cared about gas racing. So, you have the fastest cars at Bakersfield, and you also have all the big names. Everyone would go up there—Don Garlits, Chris Karamesines, Bobby Langley, Art Malone, Art Chrisman, Jack Chrisman, Ivo—anybody who was anybody went to Bakersfield, and they all wanted to win.

It was more than just a race, it was an event. It was like Woodstock. The Hell's Angels would park their motorcycles out in front, and they had bonfires and camping, and thousands of people would show up at this little track out in the middle of nowhere.

Zeuschel and Fuller stayed with me at my uncle Leonard's house. He was proud as punch to have us, and they were happy to have a place to stay too. There weren't many motels up there then. Heck, there still aren't, and in those days, it wasn't that easy to get a room because the racers would work on their cars in the parking lot the whole night, wash parts in the bathtub, and generally be loud and messy. We weren't real popular with hotel owners.

I can't even tell you now how we all knew about the race. I don't remember seeing ads or anything. You just knew: big race in Bakersfield, Fuel and Gas Championships. I think they had some stuff in *Drag News*, but really, everybody in the scene knew about Bakersfield. There were 32 qualified cars, and we went round for round 'til we got to the final.

I was so nervous the whole time that I don't remember the details. I wasn't scared of the car, I was more nervous about the guys who we were racing, because most of them were way more established than we were. We were a brand-new team; we had just got together. We would beat them, and I wouldn't even look up. I didn't do the whole, "Yeah, we kicked your ass," thing. There was no trash talking at all. I would win a round, and then come back to the pits.

People started coming around our pit. There was this big circle of people around the car, and I was right in the middle of this. And it was like, man, I've arrived, you know? I mean it was a great feeling and then we ended up winning the damn race.

I faced Ted Gotelli in the final. As I recall, they red-lighted against us. Something happened at the starting line. The guy jumped the start, and he was really pissed. I was scorching right down through there. I didn't have any problems. Well, Ted Gotelli, he was a hot motherf——er, and he says, "We need to run again." He was arguing with Fuller, and I wasn't involved. I was all, "Don't look at me." I'm just a driver, you know? But there was a little bit of controversy.

If it wasn't such a big race, maybe they would have run us again, but at this race, it was beyond that. It was a big deal just to make it run. You had to cool the engine off, get it all ready, change the oil, get it all ready to go again. At Bakersfield, they actually had rules and s—— up there. If you're out, you're out. Ted never forgave me. He didn't like me, even later on in years. He was really a piss-poor loser. Although, I guess it takes one to know one. Nobody likes to lose.

I barely remember what happened after that. I guess Fuller dealt with it. He was a pretty well-known chassis builder by then, even Gotelli didn't want to make him too mad. We packed up, I think Zeuschel put the trophy in the back of his truck, and we all just drove home. Biggest moment of my life, and then just back to your normal life. Hi, everybody! I'm home. It's not like it was on *Wide World of Sports*, or it was on the news that night or anything.

I was on cloud nine, but on Monday I went right back to work. There was no one at work who knew about Bakersfield. At that point, I was working at a Jaguar dealership on Van Nuys Boulevard. I could color match the foreign cars really well, but it was not exactly full of fellow drag racers. So, it was just regular work during the week and waiting for the next race. None of the local ones had the highs like Bakersfield. It was way different. But Fuller and Zeuschel were getting busy with other things, and running out of money, and right about that time I got the call from Keith Black.

We're racing at Bakersfield. I'm in the near lane.

I'll admit right now, I don't know who is in these cars. Neither of them was mine, but it's a good example of how different every dragster was back then: different engines, header styles, scoops, and wings or no wings. We were all just figuring it out. Later, the cars became much faster, but they all began to look the same.

If you didn't weigh down the front on those early dragsters, they would lift the wheels all the way down the track. We didn't figure out that we should be making the wheelbase longer for a few more years. This is the Fuller-Zeuschel car at Lions Drag Strip in Long Beach, California.

We won a boat with no engine in it; it was just the shell. I'm pretty sure Fuller and Zeuschel just sold it back.

In the winner's circle at Bakersfield with Kent Fuller, the trophy queen, and Dave Zeuschel.

That's my brother, Monette, kissing the trophy girl at Bakersfield. I was too shy to do it, but he had no problem with women. In fact, I think she left with him.

"Anybody who was anybody went to Bakersfield, and they all wanted to win."

In the early 1960s, we'd race other classes, including Altered and Competition Coupes. I think that's a Fiat in the far lane at Fremont Dragstrip. I must have won, since I made the cover.

From left to right: me, Tommy Ivo, and Don Moody. Moody worked for Engle cams, and he raced too. He was tough to beat!

Kent Fuller is on the floor of his shop behind Tony Nancy's upholstery place. There were several chassis builders for dragsters, but Fuller was one of the best.

This is the Zeuschel–Fuller car. Check out the push car off to the side with the big bumper on it. The guys would take their cars to Bob's Big Boy with the push bar still on, that way you knew they were racers. If you look at the front of the car, you can see the lead weights just tied on with rope. We weren't thinking much about safety. I mean, I drove the thing in just a leather jacket and jeans. Zeuschel is standing by the dragster, and that's my best bud Tom McCourry in the T-shirt to the left.

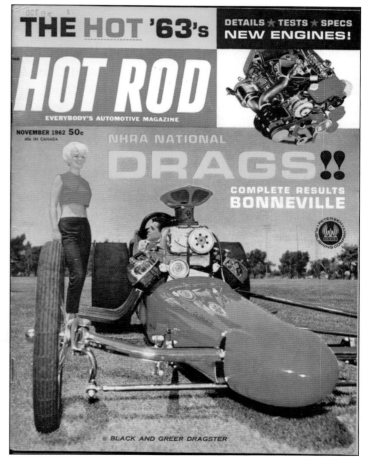

I'd been on a few drag racing newspaper covers, but being on the cover of Hot Rod magazine, that was a whole new level. We shot this in a park, and the gal with her belly showing was very risqué!

I won a lot in the Greer, Black, Prudhomme car. This is the Pomona Winternationals. You can see Keith Black's push car in the return lane.

The Greer, Black, and Prudhomme Dragster

"I thought, 'Oh my God, I get to drive this.'"

When they decided they couldn't keep running the car, Fuller recommended me to Keith Black. I can't even tell you what that phone call was like. Imagine if you were a small-time actor and you got a call that a major motion picture wants you for the lead. That's how exciting this was to me. Keith Black was already a big name. The fact that the timing all worked out so well was just very lucky. I had pretty good luck with most of my career, but this in particular was just a perfectly smooth transition to the new car—and what a car it was.

It was just amazing. Tony Nancy did the interior and the body was Wayne Ewing. When I went to go see it I thought, "Oh my God, I get to drive this." It was the coolest-looking race car I'd ever seen. I got to paint it, and although it's recently been restored in yellow, it was originally an orangey-red color like Ivo's cars. I loved his cars, and Tony Nancy had a highboy roadster that color as well, so we painted the Greer–Black car the same. I probably just had paint left over, but seriously, I did really like the look.

By that point, pretty cars were the thing to have. We were California guys, and all the hot rodding started here. All the hot rodders were painting their cars really bitchin', and that spread over to the Fuel dragsters too. Once I saw that Greer–Black car with the scoop and that body, it seemed obvious that it deserved a good paint job.

Everyone was fixing up their cars. All the junky stuff kind of came and went in drag racing by that point. The stuff you see in old photos or revival meets where guys just threw an engine in a car and left the gear shift sticking out and it was all flat black or patchwork was out of fashion. That was more the look in the late 1940s and 1950s, but by the early 1960s, paint jobs were important to have on your car. Solid colors, no jitterbug s—— on them yet. We hadn't got into the flames and stripes; that came later on.

Left to right: Keith Black, Donnie Culp, me, and Tommy Greer. Donnie was Keith's friend and he used to come to the races and work on the car, not as a job, he just thought it was fun. We all did! No one had any idea that it could be a career.

When I first started in the Greer, Black, Prudhomme car, I painted it orangey-red, like Ivo's cars. Later, I changed it to yellow. When it was restored around 2000, they chose to redo it in the yellow paint scheme. This is the restored car in Bakersfield.

Ray Brock, who worked for Hot Rod magazine, me, and Keith Black at the track. I don't know what Brock was interviewing us for, maybe a Petersen film? Pete Petersen and Wally Parks were close friends, and there was a lot of NHRA coverage in the magazines.

I got the Snake nickname from Joel Purcell on the Greer, Black, Prudhomme team. At first, I didn't like it, but it worked out well for me. This is my first Snake helmet. I went through a lot of variations, but I still have this one.

Start of the Snake

One of the important things that happened to me in the Greer, Black, Prudhomme (GBP) car didn't even have to do with winning a race; it was getting the Snake nickname, which I didn't even like at first! A guy on the team named Joel Purcell started calling me Snake because of the way I'd leave the starting line. It was sort of a compliment, sort of a jab. I think he mostly meant it as a compliment. He was a funny guy. I was not a funny guy. I didn't go around cracking jokes.

The nickname caught on, and the announcers and reporters started saying it. That was a real difference in the coverage, when they started writing, "Snake wins at Lions Drag Strip," instead of Prudhomme. At first I thought, "Oh my God, how can they do that? How would you know who Snake is?" I didn't realize that I was known more as Snake than I was by my name.

I always had trouble with my last name. People couldn't pronounce it. Even I have a hard time. When I started becoming Snake, it was so easy. And then, Tom McEwen came along and became the Mongoose, and it was Snake and Mongoose. Even today it blows me away. It was so perfect. We were Snake and Mongoose before the Hot Wheels deal. That came later.

Can't Win 'Em All

We got invited to go to an AHRA race in Green Valley, Texas. I had heard about how tough and fast those Texans were. We did really well there, but when we came up to the final round, we were racing a driver named J. L. Payne. Payne drove for Vance Hunt, and he was a real tough guy. He wore cowboy boots when he drove the race car and was known to carry a knife in those boots.

We raced him in the final round, and he red-lighted against me. I went on down and won the race. Well, he got down to the other end, idled down there, got out, and said, "Let's do that again." All these Texans started gathering around us like, "Yeah, that was a foul start, we got to run it again." So, I said, "Keith, what are we going to do?" They scared the s—— out of me.

Mongoose was there, and he said, "Well, I guess we better run them because we can't beat them in a fight." So, we went up there to run them again. On the second run, they kept me hanging out on the starting line for a long time. You know, when you're in Texas, you do as the Texans do, you don't make your own rules. They make the rules. I was running low on fuel by the time they pulled into the lights, and when I dumped the clutch the front end went up in the air and I did this gigantic wheelstand. I had to shut it off and bring it back down.

Of course, he went on down no problem and beat me. I pulled in down at the end of the course, and I said, "Okay, you beat us. Now, let's do it again. You know I did a wheelstand, so let's do a two out of three." Payne reached down in his boot and he pulled out his knife. He said, "We ain't going to do nothing. We won the race, you gone get your ass back to California." Once we saw that knife, we thought it was best to load our s—— up and head home. That was an experience for a young up-and-coming drag racer.

Later, I became great friends with the car owner Vance Hunt. I mean, even back then, I wasn't pissed. I was scared, but I wasn't mad. I was blown away by how serious this was to them. I thought racing was everything to me, but I didn't know that it'd get to the point where a guy would pull a knife on me over a race. Through the years, I'd see Hunt at the reunions and stuff. I'd bring up that thing about him beating us, and he'd get red-faced about Payne pulling that knife out.

Setting Records with GBP

The GBP car was the most modern dragster of the time. It looks small by today's standards, but it was the top dog in the early 1960s. It had a 392 Chrysler engine running on nitro and was built and tuned by Keith Black. We won races like everyone else was standing still. I got my first taste of making big news when we set a record by running a 7.77-second pass at San Gabriel. That was a huge deal because until then, no one had even run into the 7s. Well, maybe a 7.90, but having those three numbers in a row, it was like dice or a Vegas slot machine, rolling three sevens in a row, 7-7-7. It was unheard of at the time, but we did it, and everybody knew we did it. It wasn't one of those hot clock numbers.

All through drag racing (well, in the early days anyway), there were tracks that would kind of juice up their clocks so that the cars would set records because that was good for attendance. People liked to see a fast run or what they thought was a fast run. That's why there are questions as to if the Greek, Chris Karamesines, ran a 200-mph run first or Don Garlits did. You know Garlits never believed that the Greek did it first, but I think the Greek did. So, let's just say that many of the clocks were in question around the country. However, with the GBP car at Irwindale, there was no question. The car just dominated, it was way ahead, and there were a lot of people there to see it.

That run, it was all Keith Black. It was one of those cool nights where the air conditions were just great. We used to like to wait until dark, when it got cool out. We didn't know about air density or anything, all we knew was that the engine liked it when it was cool. Keith had done a lot of work on the car,

> "I thought racing was everything to me, but I didn't know that it'd get to the point where a guy would pull a knife on me over a race."

I'm in the Greer, Black, Prudhomme car racing Ivo at San Gabriel Drag Strip. He'd moved on from Buicks to Chryslers by then. He's got a Zeuschel motor in his car; mine is Keith Black's.

especially to the clutch to get it to keep performing better and better. It felt good to me on that run, but all I had to go by was the seat of my pants. There were no computers or anything like that in the car. I could tell that it was on one hell of a run, but I couldn't tell how fast it was until I saw the guys come hauling ass down at the other end in Keith's Ranchero, blinking the lights on and off. That's how we knew if we'd done something good because the crew would come hauling in fast, blinking the headlights and honking the horn, and then you knew that you either won, set a record, or were low ET. That was a thrill.

Grown-Up Stuff

The first full year of racing with the GBP car, that was really my first grown-up time period. Lynn and I were married in 1963, and the funny thing is that it cost me a big race! During the NHRA nitro ban, some guys, like Garlits, would run their cars on gas and go race there, but I wasn't interested in that. For me, it was nitro or nothing. In 1963, the NHRA started running nitro at Pomona again, and Keith wanted to take the GBP car, but there was one big problem. Lynn and I were set to get married on the same weekend that they were going to run the race.

I was just sick about it. Not about getting married but missing that race. Keith, he was all, "Oh, no. Go get married. Do what you're doing." He wasn't like, "Well, can you change the date?" He didn't think that running the race was more important than my wedding day. They didn't give me any hassle about that at all. So, I missed the opportunity to run the Nationals then. I think it was worth it.

In 1964, Lynn and I bought a house. I couldn't have even imagined that possibility when I was growing up. I think we paid $26,000. It was a lot of money. We had $5,000 in the bank; it was all from racing, and we used that for a down payment. At the time, I think our apartment payment was a hundred and some bucks a month, and the house payments were almost $200 a month. It was considerably more, and we were like, "God, how are we ever going to do this? How are we going to ever make these payments?" Somehow we did, and it wasn't a breeze, but we did it and we did it with money from racing, which is pretty wild.

I remember being proud as punch at being able to own a home at that age. From painting cars and not having an education to buying a house in Granada Hills. I stopped by that house some years back, and this guy was working in the yard. I said, "This is really a nice place you got here." He said, "Thanks. Don Prudhomme used to live here." I swear to God. I thought it was the funniest thing. It was the coolest thing ever, someone was saying that to me. The guy didn't even know who I was.

A Bad Idea

In the fall of 1964, Zeuschel asked me if I wanted to try my hand at boat racing. He built racing engines for boats too, really fast boats. He was building an engine for a guy named Rene Andre, and they asked me to drive it. It was a blown gas hydro with a wooden hull—not fiberglass. It was before fiberglass. It was built by Hallett. I said, "S——, why not."

Well, I soon found out the reason why not. That was a real short experience. I drove it a couple times, then crashed it at Marine Stadium in Long

> "Lynn and I were married in 1963, and the funny thing is that it cost me a big race!"

Beach. Mickey Thompson pulled me out of the water. He was racing a boat too. I came up out of the water, and I was floating there thinking, "God, I'm still alive." And my helmet, I remember my helmet floating next to me. *Motherf——er.* I mean, it ripped my helmet off. It felt like it ripped every bone and muscle in my body. I had a life jacket on, thank God, because I wouldn't have been able to fight to stay up on top of the water. I was just floating there until the rescue boat came.

It was one of those times where the lights went out and I was sure I was dead. I mean that's how it feels. Then all of the sudden, the lights come back on, and you go, "Oh. Blue sky. Thank God. Whatever's wrong with me I can fix. I'm alive." They pulled me out of the water and put me on a stretcher. Mickey Thompson came running over, "You gonna be all right? Gonna be all right till I get you to the hospital?" And he took his wallet out and sort of shoved it into my armpit and said, "Here. There's plenty of money in there. Whatever you need." He didn't know if I had any money or anything. I think that fortunately, I didn't need it. All I needed to do was get some rest because it didn't break anything; it just tore muscles and everything hurt. Just f——ed me up for a while.

Keith was really pissed at me. That was one of the few times we had a falling out. He thought that I shouldn't have put my life in danger driving for his competition, driving for another engine builder. It wasn't the smartest thing for me to do at all. I mean, it was stupid, actually. But when you're young, you'll just jump in anything. And it was a huge mistake.

Rene ended up driving it himself after that and flipped it again. When the boat came down, it hit him in the shoulder, and he had a dead arm from then on. He was paralyzed on one side. I think he had to have it amputated later on. That could have been me. I didn't go around boats after that. I didn't want anything to do with them.

"I remember my helmet floating next to me . . . I mean, it ripped my helmet off."

Oh sure, it looks fine here.

Looks fast.

And then . . .

Up.

And Over.

I was so stunned that I couldn't even move.

They fished me out and sent me to the hospital. That was my last boat race.

You can't appreciate how pretty the Hawaiian car was unless you see it in color with that great paint job and the wood panel on the side.

The Hawaiian

Another example of how some points in my life seemed to transition perfectly (through nothing that I did or at least nothing that I knew I did) was my luck in meeting Roland Leong. It was in Hawaii in 1963. Roland had a dragster with a Keith Black engine. Keith built the engines in Los Angeles and shipped them over there.

There was a guy there, Jimmy Pflueger, who owned a dealership on one of the islands. He had just opened a drag strip, so he wanted to promote it. He said, "How can we get Keith Black and the dragster over here?" They worked out a deal. I wasn't involved in the finances, but somehow they shipped the dragster to Hawaii. Then, they flew me and Lynn over too. It was a long flight, and a big deal, and I didn't give a s—— about going to Hawaii. All I cared about was getting out to the drag strip.

Roland picked me up and showed me around. We went to dinner with his mom and his family. He was younger than me, maybe 18 years old. The next day, he took me out with him, and we hung out all day. We went to Jimmy Pflueger's car dealership, I got to meet his buddies, and it was a good vibe. A lot of them thought that I was Hawaiian. It wasn't unusual to have different skin tones there. They all asked Roland, "Is he your brother? Hey brother. Hey brother." That's what they called another Hawaiian. I liked that part, but again, I really only ever thought about racing.

There I was in Hawaii, and I didn't learn to surf or anything, but Roland was like that too. We were total gearheads. All we talked about was drag racing. We'd go over to a buddy's house or something and other people talked about music, girls, or food, but we were just ate up with drag races and drag cars.

Speaking of food, I was pretty unsophisticated, so I didn't have any experience with the kind of food that they eat in Hawaii: raw fish and sushi. Now I love it. I remember we went to the car dealership, and they had a food truck (they call it a roach coach there). I looked inside and had no idea what to do with the options. Roland said, "Come on, Vipe [he called me Vipe for Viper]. I'll show you this." We ate some rice balls rolled up with fish and eel. He had to show me how to eat it, and he got a kick out of that.

I was over there about a week, racing and seeing the island. Roland came to the mainland right after that, which was great because I didn't know if I'd ever see him again after we left Hawaii. Then, he showed up at Keith Black's back in Los Angeles. He came walking in, "Hey man, what's up? I'm over here. I'm building a car." He'd built a car just like the Greer–Black car.

When I look at our friendship now (and we are still so close to this day), I wonder if some of what connected us was that he was unusual in the scene, being Asian. Roland looked different, and I looked different, and we both kind of bonded over that a little bit. He doesn't talk about it much, but a lot of people were prejudiced against the Japanese and Chinese. There were

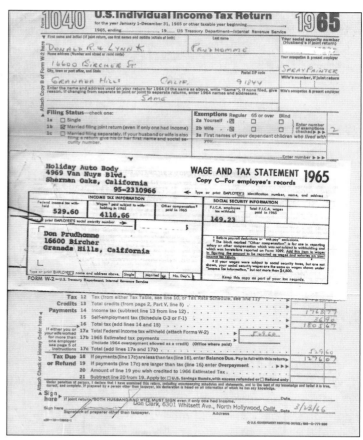

Top Left: *Our tax paperwork from 1965 shows $9,490.05 in cash from racing with Roland in the* Hawaiian.

Top Right: *So, in 1965, I made $4,000 working at Holiday Auto Body and $9,000 running the car. Well, you can guess which I did the next year.*

things happening in Vietnam, and people in Los Angeles didn't really distinguish where someone was from, they just knew they were Asian. I remember when he looked for an apartment, he wanted to move where there were other Asian families, which I didn't understand at the time, but I do now. Between that and the shared car interests, we were strongly connected. He was like a little brother to me.

What ended up happening is that he built a dragster, and we took it to Lions Drag Strip for his first runs. I buckled Roland in. I didn't know that he couldn't drive the thing! He'd been racing a dragster in Hawaii but not a nitro car. I had such good luck with the cars I'd been driving that I thought everybody could do it. He got in it and took off going down the track, but all of the sudden, the car goes right off the track.

There was a berm on the side at Lions. He got off the track and went up over the railroad tracks. He ended up right up on the train tracks, f——ed the car all up. I rushed down there and was the first one to him. He looked up at me and said, "Vipe, what happened?" I said, "I don't know. You tell me." I wasn't laughing. I was scared for him. I thought he was hurt. He didn't know what happened. Nothing, he just crashed the f——ing thing.

When we got back to the shop. Keith called him into the office and said, "Hey, I'll build your cars for you, but I don't want you to drive." He didn't want someone to get killed in his car, but also, and I didn't know this yet, he and Greer were talking about hanging up the Greer-Black car. Greer was running out of money, or at least he wanted to spend it in smarter places. Keith told Roland, "You should get Don to drive it." Roland asked me to drive it, and I said, "Hell yeah, I'll drive it. You bet." And that's how I ended up working for Roland on the *Hawaiian*.

That was a bitchin'-ass car, just a haul-ass car. It was beyond. And Roland . . . what really made it so special is that he kept pushing for more, more, more. He paid attention to the engine way more than I did. He saw that Ted Gotelli had come out with port injectors on his car, where the port nozzles are in the manifold as well as in the injector. Before that, they were only in the injector. And they went out and set a top speed that was unthinkable. We were running 202, 203; they ran 212. We were like, "Motherf——er. What happened?"

Roland ordered the stuff from Enderle and told Keith he wanted to run it. And that was bold because Keith Black was really funny about letting us

That jacket was from Lions. In those days, if you set a record, you'd get an embroidered jacket with the track name on the back and your record. The goal was to get one from all the local tracks.

People think this is a burnout, but this is what they looked like on a run. We didn't do burnouts back then; we just got up the starting line, whacked the throttle, popped the clutch, and off you'd go.

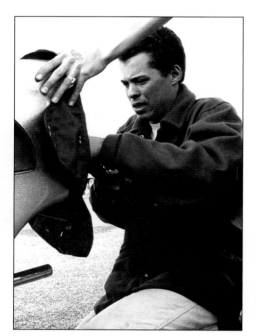

Packing the parachute on the Hawaiian. From day one, most drivers packed their own chutes. I didn't know of anyone who didn't pack their own. It was like jumping out of an airplane; you want to make sure it opens.

Roland is shown in 1965. We worked on the ground, just in the dirt or, if we were lucky, on a plywood board. Ro's pants and hands are all dirty. He'd tell you it's because he did all the work and I just sat in the car.

tell him what parts to put on it. But when we put them on there, the car immediately ran faster and quicker. Really, everything with the *Hawaiian* was good right from the start. I mean, we won the Pomona Winternationals right off the bat and several other local races at Lions and up and down the West Coast. That summer we went on tour.

Noah's Ark

We won a Ford truck and camper in Pomona, and we decided to use it as our tow rig. The first thing we did was tear the bathroom out of it because it wasn't like either of us was going to clean it. What we should have done was put a bigger fuel tank in it. It had a little bitty tank. The thing got like 5 miles to the gallon or something. It was also a huge pain to turn it around on those small tracks.

Back then, we still push-started the cars, and a lot of time there wasn't much room to maneuver. We needed a way to haul the car, and now we were big shots, so we weren't going to use a little open lollipop trailer like back in the Ivo days. I had a neighbor who did woodworking as a hobby. We didn't know anything about building an enclosed trailer because nobody had them. He built it in my driveway, and the whole thing was wood. It was so f——ing heavy. It was like Noah's ark. If the thing ever went in the water it would float, but we towed it all around the country. The camper and this huge overloaded trailer was an evil combination on the road and at the tracks.

By the time we got to Chicago, Roland sold the Ford and bought this bitchin' Dodge station wagon with wood paneling on it. It looked great. The *Hawaiian*, it fit the image. The dragster had a little strip of the same wood on the side with "The Hawaiian" written on it, where the vents were, back by the parachutes. It was very tastefully done. All of Roland's stuff was really nice. He did the design and everything, and it looked great.

On the Road Again in 1965

It was a totally different experience being on the road with Roland than it was with Ivo. Roland and I were more alike. We ate and cared about the same stuff. We talked about the car constantly. What does it need? How can

Look at Roland smoking and checking the magneto cap. Sometimes the engines would crack the cap, so he's probably looking for that. Or maybe he just was looking for an ashtray.

We won this camper and immediately tore the bathroom out so neither of us had to clean it.

we make it go faster? What do you think of this? What do you think of that? We pretty well had it figured out by the time we got to where we were going.

We had this crazy schedule: racing, driving all night to the next track, and popping pills to stay awake. The idea was that one guy was supposed to stay awake while the other guy gets some rest, but with us, I'd pop a pill, and then Roland would pop a pill to talk to me to keep me awake. So that means we're both going down the road chewing our tongues. But that's what we did to get around, just the two of us.

"The Reverend Mr. Black"

We'd talk a lot about Keith. Black said this or that. This trip, being on the road without Keith Black, that was a big deal for us. A lot of people thought we'd never make it work without him, and they weren't wrong to think that. We had almost no experience running the car all on our own. We'd get to a track or a hotel and call Keith, tell him what we knew about the track, and he'd tell us what to do. Roland and I were really tight with Keith, but it wasn't like the way we were friends with each other. We were kids. Keith was a proper grown-up; he had a shop and business plan. He wasn't what you'd call "one of the guys."

Ed Pink, a rival engine builder, would stay late, shoot dice, and gamble with all the boys, but that would be the furthest thing from Keith's mind. I don't remember him doing anything like that. His dad was a preacher, and so we used to call Keith "The Reverend Mr. Black." He was a real clean-cut guy. He didn't like our off-colored jokes. He wasn't that kind of hot rodder. We were pretty wild, and he used to kind of get on us about that. We thought he was kind of square.

One Saturday night at Lions Drag Strip, we broke something and had to go back to his shop, which was down the road. I think we had to rehone a block or something, which meant taking the engine out of the car. We put it all together, and he worked until the wee hours with us. And the next day,

"We talked about the car constantly. What does it need? How can we make it go faster?"

Saturday night at Lions Drag Strip with Keith Black, Roland, and me.

which was just hours away, we had the car all loaded up and ready to go back to Lions Drag Strip for the Sunday race, and Keith didn't show up at the track. We were really pissed.

I remember being upset at him, "What's the matter? Why aren't you here?" Well, I forgot that he was older than me; he was tired. But I just couldn't imagine someone being too tired to go to the racetrack. It was just unheard of. Later I understood. Oh my God, later I understood.

Despite him not wanting to party with us, Roland and I really respected Keith. In those early days, if the car was running good or bad, we didn't really know why. By then, we had an idea of what made a good chassis, how it had to flex right to put the power down. Keith was one of the first to figure that out. He'd take a hacksaw and cut out some of the uprights in a frame and put in different uprights, you know, where the car would flex more.

He also was one of the first guys to figure out that you didn't need to blow away the tires to go fast. Keith understood the way the cars worked, and he took care of his engines. In fact, he got pretty mad at us when we blew stuff up. What can I say? Roland wanted the records, and I wanted the wins. When I think back on it, he was really patient with us. We'd call him from the road with a report, and we didn't know to read the air or the track. No one was really doing it. So, if all of the sudden the car had set some record, going faster than it had ever gone before and Keith asked, "Do you know why?" we wouldn't be able to tell him. We'd say, "No. It just did it." We had to learn all that stuff.

Ivo at Islip

We won a lot during that trip. Not every race, but we won more than we lost. There is one loss that still kind of irritates me, maybe because Ivo tells the story so often. It was when we raced him in New York. It was at Islip Speedway, which was just a tiny eighth-mile strip. Well, Ivo told me that the top end of the track was pretty dangerous, and it would be safer if we just agreed as to who would win the two-out-of-three match race, and of course that he should be the winner. Since he set up the match, I agreed. However, even at the time it sort of bugged me. Still, I needed the money.

So, I won the first round, and he reminded me that I needed to throw the second, which I did. Well, he hadn't told his crew, and they made a big deal of it. It pissed me off, so I was like, "Screw this deal." I was going to go for it. What I didn't know is that he'd talked to the starter, so he knew that the lights were going to go down the second we pulled in to stage. As a result, he left on me and won. I was furious. I would have decked him for sure if his crew guy Tarzan hadn't been such a big dude. There was a reason Ivo hired such a tough guy to work for him! Ivo could just get under my skin that way. It's not that I ever liked to lose, but I really hated losing to him.

The U.S. Nationals

By the time we got to the U.S. Nationals in Indianapolis at the end of the summer, we had learned a lot about the car, but it was still a relief to have Keith Black come out and join us for the race. We'd run the car hard all summer, and while we had done basic maintenance, we hadn't ever taken the thing all apart or really changed much about the tune. Keith came in and man, the car was good right out of the gate.

"I would have decked him for sure if his crew guy Tarzan hadn't been such a big dude."

Indy. I think Roland and I went through a carton of cigarettes waiting for the call to the finals.

I hadn't been to the U.S. Nationals before Roland and I went in 1965. It was bigger than the Winternationals. We were shocked at how many people were there. The car was just starting to get a following because it had won the Winternationals and people were excited to see "The *Hawaiian*. A California Car." We had an advantage coming from California, not only because we had Keith Black, but because the car just looked so good. We had chrome with candy-apple, metal-flake, blue paint. The car alone would blow their minds just by how pretty it was.

The place was packed with people. It was more racers than I'd ever seen. I didn't know there were that many dragsters in the country. I can't even remember all the people we raced. They had more than 50 cars entered, and you had to go through all those cars within two days. We had beaten everyone, and we came up to the final round on Sunday. However, whoever won Sunday didn't win the race yet because there was still more racing on Monday (Labor Day).

The finals were really on Monday, but we got to sit out that day and then we'd race the winner of Monday's race. There wasn't much to it except for waiting around all day to make one run that night. We were ready to crawl the walls. We'd go up to the starting line and watch these different guys run. And I thought, "Oh Christ, I sure hope the s——doesn't come down to Ivo and us again." I was really tired of looking at him by then, and I might have still been a bit hot about that falling out at Islip Speedway. I didn't know if I'd punch him out or he'd beat me or what, but of course it came down to Ivo and ourselves on Monday, and we beat him in the finals. So, that was a

From left to right: Keith Black, Kenny Black, Wes Hanson (a friend of Keith's who volunteered on the car for the fun of it), Roland Leong, me, Miss National, Dick Day of Hot Rod magazine, and Roland's mom, Teddy. Teddy was a big supporter of us.

pretty satisfying win.

We ended up in all the papers. I should mention here that Roland's mother was a big part of our team. Not only with money, she really supported us in every way. Like at the Winternationals, she had Hawaiian leis already made up. For some reason or another, she knew that we were going to win the race. In the winner's circle, she started putting them on all of us. They were these bitchin' flowers. How in the hell did she know we would win? That would always puzzle me, but she told me, "This is the Year of the Snake." And sure enough, 1965 was the Chinese Year of the Snake. I used to think that she was even more into the racing than Roland was. She even hired a guy who worked for the NHRA, Dick Wells, and he sent out press releases. We received a lot of press coverage from Indy, but I didn't know why until much later. I thought it was just the performance of the car.

Homeward Bound

On the way home after the U.S. Nationals win, I did all the driving. Part of the deal with Roland was that I would never let him tow. After watching him drive the car, there was no f——ing way that I was going to let him tow the trailer. The trailer had really evil handling. But around Oklahoma I finally said, "I can't drive anymore." I mean, we'd already run out of popping pills. I was exhausted. I said, "You're going to have to drive this thing." And he said, "Don't worry Vipe. I can handle it." And I said, "Okay, man. Just point it straight down the road

At the winner's circle of the 1965 U.S. Nationals at Indy. I look nervous. I got better at trophy pictures as we went on. I hadn't had a lot of practice yet at this point.

It was about time I got to kiss the trophy girl! We won that Barracuda but sold it back for money to get home. Roland's mom had these Hawaiian leis ready for us. She always knew somehow when we would win. It was the Chinese Year of the Snake, she said, and you know, I always did well in the Year of the Snake.

MEMORIES FROM ROLAND LEONG

Me and Roland at Indy. I remember those Goodyear jackets—it was such a thrill to get something like that, a jacket with the company logo. It felt like the big time.

After I first met Snake in Hawaii, I figured that we'd run across each other again. After my one and only Top Fuel run at Long Beach in 1964, I called my mom and told her what happened. I was already married, and I already had my daughter (even though I think I had just turned 20 at the time). My mom told me, "Well, you know, you're married and got a kid, so you better think about what you're doing."

So, I think between that and Keith Black sitting me down, it made sense to let Prudhomme drive it. A lot of times, I tell people we were young and dumb—we did things by instinct, whatever you feel at the time.

The *Hawaiian* team was me, Snake, and Keith Black. Black was the one who knew what he was doing, but his wife only let him go to the races one day per weekend. So, if he raced Saturday night at Long Beach, he couldn't do Sunday at Pomona. For me and Snake, if you told us we could race down the 101 freeway at midnight, we'd

have ridden down there. So, Prudhomme and I would often be on our own without Keith, which often meant we'd end up hurting some pistons. It was kind of a joke with Black that when we would unload the car back at the shop after the weekend, I'd put a towel over it. If we didn't win, I'd put the Keith Black cover on it, but if we won, I just left it as Roland Leong's *Hawaiian*.

Melting Pot

Snake and I were standouts at the track. My grandparents were from China. My mom was half-Hawaiian and half-Chinese, and my father was Chinese. So, actually I'm three-quarters Chinese and one-quarter Hawaiian. I was born and raised in Hawaii, where there weren't very many White people. Hawaii's a melting pot with many different nationalities.

When I first came up to the mainland, even before I met Snake, I worked at this company down by San Diego that built race car chassis. I noticed that I was the only one different down there. Coming from Hawaii, I spoke English, but it was kind of a different type. They call it pidgin English. I never realized that a lot of people didn't understand how we talked. I felt different. After a while, you kind of get used to it.

When Snake and I went on the road, I don't know how he felt, but going to the Midwest, East, South, and other places where we raced, there weren't many people who looked like us. I was even a little self-conscious because I felt that we stood out when we went in restaurants and people kind of stared at us, but we never had a problem.

On the Road with the Snake

When we went on tour, the first race we entered was against a jet car. I'd never been around a jet car before. I remember pulling up there, and I wouldn't get out of the push car because this thing was blowing smoke and making this racket (whistling). I never heard anything like that before. I pulled up next to Snake with the car, and I remember waving him in toward the start line but not getting out of the car.

One time, we were racing in a place called Islip, near New York. We stayed in Queens, and we'd do tourist things during the day, such as the Empire State Building and the Statue of Liberty. Lynn was with us, and we went to the World's Fair. I know Don says he didn't do anything but race, but we did explore the towns a little.

When we were in Chicago, we thought we'd go see a movie, and we took the train. You know how Chicago is, all you think of are gangsters and guys with guitar cases. It was daylight when we went, and when we came back it was nighttime, maybe 9 or 10 p.m. We got off the train and couldn't find our car. Unbeknownst to us, there were two tracks. We parked our car at the southern track, and when we came back, we got in the wrong train and came back on the northern track. We thought the car had been stolen.

Helping Out a Friend

In 1972 (I think it was), my whole rig was stolen. When Prudhomme found out, he said, "Come up to the shop." In those days, we had no insurance. I went to his shop, and he said, "Well, go upstairs. There's a lot of stuff." There was a lot of stuff, good stuff that I could use. I said, "Well, how much? I want to buy this. How much do you want?" He said, "It's yours." He gave it to me.

Along the way, at different times, we were involved with our own deals, so maybe we weren't close at those times. Still, we'd always help each other. For example, in the 1990s, every few months, he'd call me and ask questions. Finally, he called to say, "Come to the Virginia and race with me." He asked me if I wanted to be on the team. I said, "Well, you and I have been friends for a long time,

and if it's going to affect our friendship, then I don't want to do it."

Fired and Fired Again!

We kind of shook hands on it, and I started running the car. My claim to fame is getting Ron Capps his first Funny Car win. When I took the car over, we were 15th in points, I think. When the year was up, we were up at number 5. I think we won a couple of races that year. Then, the next year in 1998, I ended up number 2 in the points. The 1999 season started, and he wanted to go in a different direction. I didn't agree, but he's the boss, right? So, I started in, and I knew that anytime you changed your combination there would be a learning curve. No one knows how long that can be. I guess the learning curve was too steep, so he fired me. Then, he hired me back. However, then Capps left, so he fired me again. If something happens nowadays where someone is on me, I say, "Hey, you can't hurt my feelings. I got fired by the best twice."

I think that all of us (at different times) have some luck, or people might think they have luck. But I've come to the conclusion that you make your own luck. I think Don Prudhomme was good at choosing the right people at the right time, and I still like to say to him, "Sucker, you're lucky I wasn't s—— at driving, otherwise you wouldn't be where you are."

here, and just stay in the slow lane. You don't have to pass anyone." That's another thing I learned from Ivo.

I told Roland, "You got to really be careful when the truck goes past us, this thing is going to move around, and you've got to stay with it." And he said, "Okay, Vipe. Don't worry." So, I finally get to sleep. He's driving down the road and I wake up and say, "How we doing?" He says, "Vipe, I got a handle on this thing now." Just when he said that, we were passing a truck and he lost control of it. The thing started whipping back and forth. It spun out in the middle of the highway.

Fortunately, no one hit us. The trailer broke loose from the car, the oil cans flew, and it dented the body of the wagon. It just screwed everything up, and we're lucky that we weren't killed. We limped into Jimmy Nix's shop in Tulsa, Oklahoma, and welded the trailer up enough to get the thing home. Then, Roland had a new, really nice trailer built.

I'm telling you, towing down the highway was more dangerous than running at the drag strip.

B&M

After the season with the *Hawaiian*, I was feeling pretty darn good. Maybe too good. I had gone from making $4,000 a year painting cars to making almost $9,500

That's at Bakersfield. I always look to see who's in the background, and the guy standing back is Pat Foster. He was a good driver and an unbelievable car builder.

"Keith told me, 'You know, drivers are like spark plugs. You screw one in and screw one out."

for racing. For racing! Something I that would have done for free—heck, something that I would have paid to do. I was feeling invincible. So, the universe maybe looked at me and said, "Oh yeah, big shot? Let's see how good you really are."

I was neighbors with Bob Spar in Granada Hills. He started B&M, the transmission company. We spent a lot of time together, and I really like the guy. He kept saying that I should run their car. Kenny Safford was driving at the time, and they were doing okay, but I thought I could do a lot better with it because, hey, I'm the great Don Prudhomme, right? I'm thinking I'm pretty f——ing good, so I figured I'd give it a try.

When I quit the *Hawaiian*, it really pissed off Keith Black. He was even more mad at me than Roland was to race with somebody else in a car with a Zeuschel engine. Keith told me, "You know, drivers are like spark plugs. You screw one in and screw one out." Obviously, I'm the one who got screwed out because the *Hawaiian* did great without me.

Reality Check

Roland went out the next year with Mike Snively. They won everything, and of course the first guy who called me was Ivo, telling me, "You screwed up. You know, they just won the Winter Nationals." I was destroyed when that happened. I'd gotten the B&M car, and we ran Pomona. I don't know where we went out, but we didn't win. They won whether or not I was in that car, and I really took it hard.

I went to Palm Springs—not that I'm a Palm Springs kind of guy. I just had to get away because my phone was ringing, f——ing Ivo was laughing at me, and I was gutted. I went to Palm Springs for the weekend and got a little hotel room with Lynn, nothing fancy. I found myself doing that more and more as the years went on. Sometimes you just need to get away and think, and Lynn was always able to help me get my head around things.

I thought about everything and figured there was only one thing I could do: brush myself off and get going again. I decided to build it up again, and that's what we did. We took the car and went on tour with it. It ended up being a good car, but man, there was a heck of a learning curve.

I went from the Greer-Black-Prudhomme car, which was really successful, to the *Hawaiian*, another very successful car. Then, I went to this B&M car, and it was a reality check. I've often said that it was the worst thing that ever happened to me, but really it was one of the best things that ever happened to me because I learned to pick myself up, dust myself off, go back to work, and overcome.

If I had stayed with Roland and won another year there, I might have just been a hired driver my whole life. Plenty of other guys were. Having to run this car all on my own made me learn a lot that I'd let other people handle up to that point. I was just working my way up. The Greek helped me a lot that year. He helped me with the engine. I didn't know s—— about rebuilding an engine, and he took the time to teach me.

Those days, I didn't even think about owning my own car. I didn't want anything to do with it. I cut a deal with Bob Spar for the *Torkmaster*. The deal was that I would take the car, put my name on it, and take it on tour to match race it. My name was good enough where people would book me. What I failed to realize was that there would be wear and tear on the car as I ran it. The year before, I was with Roland, and we didn't hurt anything. I think we broke one lifter. The car just ran perfectly all the time.

The deal with the B&M car was that when it came back home, it had to be in the same condition as when it left. Well, when you're on the road, it's like returning a NASCAR car after a race. There's going to be dents in it. So, all the money that I made on the road mostly went back to the Spars to fix the car back up again. We didn't have any hard feelings or anything. Well, maybe it was a little sour for a moment while we were trying to negotiate, but it was an important experience. On tour that year was Lynn, myself, and a guy named Donnie Nesland. The three of us took that car on the road behind a borrowed Dodge station wagon and raced it for a whole summer.

This was the first time that Lynn was on the road with me for the entire trip. When we had the *Hawaiian*, she'd come East and go to the races with us a lot but nothing like this. This deal, she had to push-start me. She drove the push truck and helped me tow it. Absolutely. She was staying in these motels

"On the road, you're just looking for something with a vacancy sign and a parking lot big enough to fit the trailer."

The B&M car in 1966. When we left California to go on tour, the car was silver, but it took a beating on the road. By the time we got to Chicago, a guy offered to paint it, and he did this candy-apple red. Man, I thought we had all the trick stuff back in California, but then this guy lays down this candy paint job, and I realized there were great hot rodders everywhere.

I liked this artwork; it was very hip. Anytime you were mentioned in print it was cool, and being on the cover was even cooler.

Smoke all the way down the track in the B&M Torkmaster.

On the road in 1966. We didn't have a set crew, just volunteers at each track. The car was so light that we'd just pick it up to work on it. Lynn is at the back, holding the brake so it didn't roll away.

with us, motels you've never heard of before. Believe me, there were no Holiday Inns. It was nothing that fancy. We were looking at maybe $10-a-night hotels. On the road, you're just looking for something with a vacancy sign and a parking lot big enough to fit the trailer.

UDRA National Championship

I think the biggest race that I won that year was in Union Grove, Wisconsin. It was a three-day race: Friday, Saturday, and Sunday. It was $1,000 each day for the winner, and if you won all three you received a $2,000 bonus. So man, $5,000—that's a lot of money!

We beat Garlits in the final. It was so dark at the top end that you couldn't see anything past the finish line. There were no lights, and sometimes spectators would turn on their headlights in their car to shine on the track, but once you were past them, it was just pitch darkness. So, we're coasting along in the dark, and I bumped into Garlits and got him off track. Boy, he was so mad, like I did it on purpose. He was back in the pits yelling that I tried to kill him.

The Ford Years

I first saw a Ford SOHC engine in 1966. Lou Baney was running the Brand Ford car with Tom McEwen as the driver. I wasn't very impressed with it. It was a heavy car, and I was in the B&M car kind of getting the hang of things by that point. But then Don Long said that he'd build them a new chassis to create a lighter car, and that caught my attention. At the same time, B&M was losing interest in the *Torkmaster* car. Shortly after we left town, the company decided to quit making the Torkmaster convertors, and that's what the car was all about—promoting the B&M Torkmaster.

I remember seeing the *Brand Ford Special* run a few times, but it didn't run any better or even as good as a 392 Hemi, which was the engine of choice at the time. The Ford Cammer, although it was pretty looking, was a big and heavy thing, and the car that Tom was driving was heavy and not really doing much. Then, I received a call from Ed Pink. He knew me because I had driven a dragster for him one weekend when he needed someone in the seat for Bakersfield or maybe Fremont. I think we just did so-so. It was no Greer–Black car, I can tell you.

In those days, f——, I'd drive anything. Just pull up in front of the house. "You want to drive her?" "I'm here. Let's go." Anyhow, I must have done well enough because Pink called me and said that he and Baney were building a new car, and he wanted to see if I'd drive it.

I went over to the shop, and Lou Baney was there. Baney's dragster was a beautiful car—just state of the art with aluminum heads, built so light. They were telling me that McEwen wasn't going to drive the car anymore and that I could drive it. It was as simple as that. No contracts. No "We'll pay you this" or "Pay you that." No one was paid to drive a car back in those days that I

In 1967, I became a Ford guy. Lou Baney redid his Ford SOHC dragster, and it was a heck of a car. I think this is at Long Beach. We would move the car around ourselves. There were no crew guys. We were the crew: owner, and driver.

The Baney gang in 1967: Jerry Bivens, Bill Pink (Ed Pink's kid), Janet Bivens, Frankie Baney, Lou Baney, and me. Janet Bivens was Baney's daughter, so it was really a family affair.

I don't know what the occasion was for us all to be sitting around at Riverside. It's either early in the morning or after the race was over. There wasn't a lot of downtime during the day. Among those pictured are Kelly Brown, Janet Bivens, me, Jerry Bivens, Billy Bones, Tom McEwen, and Ed Donovan.

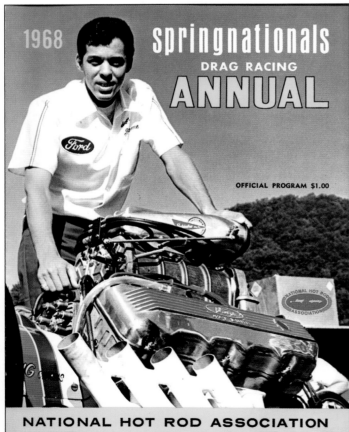

This was my first uniform shirt. Before that, it was T-shirts only. This shirt was originally a bowling shirt, ordered with our names and colors. This is one of my very favorite photos. (Photo Courtesy National Hot Rod Association/NHRA National Dragster)

Lynn, right, is talking to Carolyn Milani in 1967. Carolyn was married to Denny Milani, who was killed in a car up in Fremont in 1965. Back then, the track folks were like family, so she still came to the races even after his death.

Lynn and her girlfriends at the track. Lynn was good friends with Lou Baney's daughters, who are on the right.

know of. They'd give you a percentage of winnings and that was it.

I don't recall McEwen being upset about it at all. He already had another ride. We didn't even hardly talk about it. It isn't like he said, "Hey, you f——er, you stole my ride." I was so amazed that it didn't interfere with our friendship because I don't think I would have been too happy if I was driving a car and I got booted out for another driver. I'm sure that I would have been quite pissed, but he wasn't. He was like, "Hey, if it's good for Baney, good for Pink, and good for you, go after it. Go do it." I mean, he still wanted to beat us with these other cars, but it really cinched our relationship. We would be in the Winner's Circle with that car and he'd come hang around. Or he'd go in the Winner's Circle with us and take a picture. So, in a weird way, it made us better friends.

In 1967, we won Bristol with the car. It was the first dragster to run in the six-second bracket, and we went three six-second runs in a row with the car. We ended up beating Pete Robinson, who also had a Ford Cammer in his car.

Wally Parks

It seems odd to have gone this long without really talking about Wally Parks. Wally started the National Hot Rod Association (NHRA). He was to the NHRA what Bill France was to NASCAR. He was a big deal. I met him around the time of the Winternationals win with Roland in 1965. We took pictures together by the starting line, but I was fairly shy. It wasn't like I'd walk up to him and say, "Oh, Mr. Parks, thanks for putting this race on for us." I never did anything like that. I was just a quiet guy.

When I really got to know him was when I was driving for Lou Baney because Baney and Wally Parks had history together. Good history. Baney, Parks, and guys like Pete Petersen, who started *Hot Rod* magazine, all raced each other. I mean, they were running cars back in the 1950s. They all raced Bonneville, including Ed Pink. Wally Parks was land speed racing before the war. These guys were not just in it for a business or a paycheck; they all had racing backgrounds.

I think it was in Bristol, Tennessee, where the Summer Nationals were

Wally Parks hands over the keys to a brand-new Plymouth Barracuda after Roland and I won the 1965 U.S. Nationals. That's Roland's mom, Teddy, next to Wally. I got to know Wally better in the late 1960s, and he took on a father figure role in my life. He was proud of my wins and supportive during my losses. (Photo Courtesy National Hot Rod Association/NHRA National Dragster)

I feel really lucky that I had such a good relationship with Wally and Barbara Parks. We would even hang out outside the track. This photo was from a rodeo in Anaheim, California.

held that Baney said he was going to a party and I should come with. It was in a motel someplace, and I walked in this room and there's Barbara Parks, Wally Parks, and the who's who of drag racing. Barbara Parks put her arm around me, and I was just blown away. "Holy Toledo. Damn! This is a lot of woman here, you know what I mean?" I mean that respectfully. She was amazing, and she just made me really feel at home. Then, Wally started talking to me. I took a real liking to Wally, and it seemed that he took a liking to me. And that's how our friendship started. We didn't always agree, especially later on, but I never really fought with him like Garlits and some of the others did.

Super Snake

I met Carroll Shelby around 1962, long before I was driving the Ford-powered dragster. Everyone knows that Shelby was the man, just cool as s——. Shelby was a Goodyear distributor for drag tires. He ran the Goodyear Tires store down by El Segundo or Venice. He had a couple of different shops over the years, and I used to go down there to get slicks mounted.

One time, I was there and this Lincoln Continental came pulling up. There weren't a whole lot of people who had Lincoln Continentals back then, so when this fancy car rolled in, I looked up. I'd never met Shelby, but I'd seen pictures of him, and that's who was behind the wheel. For some reason, he gave me one of those come-on-over-type nods, so I put down my wrench and walked over.

He was a good-looking guy, and he had this good-looking girl sitting next to him. One of his henchmen was in there too. So, picture the three of them sitting in the front seat, and she's got a short little skirt on and a can of beer between her legs. I thought that was the coolest f——ing thing. I can tell you from that day forward, Shelby was who I wanted to be. I wanted to be just like that. I thought he was cool as hell.

Getting back to 1968, we were running the car with Lou Baney and Ford. The word came down from Lou that we should talk to Carroll Shelby. Carroll was getting into aftermarket parts for his Mustangs, and Baney thought he might be a good partner for the dragster. Lou told me, "Hey, we got a meeting with Carroll Shelby and Bill Doner." I was nervous as hell. I hadn't really done any business like that, where you're looking for sponsorship and had to make a good impression in a boardroom.

During the meeting, Lou was doing most of the talking, but Carroll was a pro; it wasn't his first business meeting. Halfway through, he got up and left the room. I mean, he just excused himself and went in the other room. I thought it was so rude and that it meant we didn't have a chance. Later on, when I got to know Shelby and Doner really well, Doner told us that he was

Signing the contract with Carroll Shelby for sponsorship of the **Super Snake** *in 1968. (Photo Courtesy National Hot Rod Association/NHRA National Dragster)*

This photo was in Lou Baney's garage. We kept the dragster and trailer there. Ed Pink did most of the engine work on the Super Snake. It was a complicated engine.

In the Shelby Super Snake. It looks like I might have been left on by whoever's in the right lane, but I'm going to say it's just the angle of the photo.

just jacking with us. That's the way he was, trying to get the price down. It worked too. I think he got his price. We worked together a few times after that and stayed friends until the day he passed away.

Meeting the Greats: Mario, A. J., and Gurney

Like it wasn't enough of a thrill to be working with Carroll Shelby, another thing that happened through the Ford partnership was meeting sponsored drivers from other motorsports. After they'd won Le Mans a couple times, I met A. J. Foyt, Mario Andretti, and Dan Gurney. There was some sort of Ford preview or media event in Las Vegas, and someone arranged for us to take pictures together.

Lou Baney was really the catalyst for the whole thing. He was the guy who met with the Ford people. He had a Ford dealership. He had a lot of pull, so when he said to me that we were going to Las Vegas to do something for Ford, I just said "Okay. Let's go." We had some Ford polo shirts made. Up until then we were really just wearing T-shirts. Those uniform shirts, they were actually bowling shirts with a little red stripe and the Ford logo. We all got them after that.

At the shoot, I knew who Foyt was, but I didn't know much about Gurney. I really didn't know anything about Mario because he had not won the Indy 500 yet—that wasn't until 1969. Back then, if someone was winning on small tracks, that wouldn't be nationally known. It wasn't on television. So, I knew the other guys a little, but I met Mario from that shoot. I liked him a lot, and after I met those guys, I became a complete open-wheel nut. I wanted to know everything I could about open-wheel racing, IndyCars, and Formula 1 (F1) cars.

Every once in a while, I'd have a weekend off or I'd take a Thursday off to go down to Riverside. In this case, I went to Ontario Motor Speedway to see what the open-wheel guys were doing. I stayed in touch with A. J. Foyt after meeting him during the Ford years. Here we are in the mid-1970s. He'd often invite me into the pits and show me around the car. Those Indy cars made me nervous; there wasn't much protection around the driver. They were just sitting there in a little tub surrounded by fuel tanks. We had more roll bar around us in the dragsters and Funny Cars.

I may have made an impression on Andretti too. Later in 1969, I was in Indy (not for the 500, before that) right after he had crashed and gotten burned. I went by his garage, and I was standing behind the ropes because those were the days of the old garages at the speedway. People stood outside, the garage doors were open, and there was no air-conditioning or anything. There was a crowd of people, and I was just part of the crowd. Andretti was on the payphone, but he saw me and motioned me in. I thought *Oh my God*. In my book, he just went straight to the top. It was a good lesson I learned too because it left such a lasting impression on me. I've used that myself from time to time. If I'm doing something and there's a crowd of people, I try to bring someone in, make them feel special.

Anyway, Mario had that *it* factor, and I noticed right away that day in Las Vegas. Foyt was already a big deal; he was a bigger deal than Mario. He had a good reputation with engine builders, such as Keith Black and Ed Pink, because he was a real mechanic. He worked on the car. He was like Garlits, a guy who did it all. He knew it too, but I think those guys respected the dragster and maybe me a little for being willing to drive it.

Gurney used to drag race, so he knew what it was that I did. He raced at Bonneville as well as road racing. One time, he came to Irwindale, and we talked about wings. He was trying to give us some tips; we didn't know anything about aerodynamic stuff, and he was trying to help. I don't know if someone was trying to run a wing or we had some air foils on the front of the car or something, but he would come out occasionally. I mainly got to know him through Keith Black.

When Gurney was running the Plymouth a few years later in Trans-Am, he had a driver (Swede Savage) who was my age, and we were pals. Gurney was quite a bit older than me, and he was real sophisticated, real bright. If you were going to talk to Gurney, you'd better have something to say. You'd better not act like a dummy because he would not spend any time with you.

Me, A. J. Foyt, Jerry Titus, Cale Yarborough, and the Le Mans-winning GT40. I hadn't followed Le Mans, I only sort of knew about that kind of racing, but I fell in love with the car. Later, I visited Foyt, and he had one in his garage. Even after that, I still didn't realize what a big deal that kind of racing was until much later.

From left to right: Mario Andretti, Dan Gurney, me, and A. J. Foyt. It was a thrill to get to show those guys the Cammer dragster. I didn't know if they'd care much about drag racing, but they were really interested in it. (Photo Courtesy National Hot Rod Association/NHRA National Dragster)

Guess I Didn't Want It

Dan Gurney gave me the most valuable lesson that I think anyone has ever given me. Because of Swede, I was getting really interested in IndyCar racing, and I was wondering how I could get to drive one of those things. I was a little naive, but I figured that I could just jump in and drive one. Gurney would come in to Keith's, and I would mention it to him, like, "Hey, how do I get to do that?" He didn't blow me off, exactly. Maybe a little bit. Finally, one day I came up to him again. I didn't really interrupt him, but he was working on some parts or getting some parts from Keith, and he was somewhat busy. I asked him "Hey, how can I get to drive one of those things?" He said, "If you want to do it bad enough, you'll find a way." That's what he said, and I left there thinking, "You asshole."

The thing is, he was right. I never did do it, so I didn't want to do it bad enough, apparently. I've used that a few times since when someone is asking me all the time, "How do I get a ride?" Really, that's the bottom line. It's kind of cutting through a lot of the small talk and getting right down to it. If you

MEMORIES FROM MARIO ANDRETTI

I really liked Mario Andretti's way with people. He was serious but also friendly. It's a real skill, and not one I think I had.

I feel like I've known Don forever—it's been at least 50 years. We met when we were teenagers or just about. He was one of those guys who not only enjoyed his specialty but would move around. He was part of the inner circle of racing. Indy-Car, NASCAR, Formula 1—we would see each other pretty much everywhere. The racing family's a relatively small family, but he is one of the special guys who seemed like he was always there when it mattered. A good guy in every way. Even if we haven't been in touch with each other for months, it always sounds like we just spoke or texted an hour ago. It's no big deal. It's like we're picking up a conversation we were having from six months before.

When I met Don, he was at the top of his game, but there was always curiosity and respect for what I did, which was mutual. Snake is just a cool cat—a cool cat all the way. I wish I was as tall as him. He's a guy with dimension. He's a champion, a hall of famer, and a racer more than anything. He's a true racer. I have the utmost respect for those guys and gals who do what he did. To go 300 mph, who can even fathom that? I never had the opportunity to do it at that level. It's still on my bucket list, and it's never too late.

Testing the driver's seat in the buggy down in Baja.

want to do something bad enough, you'll find a way. It doesn't matter if it's racing or something else. When Gurney said that to me, I was pretty young, and it pissed me off. I wasn't expecting that answer. Years later, I remembered it and thought "God, it's so true."

The Mexican 1000

As I mentioned earlier, Tony Nancy was an upholstery guy, a really good one. He had a shop off Ventura Boulevard, and Kent Fuller had a shop in the back of the complex where he would do the dragster frames. That's where we built Ivo's two-engine car, and we would hang out with Tony in the upstairs of the front shop.

Tony was really skilled. He did full interior work on high-end cars, such as Steve McQueen's Ferrari and some Jaguars. Most of us couldn't even touch a car like that, let alone get one and tear the seats out. Tony would do drag cars too, if he liked you. All of his work had a little seahorse logo in the back, so you could tell who he liked and who he didn't. If he didn't like you, you wouldn't even get in the door. We got along. He took care of me, looked after me, and he didn't have to. He wasn't lacking for cool friends. You'd go in there, you'd see James Garner, Steve McQueen, Tommy Ivo, or Kent Fuller. That shop was the place to go.

McQueen had been building an off-road buggy, a Porsche-engine buggy to go run a new off-road race down in Mexico called the Mexican 1000. Shortly before the race, McQueen got a movie deal, maybe it was *Bullitt*. Anyhow, he couldn't go, but everything was ready, and Tony asked me to go as co-driver. I'd never done any off-road racing, but I was pretty good on a dirt bike, so I was all for it. I figured, "No problem, it's got a wheel and tires. No s——, no problem." We didn't know anything about running off-road.

Tony said, "We gotta go down and do a prerun." I'm like, "What's a prerun?" That's how much I knew. Heck, the only thing I knew about Mexico was Tijuana and underage drinking.

He said that we would head down there, check out the course, and then have a big dinner. It was going to be great. We didn't even have a bottle of

"The only thing I knew about Mexico was Tijuana and underage drinking."

Looking over Steve McQueen's buggy before the 1968 Mexican 1000. I went down to Baja with fellow racer Tony Nancy when Steve McQueen had to back out. I was not prepared for off-road racing.

Me and Tony Nancy ready to head down the Baja peninsula. It did not go well. We didn't even last long enough to get to the dirt part.

Even though Tony and I didn't finish the Baja race, it was still pretty cool to be down there with celebrities such as James Garner (left). I fell in love with Mexico. I've been down many times since.

water when we went across the border. We ended up there, driving for miles. Finally, late at night when I'm starving, we finally see a light way off in the distance. We got there and it was closed. We ended up sleeping in the truck until the next morning when the place opened up. It was a little place with dirt floors, and they made us some tortillas and some beans and that was it. That was my big dinner. You think I would have called it off then, but nope, I was all in for the race.

When we got down there for the actual race, we looked great. We had driving suits and jackets that McQueen had made up. I didn't have my team that dressed up for drag racing; I couldn't afford it. That was the way McQueen would roll though—the best of everything. The thing is that nobody really knew much about building off-road vehicles yet. It was still the very early stages, and our buggy was cool for the day, but it was so little with little bitty shocks that had no travel and not enough filter for the engine.

So, we started out and got maybe 100 miles outside of Ensenada. We weren't even off the pavement yet and the thing goes *errrrrrrrrrr* and runs out. It was embarrassing. They loaded it on a trailer, and someone took it back. We ended up going down to La Paz, which is where the race ended—and they had a big party. I didn't know not to drink the water, so I spent the end of the race hugging the commode in a s——ty Mexican bathroom wishing I was dead. I didn't go back to off-road racing until 2018, although I did learn to love Baja as a vacation spot well before that.

The End of the Cammer

The last real race with the Cammer was in Cecil County, Maryland. It was just me and Lou Baney, and we had the Shelby *Super Snake* car and a 10-or-so race tour on the East Coast. By then, I had a pretty good name, so when the car would come to the racetrack, the ads would say, "See Don Prudhomme in the Shelby *Super Snake*." It wasn't, "See Lou Baney and Ed Pink." I was getting most of the ink, as drivers normally do.

Lou and I were at the track, and Ed Pink wasn't with us. We were having trouble with the engine. The barrel valve wasn't set right or something, and it was fluttering and missing and banging. By that time, we were really road weary. We were tired of dealing with it, and I looked at Lou and he looked at me at the end of the racetrack, and I said, "Let's go home." He said, "Perfect, let's go home!" Just like that, we were done on the road, and we were worn out. So, we loaded the car up.

We were traveling back to California when Lou said to me, "You know, you really ought to have your own car." I had never even thought about having my own car. Lou said I needed to control my own destiny, my own operation. He knew what he was talking about as a businessman who owned a car dealership. He pointed out that I could do it, that I had a big enough name to book the car around the country. If it wasn't for Lou Baney, I don't know if I ever would have run my own car. Luckily, a few other things fell into place for me too, including another chance to work with Roland Leong.

Wynn's

While I was running the Ford, a change was happening in the dragsters. People started to move from the 392 Hemi to the new 426. Like the Cammer, Chrysler developed this big new engine to win NASCAR races, but it was pushing the engine on drag racers as well. Keith Black had some of the first on the West Coast, and they were just working things out with it. I think Roland was one of the first guys to try it.

At first, nobody wanted to run it, but once they figured it out, that's all anyone wanted. When I went on my own at the end of 1968, I bought a car from Roland and went to Keith Black to talk about engines. He gave me credit to build some engines. I couldn't have afforded to buy them outright. He didn't have to, considering that when I quit the *Hawaiian* car, Keith wasn't happy about it. He could've held a grudge, but he wasn't like that. When I went back to him in 1968, he was happy to help me. Roland's car was set up

"Lou said I needed to control my own destiny, my own operation."

DON PRUDHOMME'S
WYNN'S RATTLER

Steve Swaja was a dragster designer and artist who was friends with Tony Nancy. He drew up this dragster image for me to take to Wynn's and ask for sponsorship money. On the car, we ended up going with **Wynn's Winder** *instead of* **Wynn's Rattler**.

Top Left: Keith Black, the master, is at work on the Wynn's Winder. *He sat me down and went over the engine with me so that I'd be able to do work on my own on the road.*

Top Right: This is the Wynn's Winder *with no nose on it. Back when we still used water-cooled blocks, they used to steam and dump water when we warmed up the engine.*

for a 426, and Keith sat me down and told me what he'd do for me if I ran that 426. It wasn't a hard decision to put the 426 in there. From then on, that's all we ever ran—426 Hemis.

People sometimes ask if things would have been different had Ford stayed interested in Top Fuel. Well, maybe. That Cammer was a hell of an engine, but it was difficult to work on because of the overhead cams. It wasn't built for today's racing, where you zip it apart with the air wrenches and put it back together for the next round. You've got camshafts to set and all kinds of s—— to measure. It was a difficult engine to race, but it was a wonderful engine, really powerful.

Ed Pink really made it run well, but the blocks were designed for a street car. They weren't designed to run nitromethane. It cracked the main webs in it damn near every run, so even if Ford had stayed interested, I likely would have moved to the Chrysler 426 anyway. Of course, Keith Black was generous with parts and knowledge, which made it that much easier to make the switch in 1969.

The *Wynn's Winder* came from Roland. Dodge helped him out with a Charger body, and he decided to run a Funny Car, which was not my cup of tea. Even though I quit driving the *Hawaiian* in 1965, we still remained pals. We had some times there that I think he was kind of angry at me, and I didn't blame him. But it didn't really affect our relationship for long, kind of like Lou Baney and Mongoose. We were all a small family.

Roland called, saying that he was going to build a Funny Car and that I should buy his dragster. He'd just built it, but he wanted to run a Funny Car instead. That call occurred just after Lou mentioned to me that I should own my own car. I went to Lynn and said, "Roland's got this dragster that I could buy." I think we had about $1,500 saved up, which was enough money to buy the chassis, which cost around $1,000 or so.

So, I bought the car, but then what was I going to do? It takes money to run one, and all I had was the chassis. I noticed that Garlits had Wynn's Oil on his race car, and that was about the only sponsor that was out there in drag racing. I thought, "How clever is that to have Wynn's on the car? I wonder what they paid him." I looked up Wynn's, and they were nearby in Azusa, California. I thought, "If they are sponsoring Garlits all the way out in Florida, maybe they'd sponsor a local racer." I got together with a buddy who was an artist, who painted an image of a car with Wynn's on it, the *Wynn's Winder*. Although, the first version called it the *Wynn's Rattler*.

I called Wynn's and set up an appointment. I asked them about sponsoring my car and showed them the picture. I told them what I do, traveling around the country and making runs at the different tracks. By that time, I had a pretty good sales pitch, after dealing with Lou Baney, Ed Pink, and the Spars, and I was starting to learn about business. I told them if they sponsored me for $10,000, I could really do something.

They told me that they'd have to get back to me, but they were going to think about it. And so I left there like, "Holy cow, they're actually thinking about it." I kept waiting for that phone call, and finally the phone rang. It was this lady from Wynn Oil Company. She said, "We can't pay you 10,000," and I was about to be crushed, but she wasn't done. "We can't do 10, but will you take 7?"

"Would I?" In a heartbeat! I didn't tell her that exactly, but I was so excited. We got the $7,000 and I went to Keith Black. He had the 426 running really well. Roland had it in his dragster, and he was going to put a 426 in his Funny Car also. I had enough money left over to partially buy one engine. Those engines cost about $6,000 apiece, maybe a little less back then, but they were pricey, and I needed more than one. Keith said, "I'll tell you what. I'll build you another engine so that you have a spare." So, now I had two engines. Can you imagine? Two complete engines. He said, "When you take the car on the road and you make money, just pay your bill off and send me some money." I was one of the first guys to ever get credit with Keith Black Racing Engines. Until the day he died, he and I stayed real friendly, and I always paid my bills. I paid my bills before anything else. I didn't want the nuns after me again.

426 Hemi Versus Cammer

It was a whole different ball game with the 426 Hemi versus the Ford Cammer. For one thing, I was really involved with the 426 engine because Keith put me through school. I'd go over there at night and take the engine apart, saying, "Show me this. Show me that. Show me *why* you do this." He encouraged that. He felt that if I was going to take the car on the road, I'd better learn about what it takes to run it. Of course, we ran it at local tracks too.

What Keith did with the engine was de-stroke it. It was a 426 de-stroked to a 392. The reason he did that was because when we first started running the 426, it had so much torque that when you stepped off the clutch, it would blow the tires off and the car wouldn't really accelerate very hard. It would just sit there and smoke. Keith figured out before some of the other guys that he could de-stroke the 426 and have a little less torque off the line but then run a higher percentage of nitro. The thing will just keep pulling at the top end, just keep accelerating. It was very low compression too, which allowed us to run 100 percent nitro in it. With the Ford we probably ran about 80-percent nitro.

"I paid my bills before anything else. I didn't want the nuns after me again."

A press photo that Wynn Oil Company sent out of Wynn President Wesley Bellwood presenting me with a trophy after I set an ET and speed record at Lions. This was a little later in the sponsorship. They were good sponsors for a long time on a lot of my different cars.

That's the Shelby Cobra on my helmet, but I think I'm in the Wynn's Winder. *I had several versions of the snake. I borrowed that one from Shelby. I didn't have my own version of a snake logo until Hot Wheels. Tom always had the same mongoose drawing. The snake was hard, there were so many kinds of snakes, but a mongoose was a mongoose. McEwen always said that a snake was better because a mongoose was just an "ugly rat thing."*

Even with all of that, it didn't run well until he began messing with the magnetos and started cranking lead in it. With a 392 at the time, you'd maybe run 38 degrees or 40 degrees. We ran 70 degrees and went up from there: run the car, come back, put another 5 degrees in it, run the car, add another 5 degrees in it, etc.

Keith was just going crazy. "My God! It's going to kill this thing!" But it didn't bother it; rather, the engine loved it. So, we ran 100-percent nitro with 70 degrees spark. We had a slipper clutch in it then, so I didn't really have to ride the clutch, it would do it on its own. I could just bring the revs up really high, dump the clutch, and the f——ing thing would pick the front end up and just haul ass with 100-percent nitro in it. And it sounded good. It was the best-sounding car at the track. It was so loud that I had to wear ear plugs, and then put tape over that. It was just brutally loud.

Testing, Tires, and Garlits

In 1969, I was a Goodyear guy and really well established with the company. During that year, Leo Mehl from Goodyear called me in because M&H (Marvin Rifchin) had a good tire too, and every so often we would run M&H tires. Basically, we'd race on whichever brand seemed to be better that week. Goodyear cut a deal with me where it would pay me to run only its tires when I ran the match races. That's still the only place we were making money, and it was still the biggest crowds. There was no money in the NHRA yet. Goodyear said, "We'll send you tires, you give us a report at the end of the race, and we'll pay you."

I was pretty savvy at the time about tires. McEwen was pretty good too. We used to take our tires to a tire shop where we'd shave the corners off. We had our own little tools made up to shape the tires on the side so they'd get better traction. We had our own special contour that we'd carve. That's how into the tires we were. Goodyear was trying to catch M&H, which had a really good tire. Marvin Rifchin of M&H could make a change in his tire overnight, but Goodyear was a big company, so it might take weeks sometimes to make a change in the molds.

Tom McEwen is leaving the line, I think in 1969 at the U.S. Nationals. The starter is Buster Crouch, famed NHRA starter. The box before him is the timing light; you can see the three lights sending the beam across the start.

Tom McEwen used to come up to the Valley. He had a Triumph as well, he kept it at my house, and we'd go riding together. I had a street bike and a dirt bike, and I broke my knee on the dirt bike right around this time. Fortunately, it happened in the offseason. By the time I got back in the car, I could do it with a knee brace on. After all, I only had to move my ankle. That knee still bothers me today though.

Anyhow, Goodyear said, "Hey, we'll pay for your feedback." They were paying for our travel expenses, everything. I'd get money to run the car, and they would pay all the expenses, plus I'd make money from them for running and reporting on the tires. I don't want to use the expression "rolling in dough," but money wasn't a problem at the time for us. We were starting to make it in the sport, and for Goodyear to do that, it just put us over the top. It was a good program for Leo and a good program for us because we'd give them all the information that we had. They shared it with Garlits, and he'd get some of the tires we had run. He gave feedback too.

During this testing time, if we weren't racing, we were testing for Goodyear, and we'd go to Indy or wherever to test. It was at Indy where I was watching Garlits, and I could hear a difference in his car. It sounded different, and I came to find out that he had a 2-speed transmission in his car. A 2-speed. Before that, the cars were high-gear-only, just let out the clutch and steer.

When I heard those revs drop in

Mongoose and I at the track. Tom was the president of the United Drag Race Association (UDRA), and he was probably trying to talk me into joining. I did (he always talked me into stuff), but I never went to any meetings. I hate going to meetings.

I didn't really settle on a snake logo until the Hot Wheels years. There were a lot of experiments leading up to that. King Snake didn't stick.

Garlits's car, I went, "Holy s——!" I went over to where he was pitted, and it was probably funny to watch because he didn't want me anywhere around his car, but he couldn't just order me out.

It looked like a reverser box hooked on the back of his bellhousing. And it was a 2-speed transmission. I said to myself right then and there that I had to have one of them. Garlits actually told me that Leonard Abbott out in San Diego had built it. He called himself Lenco. You never would have guessed that something so important to racing would have come out of Leonard's yard. He built me that transmission on a junkyard bench. Just greasy, full of s—— and everything. That transmission changed racing. Garlits was so mad when he heard that I got one.

1969 U.S. Nationals

In the very first race of 1969, Roland's driver crashed his Funny Car at the Winternationals at Pomona. That crash tore the car all to bits. While it was being worked on, he ended up going racing with me. I bet that he had a better time racing with me than he would have if it hadn't crashed. That year, we made it to the finals in the Winternationals and we won Indy (the U.S. Nationals)—and that last one, that's a real story.

We'd just made a run, and Roland met me at the top end. All of a sudden, here comes John Mulligan, and the car was a ball of fire. I'd never seen a car on fire like that. Mind you, we all had front-engine cars still and we had fires, but they weren't much. This was bad. We went running over there, and we could see his skin badly burned through his fire suit. Terrible.

I told Roland that I didn't want to run anymore. I said, "Let's just split what's in the trailer. I quit." For the day anyhow, but at the time I meant it. Mulligan and I were tight. He had just won in Pomona earlier in the year. I was really shaken up.

Roland told me, "Okay, no problem. I don't blame you. Just go drink a Coke and go relax someplace and let me just get the car ready."

They took Mulligan to the hospital, and we figured he'd be alright. You know, it's just a matter of healing up, and well, let's go back racing. By the time the car was all ready to go again for the next round, Roland came over to me and said, "You ready?" And I said, "I'm ready. Let's do it." So, I jumped in, and we kept going. I can imagine that it sounds somewhat cold, like a real asshole thing to do, but that's what we were like back then. I think that's true of all of us, or at least of all the folks whose names you remember. The races were everything, and your personal feelings or fears, you dealt with that on your own time—if you did it at all.

I think the first guy I raced was Pete Robinson. He was still running the Ford Cammer, and I was in the 426 Hemi. We smoked him. We were going rounds, and the big guys were going out. Garlits had already gone out.

In those days, you worked on your car on the ground or next to your trailer. If you were fortunate, there was some pavement, but usually you picked your piece of grass, went to the local lumber yard, and bought a 4x8 sheet of plywood to slide under the car. You crawled underneath the car on the plywood, dropped your pan, and worked on the engine or whatever needed to be fixed because there was really no asphalt on the racetrack. The only asphalt was the s—— that you raced on, maybe the return road if you were lucky. But most of the pit area wasn't paved.

However, at that 1969 Indy race, Goodyear had Garlits and me working in a tent. It was the only covered area in the pits. This was way before trailers, awnings, or any of that s——. But that year we worked underneath the Goodyear tent, so we were doing better than most of the guys. We weren't taking the cylinder heads off or pulling the engine apart between the rounds like they do today. We didn't have to do that. Usually all I did was take the plugs out and have a look at them.

So, before the semifinals, I took the plugs out and one had some oil on it. I thought, "Goddamn, this isn't good." When they're oily, it's a sure sign that you've knocked a ring land down and the ring's frozen. It means the piston got so hot that it collapsed the ring land. It's a real common thing. They even do it now. If you've got a collapsed ring land, that means that the ring isn't sealing that piston anymore. It only had probably 20-percent seal ratio (instead of 90 or 95 percent). So, when you're going down the track, it'll run okay until you start to build up a lot of pressure in the engine. Then, it burns the piston.

We didn't have time to take the heads off between rounds and change out a piston and rings. It was unheard of to do that. Instead, we put a hot spark plug in that hole and fired it up. The thing was oiling; it had smoke pouring out of it. I laid back from the tree so the other guy couldn't see me. I figured maybe he'd mess up if he didn't know I was hurt. I held back, did my burnout last, and stayed way back behind the start line.

The starter, Buster Couch, was looking at me like he knew what was going on. I kept revving the engine up, cleaning it out, cleaning it out, finally I staged it, and "Boom!" We went down the course, and I got the win. The only trouble was that it blew a f——ing rod out of it right at the lights. It blew the engine up. I'm down there in a puddle of oil at the end of the track.

We won the round, but there was no way that we could fix the engine or change the engine because we couldn't do that at the races in those days. Nobody did that. There wasn't enough time between rounds, and the cars weren't really designed with quick engine swaps in mind. The only thing that I had in the trailer was a short-block.

Rain Dance

While I was still sitting there, Don Garlits came to see what the trouble was. He was always curious as to what I was doing, and I was always curious what he was doing. But this time, we were wondering what the hell we were going to do because we had just blown up the engine. All of a sudden, it was like the heavens opened up. It began pouring rain, and I don't just mean a sprinkle. I'm talking about lightning and buckets of water. I jumped in the seat of the car, and we pushed it back to the pit. I figured that with the rain delay we might be able to change this engine and get up there for the final round.

We pulled up to the Goodyear tent, and all the Goodyear guys quit changing tires. They were eager to help us because we had to race Kelly Brown in an M&H car in the finals. We got the engine out, put the short-block in, put the heads on it, and torqued it all down. Went over to the rollers, fired it up, warmed it up, and just as we were ready to go to the finals, the sun came out. It couldn't have been more perfectly timed. We won the final round. If it wasn't for the rain, we never would have made it. Not even a little bit. The rain saved our ass.

Garlits thought I'd made it happen somehow. He thought that I had some magical thing. He was real superstitious. He would carry stuff on the

"I laid back from the tree so the other guy couldn't see me. I figured maybe he'd mess up if he didn't know I was hurt."

rearview mirror of his car and truck. He had all of these little carvings and all kinds of s—— he used to rub on, claiming that there was magic to them. He believed in that s——. He actually believed that I made it rain. I really think he does to this day.

Wins and Losses

I don't want you to think that I'd forgotten about Mulligan's accident. As soon as we finished at the track, we went to the hospital. They only wanted one of us at a time to go in there because they had a net over him because he was burned so badly. We didn't know anything about burns. I mean, no one did, but especially no one in drag racing. Rod Stuckey was the only other guy I remembered who got burned. Garlits got burned on his hands a little bit, but we didn't know anyone who was burned as badly as Mulligan.

We were in his hospital room, and McEwen came over said, "John, what can we do?" And Mulligan was talking. The infection hadn't set in yet, and we didn't think it was so bad. He said, "Oh, I want a Pepsi." He wanted a Pepsi, but only one from Tulsa. He claimed that they tasted different. He was from Tulsa and he wanted a Tulsa Pepsi, not one from Indianapolis. We had some Pepsi from Tulsa flown in, and we hung around there for two or three days because we still had to go race the next weekend.

While we waited, we went over to the speedway. A. J. Foyt was over there and asked, "Hey, what about this drag racer who was burnt?"

I said, "Yeah, it's Mulligan. He's in the hospital."

Foyt said, "You better get him out of there. Get him down to Houston to the burn center."

In IndyCar racing, they knew more about burns, but we didn't know anything about the burn center. Foyt said, "You better get him out of there. He could die over there. Those burns are nothing to fool with." We figured he was going to be fine, but A. J. was right. About a week later, Mulligan died in the hospital. In today's world, we would have hired a private jet to pick him up and take him to a burn center. I suspect that if we had gotten him up there, he would be alive today. But we didn't know any better. I took it pretty hard. When you lose friends, when people get hurt, it changes your whole perspective. It's serious s——.

So, that was the good and bad of 1969. After that year, everything changed when the Snake and Mongoose Funny Cars started.

Indy in 1969. We had just blown the engine up, you can see the puddle underneath of it. Roland is holding my helmet and Don Garlits is looking at the car with me, probably saying, "Gee, bad luck, buddy." Minutes later, the sky opened up with rain, and we had enough time to rebuild it and win the race. To this day, Garlits thinks that I made it rain.

4

THE 1970s

In 1970, the first Hot Wheel Funny Car appeared at Pomona. You can see the wing on the roof, which was a bad idea. That paint job was designed by Hot Wheels specifically to make it easier to put the decals onto the models.

You're sitting in the car and the body's up. You turn it over and get the oil pressure built up, and they squirt the injector with a little gasoline. Click the switch and boop, bump, bump, bump. It starts up. You can see the back of the engine while it's running, and right in front of you are the pipes playing a rhythm.

1-8-4-3-6-5-7-2, that was the firing order. You could actually see it—boop, boop, boop, boop, boop, boop, boop, boop—follow the firing order of the engine. Watch the pipes, see which is rich or which is lean. Lean it out a little bit, get some really nice rhythm to the pipes.

Then, they'd lower the body down. Roll through the bleach box, do your burnout. The smoke will billow out, come into the cockpit. The smoke just fills up the car, and you back it up as the smoke wafts out the windows. By the time you get to the starting line, it's clear. All you hear are the pipes, and all you see is the firewall. You take it down track by feel. You just know where it is. That's a Funny Car. That's drag racing in the 1970s.

Hot Wheels

I can still remember the first time McEwen mentioned Mattel to me. I was hanging out at Keith Black's. I had a little shop behind Black's shop. It wasn't much; it was more of a stall than a shop, but it was still my first place, and it felt good to have it.

Mongoose came in and said, "Hey, I've got a contact at Hot Wheels." His mom worked for a law office and Mattel was one of the accounts, so she knew some of the head people at Mattel. Tom suggested that she introduce us to them. I didn't even know what he was talking about. I didn't know about the toys, but he had kids, and they were into Hot Wheels.

That vision, he had it. I never would have thought to go outside of oil and cam companies to look for sponsorships. When McEwen came to me and asked me about it, I wasn't all that crazy about it because I already had a sponsor, and it was Wynn's. Plus, my immediate thought was, "What would Mattel want with a couple of drag racers?" Mattel was Barbie dolls, and I didn't think I needed another sponsor. I was doing fairly well, as I was getting some good money from Wynn's and getting a little more from Plymouth.

McEwen didn't need me to get it. He could see the future. He came walking in the shop one day, all pleased with himself, saying "God, I was at Mattel's. They want to meet you! They really like the idea of the Snake and the Mongoose!" Well, he would have said, "The Mongoose and the Snake." We always did that—he'd say Mongoose first, and I'd say Snake.

Now, I'd had a few meetings before, so this wasn't my first sponsorship pitch, but I still felt out of my league. Mattel wasn't the wheel or spark plug people who hung around the track and worked out of small shops; it was a big company, but McEwen was confident. We went over there, and it went really well.

They already had pictures of how they wanted the cars, and I was surprised to see renderings showing full-body cars. I thought that McEwen was talking about dragsters, but they wanted Funny Cars. That's another example of McEwen being ahead of me in understanding something. Tom already had a Funny Car. It just said, "Tom, Mongoose" on the side of it. He didn't run it that long, but he used to tow it around the country with us and do exhibition runs. He understood that the fans really liked Funny Cars.

Tom was always more into the show business part of it than I was. I was the diehard racer. I wanted to beat Garlits, and Funny Cars weren't part of that world. McEwen ended up convincing me that we needed to have Funny Cars. By the time I realized the scale of what he had in mind, I would have driven a taxi cab to make it happen. It was huge.

The Cars of Hot Wheels

I can't remember what the first drawings looked like or what kind of cars they were, but I knew some of the OEM Chrysler guys from the track. Plymouth and Dodge were out there with Sox & Martin and Dick Landy, and there were factory cars being raced by the Ramchargers. I had a relationship with Dick Maxwell, who worked at Plymouth, and Keith Black had a relationship with both Dodge and Plymouth.

With the Wynn's dragster, every so often, Plymouth would send me a set of heads for a 426 Hemi, which was a cool deal, but once the Hot Wheels thing started, we were getting whole cars, just to drive around, such as brand-new

"What would Mattel want with a couple of drag racers?"

Barracudas and Dusters. I think that was Tom's idea too, going to Plymouth and asking them to sponsor us with cars as well.

It could've been any cars, but we had the relationship with Maxwell. We could've gone to Ford, but we went to Plymouth. They drew up these images once they knew what kind of cars we wanted. It was a Barracuda and a Duster. We took those drawings to Plymouth and showed them what Hot Wheels was going to do. And immediately, they wanted their name on the quarter panel of the cars because then their name would be on all the little toy cars that Hot Wheels made. Plymouth would be a part of that. They paid us money and gave us cars to drive. I had a Plymouth Barracuda to drive with a Hemi in it. I wish I still had it!

The brilliance of that sponsorship was that everyone wanted to be on the race car, not because of the race car but because they would get to be on the toy car. We went to Coke, Federal-Mogul, and Cragar. Each company put its decal on the car and paid us. Wynn's paid us too. That's when we started Wildlife Racing Inc. We had so much money coming in that we had to incorporate.

In the Money

I don't know quite how to illustrate what a big deal the Hot Wheels sponsorship was—not just for us but for drag racing in general. Before that, even with a nice sponsorship, such as the one from Wynn's, you had to go out match racing to make enough to even cover the cost of the car. I'll round up on these numbers, but let's say that you could put together a good dragster and tow rig and some spare parts for $10,000 in 1969. Well, you'd be leaving town probably still owing some money on that before you even raced it. On

"The brilliance of that sponsorship was that everyone wanted to be on the race car . . . because they would get to be on the toy car."

That's Monette watching one of the first runs of the Hot Wheels car in 1970. Monette's support of my racing was so important to me. I loved when he would come to the track, although I wasn't ever sure that he wouldn't beat somebody up for looking at him wrong. We had such a complex relationship.

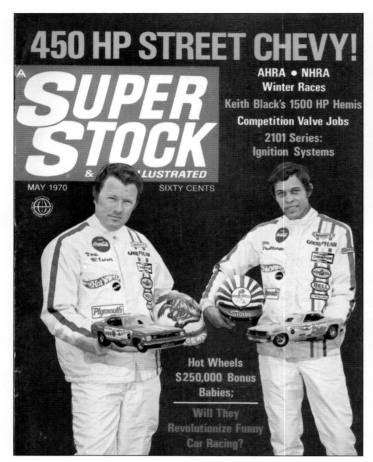

That's some early Photoshop right there. They had us pose with our hands out flat. I was wondering, "What the hell do they want that for?" Then, the magazine came out with us holding the little cars, and I thought, "Oh hell, that looks cool."

We had our Hot Wheels set first, and then they came out with models of Gurney's All-American Racers cars. I thought that it was pretty neat to be on a poster with Dan Gurney and Swede Savage.

Who would have thought those little toy cars would still be a thing even today? Well, Mongoose thought it, and good thing he did.

those tours, we were like a band going around the country playing in little beer joints and stuff, basically, small drag strips. We'd run the car as much as we could possibly run it. That's how we made money.

If you received $1,000 for a race, that was big. I remember when Garlits got $1,200 and I went, "Holy s——." If some guy wanted you bad enough, you'd have to really bargain. That was kind of a fun part about it. Someone wants you to run for him you'd say, "I don't know, what do you pay?" You'd go back and forth, and I learned how to negotiate doing that.

Anyhow, that's what it was like in 1969, but then in 1970, when Hot Wheels came in, we got somewhere around $100,000, plus some from Plymouth, Federal-Mogul, Coca-Cola, and all the smaller sponsors on the car. So even split between me and McEwen, I think we had something like $65,000 on our side of the Wildlife Racing bank account.

Now, our expenses went up too because we started to have a small crew and the trucks and stuff, but for the first time, I had the cash to do it. I bought a used truck and built the back section on it; it was expensive, but it wasn't crazy because we worked on it too. Then, we'd match race the car at the same time. So, not only were we paid well from Hot Wheels, Plymouth, and Coke but we'd also get paid to appear with the cars.

That Hot Wheels time, that was probably the best ratio of money coming in to money going out during all of drag racing. It brought attention to the sport, it brought attention to me and McEwen, and it set up the future of drag racing as a professional activity. Of course, with most sponsors, as I'd come to learn, it doesn't last. You'd get a good chunk the first time around, the second year is like, "Uh, you get half that much." And then the next year less and so on. Mattel put a lot of money into it and then they went on to the next project, and the Snake and the Mongoose got left behind. They figured that they had reached their peak in marketing with the toys. Little did they know that it would last; it's still going on.

Snake and Mongoose Chemistry

McEwen and I really fed off each other in a good way. We had a lot of energy, and we liked each other's company. We were more friends than enemies, although the announcers and reporters liked to portray us as enemies. We were truly competitive too; it wasn't all for show. I was more about the car performance and he was more about the people performance, and we used to get into big arguments about that.

When the cars were first done, his car showed up on the cover of *Hot Rod* magazine, and that really pissed me off. I had this big ego by then, and I was mad that I wasn't on the cover. He told me, "Your car's not pretty enough." His engine was all chrome, he polished the fuel tank and oil tank, and if you looked under the body, it was really nice.

Mine looked like Garlits's engine. The chassis was mostly plain black and had grease on it—okay, maybe not really. I was fairly fussy about keeping it clean, but I didn't have a polished supercharger or anything like that. The only thing that I cared about was how fast the thing was.

Mongoose had enough wisdom to make sure that his was all chrome, polished, and looked good. So, he got on the cover of *Hot Rod*, and I didn't. Add that to the list of things I learned from McEwen.

Lynn: The Brains Behind the Brawn

It's important to add that Snake and Mongoose wasn't just Snake and Mongoose. It wasn't just the two of us. We had help. For starters, Lynn was right next to me. She knew about the contracts, and she knew about what we were doing at Plymouth. She's the one who kept records. We incorporated together, and Lynn helped put the corporation together: Wildlife Racing Inc.

We used to have just one main account. However, Tom, well, he'd be buying alligator shoes and presents for everyone. He wasn't good with money, and Lynn managed to recognize that and solve it before we all went broke and stopped being friends. Lynn realized that we needed to split up the corporation because Tom was way out-spending us, so we changed our books around so we each received separate money. It went into separate accounts instead of one main account.

New Crew

All through the first decade of racing, there weren't really official crew guys. There were people who had a financial stake in the car, an engine builder who would swing by to help, or family members. When, say, Roland and I were on the road, we'd just pick some folks out of the crowd around the car and say, "Hand me wrenches," or "Go clean these parts off." They'd

"I had this big ego by then, and I was mad that I wasn't on the cover."

have fun and we'd get them a hot dog, and that was how it worked. As the racing became more serious, there started to be regular team guys, not quite like how it is now, but someone who was more official and paid to be there.

I still remember when I met Bob Brandt. It was Orange County, I think, and we had the Hot Wheels Cars, the Funny, and a dragster. Roland Leong was out there too, and he saw me working on something. He points to this buddy of his and says, "Old Bob can help you." This kid just jumped in there and started working with me. He was amazing!

I'd be working on something, and be about to loosen say, a 9/16-inch bolt, and before I could even look up, there would be a 9/16 wrench in my hand. It was like doctors operating, you had someone there handing you the tools. He was brilliant. He was worth two hot dogs. He was worth buying a steak dinner for, and in fact, I think I did buy him dinner that day. After that, I said, "So, you wanna go to the races next week?" And that was that. Bob Brandt was on my team for the next 15 years. I guess I sort of stole Roland's crew guy, but he never complained about it. Brandt and I were just meant for each other.

Hot Wheels on the Road

"When those two ramp trucks with the Hot Wheels cars at the back came to town . . . kids gathered around the trucks like we were rock stars."

When we got the Funny Cars, we needed a way to tow them. When you had a dragster, you could just pull it with a little trailer. Funny Car guys started using small ramp trucks. You'd see those guys up and down the highway with the car up against the cab. We wanted our trucks to be different; we wanted them to really stand out.

It's funny though, because even though Hot Wheels was the biggest sponsorship I'd ever had, and we were two of the biggest teams in drag racing, we still didn't get brand-new trucks. Mine came from Richard Petty. It was what they called a cab and chassis. Dodge would loan you the cab and chassis, and then you'd put a back section on it. Then, you'd take that back section off and put it on a new truck and turn in the other one. Well, when Petty got his new one, I bought his old one from a dealer in North Carolina or wherever it was. They shipped it to us, and we put a back section on it. McEwen got his from Sox & Martin in a similar deal.

Once we started going on the road with the Hot Wheels cars, it was huge. We would go down the highway together, stay at the same hotels, and work on our cars together. When those two ramp trucks with the Hot Wheels cars at the back came to town, it was like the Charlie Daniels Band or something. When we'd pull into a little drag strip in Des Moines, Iowa, or someplace like that, kids gathered around the trucks like we were rock stars. The thing is, we really were good racers. At least I considered myself a damn good racer. I wasn't there just to put on a show. We were there to win the race, and putting on a show was just part of winning the race.

Jim Nicoll

I'm a pretty emotional guy about crashes. I might act tough, but I took it pretty seriously when people that I knew well would get hurt. In all forms of racing, I think it makes a mark in the mind of drivers when someone is injured or killed. When Dan Wheldon was killed in 2011, I was at the race. You could look at the faces of the other IndyCar drivers and tell that they were probably asking themselves the question, "What the hell are we doing here?"

Every accident is different. Back then, it was just luck if you walked away or not. We knew so little about safety. Back in 1967, Mike Sorokin was killed when his car was cut in half and he hit the guardrail full stop. We all took that really, really hard. That was probably the first big crash that I was around. We only kept going after that because of Keith Black. As soon as he saw what had happened with Sorokin's clutch, he stopped everything and said, "Hey, we've got to redo these clutches." That's when we went to a three-disc clutch instead of a two-disc clutch.

I was so lucky that I worked with people who took safety seriously, especially Keith Black. Those crashes when someone got hurt really bothered him, and they bothered me too. In those days, it seemed like there was at least one really bad one every year. At least.

In 1970, it was Jim Nicoll who made the news. It was the final round of the 1970 U.S. Nationals, and I was racing Nicoll. He was a real tough competitor, not someone you take for granted. I remember doing the burnout and seeing him do his out of the corner of my eye, and he looked quick. I thought, "Holy s———. Man, I've got my hands full with this guy." I think he left a pinch ahead of me. Just a little bit. Getting down the track, it was a dead heat. All of a sudden, there was this big explosion. I didn't know if it was my car or his at first, but then I saw the whole front of his car spinning out in front of me, right in front of my front axle. The explosion severed his car from the engine, and there was no roll cage, no back at all. I thought it was his body dragging behind the motor because of all the flames and the debris.

I got my car stopped and just sat there for a minute, thinking, "Boy, this guy's dead." I had all these thoughts going through my mind like, "Why didn't I get to know him? Now, it's too late." Then the crew came to pick me up and said, "Hey, he's okay." I was shocked because I was ready to quit.

There's a famous clip from Wide World of Sports that still gets played, where I say I think I should quit. I didn't know it was being recorded. There were so many people down there and I was sitting on a hay bale and I was totally spent. Remember, we were running a bunch of match races, towing the car around the country, working on it. I was skin and bones, and I was just completely exhausted because of all the work that it took to do what we were doing. During that time when I was sitting there, honest to God, I thought,

> "Every accident is different. Back then, it was just luck if you walked away or not."

The **Wild Wheelie** *dragsters. McEwen had a blue one, and mine was white. The toy versions would do wheelies, and the real one ran pretty well. Don Long built it. It was similar to the* **Wynn's Winder** *but with a full body around the back. Tom Hanna built the body.*

*In the cockpit of the **Wild Wheelie** car. It's a tight fit, but at least by then I was wearing more than a leather jacket. (Photo Courtesy National Hot Rod Association/NHRA National Dragster)*

This was the first time I ran the John Buttera-built Funny Car. I put the yellow paint scheme on it, and it was a badass car. Later, we painted it white with a new Hot Wheels scheme on it.

"I don't want to do this anymore." I didn't know what I was going to do, but I knew that it just wasn't worth it, someone getting killed. I was completely drained from it. I'm glad he wasn't killed, and I'm glad I didn't quit.

Flopper Flops

Even after the first year in a Funny Car, I still liked dragsters better. They were faster, and so much more fun. The yellow Barracuda had an automatic transmission, and it was a real bummer. I hate to say it because it was a B&M automatic, and those guys were really nice to me. It wasn't their fault; it just wasn't as much fun to drive. Plus, the cars were all the same: boring, cookie-cutter. Here's your Logghe chassis, or in our case a Ronnie Scrima chassis, but same thing: here's your 426 Hemi, here's your automatic transmission. It didn't do much for me. I would always rather be in my dragster, but that changed in 1971.

The White Hot Wheels Hemi 'Cuda

It was probably in late 1970 when I had the shop in the back of Black's when I was working on the 'Cuda, and this guy pulls up in front of the shop. It was John Buttera. I didn't really know him, but I'd heard of him. Keith knew him. Honestly, I didn't really know a bunch of people. It wasn't that I wasn't friendly. I mean, people would probably tell you that I wasn't friendly, but I was just really concentrating on what I was doing.

Anyhow, Buttera said, "Hey. Come out here. I want to show you something." When I walked out in front of Keith's shop, there was a Mach 1 Mustang Funny Car on a trailer. It was a Mustang body that Buttera had just built for Mickey Thompson and Danny Ongais. I looked at the chassis and the car. It was so cool. It was the coolest thing I'd ever seen.

It had a roll cage like a dragster. The headers on the engine went over the top of the frame rails instead of down. In our Funny Cars, the headers would

One of the things that made Buttera's Funny Cars so much better than the 1970 car is how much easier it was to work on. You can see how the headers are above the frame rail, which made it possible to take the head and header off in one piece.

The early Funny Cars had shocks on the front end. We didn't know much about setting up suspension back then.

go down, over, and out through the frame. It made them a bitch to work on. The headers were sandwiched underneath the frame. On this car, it went over the top of the frame just like a dragster. So, when you took the heads off, you just pulled them right off. You could take them off with the headers on there and everything.

It was a f——ing amazing car. It had a 2-speed transmission in it. No automatic. It was just so beautiful. It wasn't even painted or anything, but I said, "I've got to have one of these." Buttera got busy right away and built me a car

I didn't really start liking the Funny Cars until 1971, when Buttera showed me how light and trick a Funny Car could be. It was more like a dragster with a body. Way more interesting, and a lot faster.

Behind Keith Black's shop during the second year of the Hot Wheels deal. The Buttera car is white here. Those pants were part of a promotion Coca-Cola was doing. They were a secondary sponsor on the car. I didn't like the pants, but I liked the money. Also here is Bob Brandt and Steve "Okie" Bernd.

Look at that wing. We didn't know anything about aero. It's like a board up there.

with a Barracuda body on it. It was a lightweight body, the white Hot Wheels Hemi 'Cuda, and I fell in love with the Funny Cars after that.

Aero-Oops

We knew little about aerodynamics when we first got the Funny Cars. If you look at the first photos from 1970, we had spoilers on the roofs, right by the back window. I think the only reason we did it is because we thought it looked cool. Most guys had them on the trunk, and we thought we'd be different. We went, "Eh, let's put ours on the roof." That's how little we knew about air.

I remember racing it at Pomona that way. I got down near the lights, the back of the car came up off the ground, and the tires started spinning at the top end. If you can picture the back of the roof, the air would come over, hit that spoiler, and start churning above the car. What it's supposed to do is hit the spoiler at the end of the trunk and churn behind it, and that sucks the back of the car down. The way we had it, it would lift the back of the car up. McEwen's was the same way.

I called Dick Maxwell, or maybe Maxwell called us. He said, "What are you doing with that spoiler on the roof? You've got to put it on the decklid, and here's why. . ." The Plymouth and Dodge factory guys knew all that stuff because they'd been working on those big-wing cars for NASCAR. They'd been in wind tunnels. We put it on the back, and all of a sudden, *bam*, we were right in the hunt.

That roof wing was early in 1970, but it wasn't like we figured everything out right away after that. We were still doing it by trial and error. The factory guys were using technology like wind tunnels, but I don't think that Tom and I knew such a thing existed. We never really paid attention to that because at the time, all the cars were kind of a copy of what somebody else had. Who's going to put our car in a wind tunnel? We weren't thinking that big. Dodge probably would've done it at the time, but we didn't think to call Plymouth and say, "Hey, we'd like to get in your wind tunnel and lower the car to the ground and try all this stuff."

I wouldn't call Mongoose or myself big innovators, at least not back then. That was the kind of thing that Mickey Thompson or Bob Skinner from the Surfers would do, not us. Mickey was the first guy I saw lean the headers back—the zoomie headers. Before that, they just came straight out. We called them weed sprayers. They looked bitchin', but if you put a cylinder out, it would move you side to side. When we changed to the zoomies, it changed the whole way the car ran.

If we had known more about aero, it would have saved me some trouble. We ran the early cars so high off the ground, it's a wonder that they went down the track. In 1971, I was in Seattle for the Hot Wheels Northwest National Open, and the car blew up. The body flew off it and flipped right off the ground. It left the start line really well and transferred weight great, but when we got down at the other end, it rode pretty high. It wasn't real stable, which meant that if something went wrong, it went really wrong.

Flying on Fire

It all started with an oily plug, like the dragster back in 1969. We didn't have time to change it, although by then we were starting to take the heads off the engine to service it between some runs. But we really didn't have time because they wanted us on the starting line, and it was getting late. We had to race a car called the *L.A. Hooker*, which was Gene Beaver's car.

It was the final round, and we were running better than anybody, so I wasn't worried about beating them. Although, I was concerned about that oily plug. We left the line, smoking down the track, but it ran well, and we made it through the lights. I was just fixing to open the parachute. I hit the lever, and all of a sudden, the lights went out. This thing immediately just burst into flames. The minute it did, it went dark, and I couldn't see anything. It was just all fire.

Things got real quiet for a minute. The back wheels were off the ground,

"I couldn't see anything. It was just all fire."

Wheels up in 1971! We didn't run big wheelie bars on the first Funny Cars, and they would pick up the front tires. This is a little excessive. I'm sure I had to get out of it right after this shot. I must have been watching Dick Landy and the Pro Stockers or something. (Photo Courtesy National Hot Rod Association/NHRA National Dragster)

The scariest thing to a Funny Car driver is a fire. People were injured and even killed because once those fiberglass bodies caught, they became an instant fireball. I was very lucky that the body came off the chassis, and I was able to get out just a little warm. (Photo Courtesy Al Kean)

the front end was off the ground, and it was floating along. The next thing I knew, the body had blown off it. So, I'm just sitting in this cage, and the chassis came banging down on the ground, driving my spine up into my neck. It was just *Bam!* Hit the deck. By then, the fire had gone out. I think the fire went with the body, so thank God it blew the body off, otherwise the whole thing probably would have turned over backward.

That's when we first started learning about aerodynamics. The Dodge guys, or rather, the Plymouth guys, had to explain it to me. Because the car rode so high in the front, when it caught on fire from burning the piston, it put pressure on the oil pan and on the dry-sump tank and blew oil out that caught on fire. The fire ate up the oxygen that ran underneath the car, and it just lifted it right off the ground.

Garlits and the Rear Engine

Is there someone in your life who you respect completely but also don't really like? That's me and Don Garlits, and I think he would say the same about me. We didn't really race each other as much as people might think because when I was in dragsters, I was mostly on the West Coast, and if he came out here, well, he was a big deal. He was, you know, "Excuse me, Mr. Garlits." He was like the biggest name by far in those days. Bigger than Ivo. I was just a kid back then. Later, I was in a Funny Car, so we weren't matched up together.

I thought he was a genius. I admired the s—— out of him then, and I still do. I never thought I was as good as him, and I still don't to this day. I mean, he's about the only guy that I would honestly say that I don't think I was as good as him. If you want to talk about the ultimate driver, and the ultimate car builder, engine builder, everything in one package, it was Don Garlits. The ultimate.

By far the most amazing thing I've ever seen was watching Garlits work out a problem. When he really amazed me and everyone else was when he put that engine behind him. That was like the shot that was heard 'round the world. He was so far ahead of everybody to figure that out and to make it work. People had tried it, but the idea of a rear-engine dragster was practically a joke after a while. It just didn't work. They would crash and turn over. Then here comes Garlits, and he figured it out.

In 1970, at the finals of the AHRA at Lions, Garlits crashed and his foot was cut off. After that, we thought he was done. I was there when that happened, and after the race was all over with, I went with Mongoose to the hospital, and there he was still all wrapped up. I told 'Goose, "That son of a bitch is done. He's retired. He's gotta be done." I mean, if I cut my foot off, I think that would be the last time I drove. I don't think I would be jumping back into a car right away. But this guy, he goes home and heals up and builds his rear-engine car. It was like the moon landing or something. It was beyond anything I'd ever seen.

After that, I followed and watched him and tried to learn from him. I picked up some of his bad habits too. You know that temper I'm kind of known for? He has a horrible temper as well, so we weren't ever friends, but I respect him so much. There just wasn't anyone else like him.

The Wedge

Sometimes in racing there's something that looks like it's gonna fly, and it just sinks. The wedge car was one of those for me. Garlits came out with the rear-engine car in 1970, and we could see the writing on the wall that we were all going to be in rear-engine dragsters. The only question was whether we could outthink Garlits and make a better one.

Buttera built me a bodied rear-engine dragster that we called the wedge. It just didn't work very well. The design was pretty good, but we never really got a chance to run it all that much. We couldn't work out the aerodynamics to it because we were hindered by the weight. The idea of a dragster with a body on it was something that a few people were trying out at the time, but the problem was weight. It looked great, and it was built well, but it didn't work.

We towed up to Continental Divide Raceway in Denver to race Garlits. He was probably on tour and we were asked to race him. Don't ask me who won. He probably did. Back then, a track would call and say, "We got Garlits booked, you want to race?" Of course, we always wanted to race.

MEMORIES FROM LYNN PRUDHOMME

Don remembers meeting me in class, but to be honest, I don't remember that. However, I do remember seeing him at the skating rink. Don and Tom McCourry were wonderful skaters. We weren't real serious at the time, so when he went on the road with Ivo, it wasn't such a big deal to me. I had other things to do; my girlfriends and I would try to sneak into jazz clubs and generally just do crazy teenage stuff.

Don and I became more serious as things with his family got worse. I didn't really want to be around it. He didn't either. Their house wasn't a place you wanted to go over the holidays. I could see how different Don was from his parents—it just didn't seem like he belonged there. He had to drive. I thank God because I think that is what got him out.

Paychecks

Both Don and I always worked—at least until the car started paying our bills. I was a hairdresser, and we would use my tip money as spending money. Everything else we either saved or used to pay rent. We were lucky because other than the very first Road Kings car where Don paid the expenses, he was a driver and not an owner, so he didn't pay to run the car. We missed that struggle that a lot of racing families went through.

Racing is an obsession. I've always said that drag racing is not a sport; it's a disease. Once it gets under the skin, people will spend all of their money and energy on it. Look, at the time of this writing, here's Don 10 years removed, and he's back in, working with John Force and Austin Prock, and he's just as serious as he was then. It's like, "Oh my God, I thought it would all be gone by now, but it isn't." So, what can I say? I repeat that I'm lucky that he was always sensible about money. It's not like I didn't like the cars. I didn't race, but when Don and I were married, I had an Austin-Healey, which was my pride and joy. Don painted a blue racing stripe down the center of it for me. I thought I was really cool.

Crewwoman

When Don took the B&M car on tour, I went along and helped as much as I could. I didn't know how to tow a trailer, until one night, we were on the New Jersey turnpike, and Don said, "I just can't go anymore." I was so worried about paying the bills that I decided that I could drive, and he went to sleep in the back of the station wagon.

I got behind the wheel, and I'm sure that I was doing 20 mph the first half hour because you had to go through these little toll booths with a big trailer, and I was scared to death. However, by the time we made arrived in Maryland the next day, I was pretty good at it. So, I had the night shift from then on. He had the day shift.

The role of wives and girlfriends in the early days was to help, make sandwiches, and do this and that. When they got paid crewmembers, the crew would do all that. I never did any backup girl stuff. If I had stepped out in front of the race car to help him with a burnout, he would have run me over. He was not into having the women up there doing the backup.

There weren't many women racing back then, but there were a lot at the track. However, it wasn't always easy to make friends. In the very early days in match racing, most racers (other than a few regulars) you'd meet at a match race somewhere you wouldn't see again for 3 months until the next one. So, it wasn't like we girls formed close relationships. Later in the 1960s, I'd go to the races and meet my girlfriends there. In the first years on tour, you very rarely saw the same person twice. Patty Garlits is the only one I can really say that I was friends with in the early days. We remained friends throughout her life.

Social Life, Stardom, and Scares

We tended to have friends who were also in racing because you're busy every weekend. If you have non-racing friends, they want to go out on weekends because they work all week. That made it hard to maintain close friendships. That doesn't include Tom McCourry of course, but he lived nearby and understood us. So, we had friends who were also in racing, such as Dick Landy and his family. We saw them all the time.

There were times that were hard and lonely, especially when Donna began school and I had to transition from going to all of the races to staying home. Fortunately, by that time, we had enough money where Don could come home more often. He would be gone for maybe a week and then fly home. So, it wasn't quite as bad as some of the guys who couldn't afford to come home. My girlfriend's husband, he'd go on the road for a month and she wouldn't see him.

I never had a moment where all of a sudden I realized that Don was famous. When we had Donna, I don't even think she understood what her dad did. I remember once the little boy next door and Donna—they had to have been maybe 3 or 4 years old—were playing in the sandbox and I was at the kitchen window, and I overheard him ask what her dad did. She replied, "I don't know; he drives cars." She didn't even know it was a race car!

The rise to fame was so gradual that I didn't think of him as a rock star. Now I do, but in those days, it didn't seem like it. We were so serious—well, Don was so serious—that we could have a great year, but if there was one bad weekend, it would feel like, "Oh my god. We're not going to make it." It was very dramatic.

The scariest moment was seeing the photos of Don in Seattle with the Hot Wheels car because I wasn't there and later seeing that wreckage was terrifying. I never really worried much about Don's safety. He was such a nut about making sure everything was good on the car that I didn't have that fear like a lot of women did. Seeing that aftermath was very frightening. I guess I learned to drink more wine in those days. I don't know. You just dealt with it. It was part of your life. I wasn't quite as nervous about that as maybe I should have been. I was always confident that he would do the right thing and he would be safe.

I am just thankful for my life, his life, and where we've ended up. I don't have any regrets. A lot of times were harder than others, but I feel blessed. I have a beautiful daughter who I love, my dogs, and a gorgeous house. What more could I want? I feel very lucky. We worked hard, but we got lucky.

The wedge looked better than it ran. It was heavy. Buttera was experimenting, but it wasn't a successful direction.

Nye Frank and Quinn Epperly built the aluminum body, and those guys were well known for their metalwork, but just because something looks like an IndyCar, doesn't mean it will run like one. It was my first rear-engine dragster, and it didn't do much to win me over to the format. One thing that's sort of funny looking back is that I was such a diehard racer that it didn't even occur to me to ask Hot Wheels how they felt about me building a new dragster. I didn't ask anybody's permission, I just went ahead and built it. I put the Hot Wheels name on it, and I guess they liked it because they built model cars of it. They built one for McEwen too. He never had an actual wedge car, but they built Snake and Mongoose wedge dragster toy models. I think they went better on the Hot Wheels tracks than they did on the real track.

The *Yellow Feather*

The last straw for the wedge was when we were back East. I'd been dragging it around on tour with us. We were in upstate New York at some track. I don't even remember where. I was at the starting line, and I go *Jhooom* and left the line. All of a sudden, I saw Garlits in this little, bitty, rear-engine car with no body, just aluminum wrapped around the cockpit of the car. It squirted off and beat me by half the f——ing drag strip.

I put that wedge son of a bitch in the trailer, went home, got rid of it, and built the *Yellow Feather*. That was the start of the end for my relationship with Buttera. I went to Kent Fuller, and he built me the *Yellow Feather*. Garlits named it. It was a light, little, yellow dragster like the GBP dragster, and it ran well. The thing only weighed 1,280 pounds. Everything was super light after that.

We had some good races in the *Yellow Feather*. At Lions Drag Strip in January, I defeated John Wiebe with a 6.174 over his 6.175. It was the first time two cars ran under 6.20 elapsed times. It's not like I won every national event in the world. Although we won a lot of them, I lost a lot of them too. That was a strange time, 1971 and 1972. It was my first rear-engine dragster experience. I was trying to learn about it, and at the same time the Funny Cars were taking off. But at that point, mostly the Funny Car was still more of an exhibition car, and the dragster was for NHRA competition. It was almost like having two totally separate racing jobs.

The Yellow Feather at Orange County. We were always trying different wings. If you look at later photos of the car, the wings are a little smaller and painted.

The Yellow Feather *in the lights. You can see the chute just starting to come out.*

We built the Yellow Feather after the failed wedge dragster. That's my cousin Mark Prudhomme in the background. He worked for us on and off for several years in the 1970s. He was really the only family member aside from my cousin Harold who liked racing and cars.

Don Garlits named the Yellow Feather. He inspired it by beating me with one of his super lightweight Swamp Rat dragsters when I was in the heavy wedge car.

Pushing the Yellow Feather around the track. You can see the push truck has a corresponding number to my competition #712.

Match Race Madness

The fans wanted to see Snake and Mongoose race each other more than they wanted to see just the Snake or just the Mongoose. At a national event, I didn't know if I was going to race McEwen, Garlits, or some guy no one had ever heard of. Also, there was no money in it. If you went out in the first or second round, you might make a few bucks, but it certainly didn't cover your expenses. Running match races was equally as important to us as running the national events, maybe more back then.

We had some regular crew by that point, as well as guys who'd come along for fun. We'd take the pickup truck and trailer and the big truck with the Funny Car. We had a guy, Big Hermie. On one trip, he was driving the Hot Wheels truck, and we were pulling into U.S. 131 Dragway for a match race. He was coming down the off-ramp going into Martin, Michigan, and a car stopped in front of him. Hermie couldn't stop the truck in time, and he plowed into the back of the car and hurt the guy. There was a lawsuit over it. Fortunately, not with the sponsor—just with our insurance company. It was the first accident that we ever really had on the road that involved hurting someone. We were lucky that we didn't have more with the hours that we'd keep going up and down the road. We got the guy off to the hospital, and then we went over to the dragway and won the race. I think that was 1971.

Even now I need to thank Lynn for that one, because she was the one who made sure we had insurance and permits. In those days, we didn't have to stop at the scales, but we were going through toll booths and things like that, and she would make sure that we were prepared. We were covered as well as anybody out on the road. I certainly wouldn't have thought about that and would have ended up missing a race for lack of toll money or something.

Every so often we'd get pulled over though, and we always made sure that we had an extra T-shirt and baseball cap to give the officers. Usually they just let us go because they only wanted to look at the car. It didn't hurt to have an extra little Hot Wheel toy in the back in the sleeper to give a cop when he pulled you over, but you couldn't count on everybody being a racing fan. Later on, when we started going through scales, you'd better have a cap and T-shirts because you'd be overweight for sure if you didn't.

Drag Racing was Faaaar Out

There were all kinds of personalities in drag racing. McEwen and I, we were kind of clean cut and family friendly with the Hot Wheels sponsorship, and that always stuck with me. I was always focused on trying to appear as professional as possible. On the other end of things were the real wild guys, guys like "Jungle" Jim Liberman with his long hair and crazy paintjobs. I raced him a few times in match races, but he was far East Coast and I was West Coast, so we didn't

Some tracks would send you a certificate in the mail after a record run. It didn't happen often, but it was always very nice that someone took the time to do that. This was for a 204-mph run in Utah in 1971.

overlap very often. It's not that I didn't like him, it's just that we looked differently at drag racing.

Jungle, he lived like a hobo on the road, and they partied and smoked dope. I was thinking more about building up the sport and being part of the big picture. Jungle lived for day to day; he was a wild character, a real wild-ass guy. His car had this big face painted on it. I wanted a corporate-looking paint scheme like I had with Hot Wheels. I wasn't too big on the idea of having a big picture of me on the car because that didn't pay any money. I respected Jungle Jim; we just weren't each other's kind of guy.

One time, there was a race up at Fremont Drag Strip. Bill Doner was putting it on. We went out on this boat and Jungle was with us. I knew him and his girlfriend, Pam. She was so hot that she kind of scared me a little bit. She was a little intimidating. Anyhow, we're on the boat and Jungle whipped out his harmonica and started playing. He was pretty goddamn good with it. I thought, "This guy's okay. This guy's pretty cool." But that's the closest we ever came to hanging out together.

Paint or Primer

Remember that flying Funny Car fire where we blew the body off and burned it up? Well, that wasn't the end of the racing season. We had to scramble to get a new body and get the car back together. It wasn't very easy to get something painted. You put it in the paint shop with Bill Carter or one of those guys, and then you had to wait until they were ready to spray it and stripe it up. Painters have always worked on their own schedule. As a painter, I should know.

We had to race that weekend, so I didn't have time for stripes and waiting. So, we just got the body mounted, and it was probably about Wednesday by then. It wasn't like me to take a car out that wasn't painted. Guys would work all night long in the paint shop. I mean, we'd get to the races, and the car would still be wet because I thought it was really important to present a nice car. However, in this case, there just wasn't enough time, so I said, "You know what? F—— it. Let's just go with it."

We sprayed primer, just black primer, and put the decals on it. I thought people would probably laugh at me. I was a little worried about it but not

"[Jungle Pam] was so hot that she kind of scared me a little bit."

After we burned up the other 'Cuda body, there wasn't time to paint the replacement. I was worried it would look shabby, but the all-black 'Cuda ended up being one of my more popular paint schemes!

too worried because, first off, the car was lighter with no paint on it. We only ran it like that for a couple of weeks, but it was a big hit. People liked it, but I didn't realize they liked it until much later. I only did it because of the necessity of getting out to the track and being able to race. That ended up being one of the most popular cars that I had.

When Opportunity Knocks

The fact that Lynn and I could pay our bills with racing never stopped amazing me, and after the Hot Wheels deal, we weren't just paying the bills, we were making a living. We were paying our bills, and I was even able to help out my mom and my sisters, which felt pretty good to me. I always felt guilty about leaving them behind when I first moved out.

We sold the little house, and we got a place in Granada Hills. It was a nice house off the beaten path up against the foothills. There was a piece of property behind us, right next door. The kids in the neighborhood would ride their dirt bikes over there, and I would ride sometimes too. One of the kids' dads had a tractor, and he built jumps. We had our own motocross track right behind us. Well, I thought it was wonderful, right?

The problem was that there were other neighbors in the area, and they were complaining about the noise. The woman who owned the land lived in Malibu, and she got these phone calls. So one day she came over and knocked on our door and told me she's getting all these complaints. I'm going, "Oh, that's too bad." I'm listening, but I'm not really listening, because it's not my property or my kids. Then she said, "Why don't you buy that property?"

I thought, "Are you kidding? We already get to use it for nothing." I wasn't being a smart ass, I was just being logical, right? She wanted almost as much for the property as we had paid for our house, and we still had big payments on the house. I said no and kept riding motorcycles, and I forgot

"When opportunity knocks, you need to learn how to take advantage of it."

From left to right: That's Okie, some cute girl (maybe Miss Orange County), me, my cousin Mark Prud-homme, and Bob Brandt in the winner's circle. I'm about 90-percent sure it's Orange County. We had beer in cups because at the time they were trying to clean up the sport and not have booze in the photos.

My cousin Mark Prudhomme was Leonard's kid. He worked for us for a few years and I was sort of hoping he'd really get into it, but he had other interests. Too bad, he was really good with the car.

about it. Then, one day I was back there, and I saw surveyors working on the property. I called the owner back, and she told me that I was too late. The property had been sold, and they were building houses there. She paused for a minute and said, "Young man, I want to tell you something. When opportunity knocks, you need to learn how to take advantage of it." She was so right. They built the house and blocked our view. No more motorcycle riding. I was crushed, but I never forgot that. You need to recognize when you have an opportunity.

Not So Carefree

Eventually, I didn't have time to split between dragster and Funny Car. The way we were racing was changing, and the expectations the sponsors had were changing. The Hot Wheels situation was running out. That started to go away, and Carefree came on board. That was a deal that Mongoose put together, and the only thing we got out of that deal was chewing gum. I'm not kidding you. I guess we could use the chewed gum to stick our bills up on the wall, but it sure wasn't enough to pay to keep up with a dragster and a Funny Car.

I think that was the beginning of my first slump. Before that, even if it was not as successful of a year, I still felt like I won more than I lost and made more than I spent. The Carefree car was anything but carefree.

Out of the Slump

By the 1970s, most of our friends had kids. We didn't have any kids, but it wasn't that we didn't want them. In fact, we were trying, but it wasn't happening. I did tests, Lynn did tests, and nothing was wrong, but it seemed like it just wasn't going to happen for us. We were ready to adopt, we were even talking about it on a trip up to Yosemite, but then we came home, and Lynn said, "I think I'm pregnant." Get the hell out. Sure enough, she was pregnant, and that changed our lives completely. It was a really cool deal.

I remember everything about that weekend in 1973 when Donna was born. It was during the slump, when I wasn't winning much. I had an out-of-town race in Michigan and then rushed home to be with Lynn at St.

A few guys were getting their hands burned even through the Nomex gloves. The material would get so hot, they'd get burns from that. Someone figured out that if you wore a cotton glove under the fire glove, it would add more protection. Now they have much better fireproof gloves.

Lynn used to wear white jeans to the track. Actually, a lot of us wore white pants. It sounds crazy, but she says the only way you could get them clean was by bleaching them. Blue jeans would get ruined by the bleach.

Joseph's Hospital in Burbank. Donna was early, very premature. We resigned ourselves to the fact that Lynn was going to have a miscarriage and Donna wasn't going to make it. Man, that was a bad deal. The doctor wasn't very encouraging, but one nurse leaned over and said, "No, this baby is going to be fine, she's going to make it."

Sure enough, she made it. She was 4 pounds, 4 ounces. I went into the room afterward because they didn't want me in there during the birth because they thought she was going to be stillborn. Donna was in a little crib, just a tiny little thing, and she had tubes sticking out of her, but she was healthy. I knew right then that everything was going well. I was so thrilled that I had a kid. At the time, Ritchie Valens had a song out called "Donna," so we named her Donna. I had to leave the hospital, get on a plane, and go back to Martin, Michigan, and I remember singing "Donna," to myself in the car on the way there.

I got back to the race and we won the whole thing, set a new record, and did everything right. I contribute it to Donna. She changed my luck completely. All of the sudden, there was this other person who I brought into this world. My racing went straight up after that as far as working hard, hitting sponsorships, and making money. It was pretty cool. There's a connection between feeling good and doing well. It's not always something you can control, but it's there.

Out of the Black and into the Pink

I was working out of Keith Black's place. Mind you, I lived in the San Fernando Valley and I drove every day down to South Gate, which was more than 40 miles away. So, it was a lot of time just driving there and back.

By that point, Keith had started getting to where he was more of a manufacturer than a race engine builder. He was doing these aluminum blocks, his business was growing, and he didn't have time to be going out to the races with me and Roland or Bob. He wasn't that old, but he was old for his age, the Reverend Mr. Black.

At some point, I was talking to Ed Pink about it. He was building these 426 Hemis that were badass, and he was based in Van Nuys, which was just down the street from Granada Hills. Pink had some little shops in the back of his place, and he offered me a stall if I wanted to move my stuff there. I told Keith, "Hey, I'm going to move out there and, you know." He just said, "Well, I wish you luck." That was it. It didn't really bother him much.

One of the reasons that he didn't care when we left was because he wasn't dependent on us for work. In the early days, he would build the whole engine for someone, and most of his customers would blow it up and then send it back for him to rebuild it. Roland and I couldn't afford to do that, and Keith was really good about teaching us how to maintain the engines, how to disassemble them, troubleshoot, and reassemble them. No one could afford to go to Keith Black every week and bring an engine there to have it worked on. You had to work on it yourself unless you were a multimillionaire, and I didn't know too many of those. So, when I moved out, it wasn't a problem for Keith, he probably appreciated getting the space back.

When I got to Pink's, oh my God, Ed Pink was amazing. It was a whole new world. To start with, he was a totally different personality than Black. He would shoot craps with the guys at night. He'd pull out the card table and have a couple of beers. He was one of the boys and was really fun. Most of all, he was really on top of the 426 engine.

His engines looked like a Rolex watch when they were taken apart. He painted the inside, the pistons were all polished, and the valves were all perfect. Plus, he built his own superchargers. We were able to get all of that stuff that he had and it put our car right at the top of the heap.

I learned a lot working out of Pink's place. He did work for a lot of the fast guys, including Barry Setzer, Don Schumacher, and Richard Tharp in the *Blue Max*. They were all running Ed Pink engines. Bob Brandt and I were running the same engines at first. Pink built the first one. Actually, I think he built two of them. He showed us how to maintain them, and we'd still buy parts from him. Eventually, we would just buy rods from the same place he bought them from, or we'd buy our own pistons. We had to (to save money). He understood but didn't love it.

Flow Bench

Pink had a flow bench in his shop, and no one else had flow benches for the fuel systems. Maybe the fuel system companies like Enderle and Hilborn had one, but there weren't many flow benches around the regular shops. We would take our pump up front each week to have it flowed and get it back. We'd have our blower tested by Pink and so on. Finally, in our back shop there, Bob Brandt said to me, "Hey, why don't we build our own flow bench? Then we could do our own s—— the way we want to." And I said, "Well, who's going to do it?" He says, "I can. I'll do it."

So, Bob Brandt built the first flow bench that I ever had. Pink didn't like the idea because we stopped taking our fuel pumps to him. We started finding stuff out about our own fuel pumps that was different than the way he was doing it. And it gave us an advantage down at the racetrack.

We'd run stiffer idler springs and have the pumps redone by Enderle. We were keeping secrets from Pink because we didn't want his other customers beating us. We'd go out to the racetrack, Pink would be working on Barry Setzer's car, and we had to race him. Well, we wanted to kick their ass, you know? And they wanted to kick our ass. So, we became not enemies but competition.

That's baby Donna. She's maybe 3 months old there. There was a double foldout in Drag News congratulating us on her birth. All the sponsors pitched in to celebrate.

Ed Pink was really good about sharing his engine knowhow with me as I was learning. Maybe too good. He might have regretted that later when Bob Brandt and I beat his other customers.

Bob Brandt built us a flow bench to test fuel pumps, which made it possible for us to really get ahead of the competition. It led to four championship years in a row. This photo is from later (in 1994). It's a mess because we had just had a big earthquake in Northridge.

Working on the cars in the Northridge shop. You can see the naked Funny Car chassis and a spare engine block against the back wall. I visited that shop a few years ago, and it's all different of course; it's no longer a race shop, but that loft storage area is still in the building, as are the stairs, which Bob Brandt and I built. (Photo Courtesy National Hot Rod Association/NHRA National Dragster)

Taking Names and Cashing Checks

It probably wouldn't have mattered, except we started kicking all of his customers' asses. I mean, big time. His customers were thinking, "How are these guys so fast?" We were still working out of the back of Pink's place, but things were getting a little hot and heavy over there.

It's not like I tried to make it better; I'd start stuff. In the morning, I used to go in, walk up to the front shop, and say, "Hey, chief [that's what I used to call Pink]. What's going on?" And he'd give me a dirty look. He didn't like for me to call him chief, but I liked to kind of rattle his cage. Then, I'd go over and get myself a free cup of coffee from his coffeepot. That would really piss him off because I wasn't spending any money with him anymore since we were doing our own stuff.

Finally, one year for Christmas (the last one we were there), he said, "Hey, you've done such a good job racing and everything, so the guys and I bought you a Christmas present." I thought, "Oh s——, that's really nice." So, I went up there, opened the present, and it was the old, used coffee pot. Message received. I wouldn't be drinking their coffee anymore. They didn't even want me in the shop. And so, about that time we bought our own shop.

Enter the Army

Picture this: I've got bills to pay, crew guys, and a shop and house mortgage. I'm sitting there chewing my free chewing gum and wondering how I'm going to pay to run my car because that Carefree sponsorship wasn't cutting it. I still had match races, and I still had a deal with Wynn's and some

The very first Army car, the Vega, at Bee Line Dragway. It didn't work very well, and I got rid of it quickly. It had that slot in the roof so I could see out of it; it was so low.

associate sponsors, but mostly we made the money going 'round and 'round the country to different tracks. We booked in Fremont or Chicago, you name it. Wherever there was a racetrack, we'd be on the road running there.

On Each Other's Nerves

McEwen and I were getting on each other's nerves. He got the Hot Wheels deal and got us all started, and I think he blamed me for losing the Hot Wheels deal by not being promotionally minded enough. I blamed him for not running well enough so that they didn't want us.

In his opinion, I was a real hard-nosed racer and I wasn't nice enough to the fans or to the Hot Wheel guys. And I guess, looking back on it, he was probably right. I was all about racing, and I wasn't about doing the public relations side of things like he was. It's not that I thought that I was too good for it; it's more like when the teacher asks for an answer in school, and some kids raise their hands up real high. I was the guy who kept my head down. I didn't want to deal with that stuff. I'd let him deal with it.

I thought he was too casual about the racing. You know, I'd be in the parking lot honing my cylinder walls because I was going to race his ass that night (and I was planning on winning), and he'd be in the hotel room with the air-conditioning going, peeking out the window and laughing at me because I've got sweat rolling off me with no shirt on.

So, I got pissed off at him because he wasn't working on his car, and he was pissed at me because I wasn't working on the sponsors. That broke up the partnership. His next move was to go out and get the U.S. Navy. But it was like the Carefree thing, where there was no money involved. It was just an advertising thing he was doing.

A friend of mine, Bob Kachler, was an artist in Long Beach who dabbled as a promoter as well. He said, "Why don't you go to the U.S. Army?" I thought he was nuts because everyone knew that was government money and it couldn't be spent on racing. I said, "I'm not going to do that because I need to get paid. I had a dry year with McEwen and Carefree, and I don't want to do that again."

Kachler said we should talk to the U.S. Army's advertising agency, since they were taking out ads in *Hot Rod* and in sports magazines. He got ahold of them and started talking about them doing some advertising on our race car, and us working with the recruiters in high schools and even at the racetrack.

NATIONAL HOT ROD ASSOCIATION
10639 RIVERSIDE DR., NORTH HOLLYWOOD, CALIFORNIA 91602 • (213) 877-2751

September 24, 1974

Mr. Don Prudhomme
11564 Lerdo
Granada Hills, California 91344

Dear Don:

Enclosed is a little extra memento of your
victory at the 20th Anniversay U.S. NATIONALS.

Your having won in a field of such tough competition is one more verification of your
capability and we are proud to have you as
one of our champions.

I hope I will see you again, under similar
enjoyable circumstances.

Best regards,

Wally

WALLY PARKS
President

WP/mz
encl.

I don't remember what the memento Wally mentions in this letter was; it was probably a photo. He would often send little letters when we did well.

"I didn't graduate high school and was so dyslexic that I could barely read, and here I'm being invited to stand up with a microphone and talk to a room of people."

And the agency said, "Great idea. We'll treat this just like we do if we're running an ad in *Hot Rod* magazine. We'll pay you guys to basically run an ad on your race car." That's how we did it. It was the most fabulous thing ever.

Recruiting

With the U.S. Army deal, we would send the recruiter our match racing schedule, he would see that we were running in Union Grove, Wisconsin, and he'd have us meet him at a high school nearby. We would bring the race car by the high school and unload it (not start up or anything, just unload it), and the kids would gather all around the car. By the time we left, the recruiter was a cool guy. Before that, he used to walk into the school and the kids would all duck their heads because they didn't want to be involved. But all of a sudden, the recruiter became a hip guy and someone they could talk to about joining the U.S. Army. Now they paid attention to what the army had to offer. It ended up being a tremendous program, and the best part is that we got paid for it.

I got to meet a lot of different recruiters and high school kids, and my attitude got a lot better about dealing with people and dealing with young people. I felt like I was giving something back, like I was giving some kid some opportunity that he didn't realize was out there, whether it was motor racing or working on engines—things like that. I still get people coming up to me and say, "Hey, you were at our high school when I was just a young kid. You came by and showed us your car."

Public Speaking

Hot Wheels was mainly with little kids. They were real little kids, and they had their Hot Wheel cars, and that was cool, only I was kind of clumsy around young kids. McEwen had kids, so he was better at joking with them and playing with them. I had an easier time with the older kids at the high schools. The most important part of it for me though wasn't the money or even getting over being shy, it was getting up in front of a bunch of people and talking. I'd never done that before. I certainly didn't have to do it with little kids who were buying Hot Wheel cars.

I didn't graduate high school and was so dyslexic that I could barely read, and here I'm being invited to stand up with a microphone and talk to a room of people. I spoke about highway safety, how not to speed on the highway, and why you should go to the drag strip if you want to drag race. I learned to speak in front of people, which really helped me a lot later on.

I never really wrote things down. I just memorized the main points, and then I was pretty good at winging it from there. I'd go into a room and not even know what the hell I was going to say until I got there. It might have been, "Hey, how many of you guys have a GTO?" "How many of you guys have a car?" or "Who's got a driver's license?" Even today when I do speeches and different things, I pretty much wing it.

The Recount

I know that a lot of guys didn't like me, but for the most part, I didn't dislike most of the people I raced. I just wanted to beat them, not drink beer with them. One guy I did dislike was Billy Meyer. He was an archenemy, and not just on the drag strip. One of the big drag racing papers was *Drag News*. *Drag News* had this award for "Driver of the Year," and winning that was almost like another championship.

I liked that jacket. I'm wearing it in a lot of photos from this time period.

We were competing for the award against Meyer, and I had to run against him at the 1974 U.S. Nationals in the final round. We got rained out and had to come back on Tuesday morning. Meyer was really running well in the event. As a matter of fact, he'd run a little bit better than us. Brandt and I loaded our car on the trailer and took it back to the hotel because we had to figure out why it wasn't performing like it should. It was raining like hell at the track and, no surprise, it was raining like hell at the hotel too. We didn't even know if we were going to be able to run the next day.

We spent all night working on the thing, and while we were working, Meyer and all those guys were in the bar partying it up because all they had to do was just show up and beat us that next day. So, they were having a grand old party, and we were out in the trailer working on the car. The next day at the races, we did our burnouts and staged and he smoked his tires. We ran down through there and won the race, and I bet they regretted partying all night long. Anyhow, I don't think he was too happy with us.

When the time came for the *Drag News* "Driver of the Year," I kind of thought we were a shoo-in. Then I got a call and it turned out that Billy Meyer won it. I said, "How the f—— did he win it? I mean, I beat his ass. How did he win it?" They said, "Well, all we can tell you is these are the votes." I jumped in my car and I smoked it over there and said, "I want to count them all. I want a recount."

They pulled out the ballots, and it became clear that someone over at Meyer's had made copies of the ballot. Like, not the original page in the magazine but a Xerox copy of it. I think Meyer's dad owned a printing place, and they sent that copy to people who worked for his dad to get them to vote for Meyer. It was cheating! When they took out all the copies, I'd won it hands down.

Billy and I went to fisticuffs over it. I was really hot about it, and I slapped his ass around. We weren't too tight after that for many, many years. We're okay now, but we weren't then. That's when the big money came in to racing, and it wasn't a game to us anymore. Brandt and I had to win to keep racing, and a kid like Meyer gets his daddy to pay for the parts and get him wins. I never did care for those guys—the rich kids whose dads bought them engines, superchargers, and fancy trailers. I never was buddies with those guys. Maybe I was jealous. Maybe I still am.

The Championship

Until 1975, the national events were not as much of a focus for me because there was not much money in winning and no championship. You'd win the trophy and some money, and

Drag News's *Driver of the Year was a big deal. I won it several years in a row—not without some drama. Getting voted for this or for the Car Craft All-Stars was almost like winning another championship.*

the best part was that you'd be on TV. Basically, you did it for the television exposure.

To win a championship, you'd have to run in a division race. You would get points for running that, then you'd go run a national event. They would determine who the champion was that year by the amount of points from the divisional race and then the amount of points you get at a national event.

We didn't run any divisional races because they didn't pay, and we were too busy barnstorming up and down the road, getting paid to run the car. In 1975, it all changed when Winston cigarettes with Ralph Seagraves came in as a title sponsor for the NHRA.

Shirl Greer had won the championship in 1974, and I raced him in 1975 at Ontario. He caught on fire, he burned up or something, and I lent him some parts. Someone said to me, "Don't you know this is for the championship? If he goes on and wins, it's for the championship." And said, "What? What championship?" He said, "The world championship." I didn't really know there was one.

From left to right: Bill Jenkins, Marvin Graham, me, and Wally Parks (top right) in the winner's circle of the 1975 Springnationals. You can see how the Winston sponsorship of the series made everything look so professional.

It didn't really dawn on me that that was a big deal. I'm not being snobbish or anything, but we had to make money by getting paid going into races and match racing. So, Shirl won the championship and then I thought, "Jesus, maybe that's something we should do." At the same time, Winston came into our sport and put up $25,000 for the world champion. I thought, that's definitely something we should do. I want a piece of that.

There were a bunch of us who used to go riding. Sometimes we'd ride on Pete Petersen's (from Hot Rod magazine) ranch. It would be a mix of racers. Pro Stock racer Dick Landy would go a lot, as did guys from Plymouth and from some of the parts companies. It was a lot of fun.

Winston

I remember meeting Ralph Seagraves. He had a cigarette coming out each side of his mouth; he was a chain smoker. And he had on his red-and-white Winston outfit that he'd wear everywhere; he was like Santa Claus. He's at this NHRA function, and Winston absolutely changed the sport.

They started painting up the tracks and putting Winston signage all over, and it looked real professional. I smoked at the time. You could get as many packs of cigarettes as you could carry in your pockets. Roland and I both smoked like chimneys. We loved having the Winston cigarettes, but most of all we liked having the $25,000 put up for winning. That year, I went out and won the championship and made $25,000 extra. That was a lot of money.

They spent a lot of money promoting the sport. And when they promoted the sport, they promoted me too because I was a Winston world champion. I mean, the Hot Wheels deal was a big deal, but winning the Winston championship was the thing that really kicked off my career. And from then on, we won it four straight years, Winston along with the U.S. Army sponsorship.

The Monza replaced the Vega, and wow, what a difference. With this car, we won the first and second championships and seven of eight national events.

Lynn, Wally, and me celebrating my first, and the NHRA's first, Winston championship in 1976.

First Funny Car in the 5s! You never knew when you would get a plaque or a ring for setting a milestone or a record, but it was always a nice feeling to stand up there with a sponsor and Wally Parks (right) to be recognized.

Here's an advertisement for Federal-Mogul. I also had a deal with Suzuki at the time. They used to give us pit bikes and street bikes to use at the track.

Two of the best-known names on four wheels introduce three great products for two wheels.

I asked Niki Lauda if he wanted to swap cars, but he said Mr. Ferrari wouldn't be pleased. He did give me a ride in a Ferrari 308 though.

"Niki, Wanna Drive?"

"If I didn't know much about Formula 1, [Niki Lauda] knew even less about drag racing."

The year 1976 was a good one. We were really on a roll with our Funny Car as defending champions on the way to a second championship. Goodyear did a promotion with us in Europe. They shipped the car over to Bologna, Italy, and that's when I first discovered how the other half of the world lives.

Formula 1 was eye-opening. The Funny Car was on display, a group came over to look at it, and one of the guys was Niki Lauda. I hadn't met him before, but I had certainly heard of him. And if I didn't know much about Formula 1, he knew even less about drag racing, but he came to the Bologna show, kneeled down, looked in the Funny Car, and was obviously interested in it. I asked him if he wanted to drive it, but he said that Mr. Ferrari wouldn't like that at all. He wasn't allowed to drive anything else under his contract—especially not a Funny Car. I liked him though. I thought he was very cool.

A Ride with Niki Lauda

Later on that trip, we went over to the Ferrari plant, and the Goodyear guy, Bernard Cahier, took me to meet Enzo Ferrari. I may have been focused on drag racing, but even I'd heard about Ferrari, his son Dino, and how he kept a photo of Dino in his office with a flower in front of it. Sure enough, I walked in the office, and there was a picture of Dino and a flower in the vase and there was Enzo Ferrari there to meet me.

Enzo didn't speak English and I didn't speak Italian, but Bernard translated and told him we were going across the street to watch Niki run his car. Enzo must have approved because he gave me a book and a scarf for Lynn, and he came over to the test track with us. I can still picture him there, standing in his long overcoat, watching Lauda drive. He always wore this big, long

Goodyear shipped the Army car over for exhibition.

In 1976, Goodyear took a bunch of its racers to Italy for a big event. I got to meet a lot of the European Formula 1 racers, such as Jackie Stewart.

Nobody in Italy had ever seen or smelled anything like a nitro Funny Car.

All the Formula 1 guys start in go-karts. I didn't fit well in them, maybe that's why my road-race career never took off.

We left the car on display and the Goodyear rep took us on a tour of the Ferrari factory.

They wanted me to do exhibition passes, but it turned out that there wasn't enough room. I ended up spinning the car out at the end of the parking lot, and then they wanted that every time.

That trip to Italy really broadened my mind about racing, about style, about everything. I arrived home as a huge Formula 1 fan.

"The other thing I came home with was the desire for a Ferrari."

overcoat. He was definitely the main man. You could tell just by looking at him and by the way his people responded to him. He was quite a guy. I guess it's a good thing that he didn't know I was friends with Carroll Shelby, otherwise he might have thrown me out of the office.

This was right after Lauda had been burned in that bad accident in Germany. He recovered enough to be testing, but he was still running the car in bandages. There was a Ferrari 308 there at the track, and he offered me a ride. I'd been around a road course a little bit before that but never with someone who knew what he was doing. Oh, it was amazing. I mean, he'd run the car right up to the corner, and I'm going, "We're not going to make it—we're not going to make this," and . . . *shoop*, it goes right around the turn. He was amazing. It made me wish that I was doing that for a living, that I was a Formula 1 driver, a road racer. After that, I always followed the IndyCar racing and the Formula 1 racing. Those guys were my heroes: Niki Lauda, James Hunt, and later, Ayrton Senna.

Italian Stylin'

I couldn't be a road racer, but I did try to bring some of that European style back with me to drag racing. The Formula 1 guys used to have these bitchin' jackets, built and fitted way nicer than the s—— we had over here. I started getting some of our jackets and uniforms made like the Formula 1 guys had. It's a little like when I met the Ford guys back in the 1960s and they had these nice, clean button-up shirts, and that look always stuck with me. Professional.

The other thing I came home with was the desire for a Ferrari. So, it was an expensive trip in the end! I'd never thought about having one before then or even being able to afford one. As it turns out, there was a collector in Nevada, Bill Harrah, who wanted the Chevy Monza for a museum he was building. Wally Parks thought I should do it because it reflected well on the NHRA, but I didn't really want to let it go. I would really get attached to the cars, and that one (with all its wins and records) was especially cool.

Harrah said, "Well, what would you want in exchange?" And he had a Ferrari dealership, so I said, "Well, how about a Ferrari?" I traded him the Monza for a brand-new 308 GTB Ferrari. When I look back on it after all these years, Harrah got the best deal. I wish I had the Monza back. It's worth more than the Ferrari to me.

Building a Team

For the first decade, heck, maybe for the first two decades of racing, aside from a few key guys like Roland or Bob Brandt, the teams would kind of

MEMORIES FROM BOB BRANDT

If you want to understand what Snake was like as a racer, picture this: I was at the track in Canada for a race, and this van pulls in. Inside were Lynn and Donna, and Snake was lying in the back on a mattress with a doctor working on his back. In the hotel, I guess he went to pick Donna up out of the bathtub, and he threw out his back. When they got to the track, he could barely get his fire suit on, let alone get in the car, but he made all the runs and we won the event. The thing is, anybody else would have said, "Pack it up, we're heading out. We're not going to run this race, you know. He's hurt." But he did whatever he had to do to get down that track every time. Amazing.

I was used to it; that's just the way we rode, you know. Something went wrong, and we went over it. I wasn't ever starstruck by Snake or drag racing because it wasn't like I was looking for a job to be a crew chief. I was doing heating/air-conditioning over in Azusa when I first met Snake. I was a tool and die maker. That's how Snake and I first hit it off. There was stuff that needed to be done outside of the racing. The radiator went out in the truck, I could fix that, and Snake was impressed.

We figured things out on our own. When we first had the *Yellow Feather* dragster, we needed a wing, a good wing that would go back down after it had done its job, one that would release and allow us to run faster at the top end. Tom Hanna built this test wing for us. He had a Ford Falcon Ranchero, and he built a bracket out front and put the test wing on there. He tested different springs by taking it on the freeway, and at a certain speed, the thing would fold down. So, they kept changing the spring until they got it just where they wanted it, and then we ended up running it on the car.

We were always so involved in every detail of the cars during our time together. When we built the Arrow, we got a body in white from the factory delivered to us in a box truck so that nobody could see it. We took it right to the fiberglass shop, took a splash off of it, and then we built a buck, a mold, the plug, and stretched it. Snake and I were there every night working that fiberglass, tweaking it until we got the whole thing perfect.

That was the year we went to Italy with Goodyear. We had lunch with Enzo Ferrari in his own private luncheon room. Jackie Stewart and A. J. Foyt went with us. I have a photograph of myself with Enzo in his office. But while we were there, they had to take me to the hospital because my eye was bleeding. In the picture with Enzo, my eye's all bloody. The doctor couldn't find anything in my eye. Two or three different times they looked. Finally, we figured it out. It was fiberglass from working on the Plymouth Arrow.

That wasn't the most dramatic story of the trip. Goodyear shipped the Funny Car over, and Snake was doing exhibition runs with it. It was really cold over there, really cold. He was supposed to do a burnout and then pull the chute. All these people, they'd never seen tires this big, and they'd never seen nitro. There were so many people there, thousands of them. Snake got in the car, we started it up, and when he got down to the other end, the parachute didn't deploy. He was headed right into the crowd, and there was nothing but gravel at the end. Suddenly, the car spun around and stopped.

I got down to where he was at and said, "What the hell happened?" He goes, "There was no way to stop. I had to spin it out to keep from crashing." We got back, and the first thing they said is, "Can you do that every time?" He said, "Not a chance." Every day after that, when he left the starting line, he already had the chute coming out. No more spinouts.

It was impressive but not surprising. Snake can drive anything . . . except a golf ball.

come and go. Maybe a local guy would help you at an East Coast track, some other guys would help for a few races at home or maybe stay at the shop and do work, but it wasn't like today with full-time jobs for 20 people or more. I hope the guys who helped me over the years forgive me for not mentioning them all by name. There is one kid though, who I have to put in this story.

At this time, we were still working out of Pink's place, and I'd leave the trailer parked outside. One morning, we got to the shop and the trailer was open. Someone had broken the lock on the door and stolen a fire suit and some other stuff out of the trailer. Well, I went f——ing crazy. I was just pissed off as could be. "Who would do this?" I thought. I was really upset. Not long after, some kid comes by the shop on his bicycle and he said that he knows who stole my stuff because the kid who did it wore the fire suit jacket to school. It was a two-piece fire suit, and the jacket had my name on it.

It wasn't too hard to find out the kid's name: Billy Bevel. I ended up talking to his mother. I said, "Your kid's a thief." I was really on her ass about it, and she said, "Well, I'm bringing him over. He's really a good kid." She marched him over to the shop with the fire suit, and right away I took a liking to him. Although, I was still pretty peeved. I said, "Hey, your dad ought to kick your ass." He said, "Well, I don't have a dad." I said, "Oh, okay. Well, somebody ought to kick your ass." But I really wasn't mad at him anymore. I wanted to be mad, but the poor kid didn't have a father—it was just him and his mom doing the best that they could. I felt bad for him.

So, I gave him a choice. I said that I could go to the cops over this, or he could come by every day after school and sweep our shop out, clean up, clean the race cars off, and basically be a gofer. I figured that he'd come for a week or something and blow us off, but every day after school he'd be over there cleaning the race cars. That turned into going to the track with us, and eventually he became a good mechanic, and he stayed with us for years.

Monette's Death

Well, 1976 should have been one of the best years of my life. We'd won the championship, and we were on the way to win it again. Heck, we had won seven out of eight national events that year. Racing-wise we were incredible, but it was a terrible year for me on a personal level. My brother Monette died very unexpectedly, and it made me revisit a lot of my thoughts about my family. I felt a lot of guilt about how I had escaped from what to me was a bad place, but I always worried that I had left all of my sisters and brother to deal with it.

During that hyper-focused, win-at-all-costs time period, I heard that my brother died. Dropped dead at a truck stop. He was a long-haul trucker, and he had just been to the doctor in Los Angeles because of chest pains. The doctor wanted him to come back, but he had a trip to make back in Ohio. So, he went back to Ohio, and that was it. He never came back.

It turned out that he had a condition, diseased arteries, and he never knew. He was a young guy, not even 40. Who would ever think you'd drop dead of a heart attack at that age? My folks were still together at this point, although I couldn't tell you why; all they did was drink and fight in this little apartment over in Van Nuys. I can't remember who called me about Monette, but it wasn't either of my folks. They didn't know yet, and it was up to me to go over and tell them. I'll never forget the way my mom screamed when I told her. It went right through me.

"I'll never forget the way my mom screamed when I told her. It went right through me."

I wasn't close to him by that point. When he died, he was doing his thing and I was doing my thing, and I was kind of selfish. I cannot tell you how hard it is when you're young and you find a spot of light out in the distance and you're just trying to get there. When I first found drag racing, it was like I had been buried in a hole my whole life and I saw a light and was just digging to get out of the hole and nothing else mattered. That's how I was for all those years. Even when I was doing well, I never thought, "Hey, I've got it made, I should relax and spend time with my brother, see what I can do for him."

My whole life was drag racing, and I wish I would have spent more time with Monette, like you always do when someone's gone. When he died, it made me not like myself so much. I had just been thinking about me, me, me, winning races and winning races. I was just totally into that, until it was the whole world to me.

Snake Health

I'll tell you, Monette's death f——ing freaked me out big time. I was sad, I felt bad that I hadn't been there, and I was worried that it would happen to me too. We were racing our Funny Car, and you can imagine how busy we were and how stressed I was. I was at a match race and I checked myself into the hospital because I was so freaked out about my brother dying. I couldn't stop thinking about it.

The doctor gave me a stress test, and it all went pretty well, but the guy said, "I can't guarantee you that you don't have a problem that I can't see." Well, gee thanks. What am I going to do now? He said that the only way to know for sure was to do a heart catheterization. I figured that if I need my engine at 100 percent, then I need myself the same way—not 99 percent, all the way. You don't 99 percent win something; it's all or nothing. Of course, had I known what a big f——ing deal a heart catherization is, I might have settled for 99 percent, but I didn't know how dangerous it was.

They shoot dye up into your heart, but it's possible to have a bad reaction to the dye, and guess what happened? I died. I'm not kidding, I died right there on the table. When I woke up, they had a pacemaker they had stuck in me, and they were beating on me calling, "Don, Don, wake up, wake up," and there was blood everywhere.

I walked in there, but I left in a wheelchair. It knocked the s—— out of me. I was in there for about, oh man, about three days healing up from it. When I got out, we had a match race in Oregon, and I flew there to race but I was really weak and out of it. I put my fire suit on and passed out in the trailer. I still managed to run the race, but I took about a week off after that.

Something that happened at that first

Donna is around 4 years old here. She hadn't started school yet, so she and Lynn would come to almost all the races. It was hard sometimes with the late hours, but I always enjoyed having them there.

Taking Donna for a ride.

At the house in Granada Hills soon after we bought it. Lynn, me, Donna, and Pepper and Geoffrey. It's funny how many parallels I had with Garlits. He had the same kind of dogs: Yorkshire terriers. We used to take them on the road with us and so did he, and the dogs would play together.

I wish I had been able to spend more time at home when Donna was growing up. Missing out on family milestones is my biggest regret.

Lynn was behind the scenes of every contract, every paycheck we signed, every part we ordered, everything. Those trophies are as much hers as they are mine.

doctor visit is kind of funny in retrospect. When Lynn and I were waiting for the doc to get the results back, he was making small talk, and he said, "I don't see too many interracial couples." Lynn and I were both like, "Huh?" We had no idea what he was talking about. Even then, I still didn't acknowledge or understand my own history.

Under Pressure

I can look back now and pick some years that were more fun and others that weren't. It was more than just if we were winning or not . . . although, it was always better to be winning. Still, no matter what time period we are talking about, I was a pretty tightly wound guy at the track, and it resulted in stomach problems, not eating, and ulcers.

Even when things were going well (winning races and getting accolades, glory, and awards), that's still not easy on your system. People handle it differently. Some people just laugh it off and have a great ol' time. I took it really hard, and I wasn't alone. I remember hearing that Richard Petty had half of his stomach removed because of ulcers. He may not have shown it, but he was a stressed-out son of a bitch, and I was pretty close to the same.

Chatting with Garlits at the track. That's the Goodyear rep, Leo Mehl, in the background. He was an amazing guy who deserves more credit for drag racing becoming such a successful sport.

Even though drag racing was growing and becoming more professional, we still worked on the ground next to the trailer. There wasn't much separating us from the fans. It's less stressful the way they do it now because you don't get interrupted, but I think that access back then is what made people love the sport. They felt connected.

Ed Pink is talking to me about the tune-up of the engine or something. Pink was almost done with drag racing by the late 1970s, and he'd go on to do very well in Indy-Car and sports car racing.

For the most part, Shirley Muldowney and I didn't run the same category at the same time, so we didn't race in competition all that often, but I always had a lot of respect for her. We spent a lot of time on the road together. I like her. She had a hard go of it, and she was brave to stick with it and do so well.

Mongoose, Garlits, me, Ed "the Ace" McCulloch around 1978.

Bob Brandt, Mike Pelequin, me, and Billy Bevel. Mike was Bob's relative, one of those girlfriend's brother's sister's kid type deals. He was a good kid and a good worker. Bill Bevel and I met when he stole my racing suit from Pink's shop as a teen. He ended up giving it back and working for us for years.

In 1977, we built the Plymouth Arrow and won two more championships.

Secrets and Stress

After two championships, the car dominated again in 1977. We were still on top of our game. Winning felt different in the 1970s than it did back in the 1960s. Teams were still friends away from the track, but at the track, it felt like we had a target on our backs. We had to be very protective of what we were doing technically, and it was socially isolating. It was just Bob Brandt and me mainly.

When we were working out of the back of Ed Pink's shop, we were there day and night, and we weren't chitchatting with the people who stopped by. I wasn't trying to be unfriendly, but I sure wasn't going to go start a conversation with someone and start talking about what we're doing on our car.

In 1978, we won the championship for the fourth time.

Adding oil to the Plymouth Arrow Army car. That Cam2 oil really worked well. It was developed by General Motors, Sun Oil, and Roger Penske, and they sponsored a lot of successful racers. At first, Beadle and those guys thought I was crazy to run an off-the-shelf oil in the car. They ran a 70 heavy-weight that was just for race cars, but I swear, the Cam2 worked great!

I never was a guy who would go out and run well, and then tell everyone, "Hey, we found this really trick thing." I was the opposite; I didn't tell anybody. And being isolated and feeling that pressure, it was pretty stressful. Although, at the time I also enjoyed it.

Once you establish that you're capable of winning championships, there is just a lot more in the tank to draw from. I wasn't empty. I was building on it, and we were starting to get more recognized by sponsors. That's how you build a career. It's a good pressure.

It's a good thing, but it comes with expectations, and I didn't have a great way of handling that internally. I felt that pressure to keep winning. I had the fear of losing all the time and that's what drove me. It may have been productive, but it was a horrible feeling. Winning was great, but losing felt a lot worse than winning felt good to me. When you won, you would celebrate, it was great, and then it was over. But losing, oh, that hurt. That hurt stays with you. It eats at you. Winning doesn't eat at you; losing eats at you.

Looking back, I can see how grouchy I was starting to be at home with Lynn and Donna and grouchy at the track and at the shop with my crew. I was very touchy, and I was always on edge. I would get into someone's face because they did something wrong or didn't adjust something right. That would haunt me a bit going forward. I picked up a bad reputation for that. Once you're grouchy and s——ty to people, you can never put that behind you. They always remember, and there were worse days ahead.

The Greatest Loss

In the mid-1970s, a lot of the friendships from when I was younger suffered from the increased pressure we were all under. In particular, my relationship with McEwen wasn't great after Wildlife Racing ended. I think that we both had some hurt feelings. We would see each other at the track, but we weren't very close.

I got really busy racing, and my racing was going better than his. We were winning races with the Army car. I was on top of my game, and he was probably at the bottom of his game, so that is a hard place for two competitors to be at and still be friends. But then his kid got sick.

I liked his family. His 15-year-old son, Jamie, used to come to the track and hang out. I'd see him on the road. When Tom lost Jamie, I heard about it. When I saw him afterward, he was pretty down, and we just started talking about all the things that we've been through.

Brandt and I were running well at that particular time. When you are running well, you go into a race already thinking about who you're going to race in the semis or the final, versus back in the old days when we were just worrying about if we were going to qualify. So, at the 1978 U.S. Nationals, I was not betting on Tom McEwen as the guy I'd end up racing in the final round. I figured we'd end up against Raymond Beadle, who we were racing for the championship. But then McEwen took out Beadle. He beat Beadle!

Some people were surprised that McEwen was at the race because he had just lost his son only a few weeks before, if that. I was a little surprised. I mean, it made sense to me to race, but at the same time, I never felt like he was that focused on the races, so it wouldn't have been odd for him to skip it so soon after that tragedy.

When I checked in with him, though, he just acted different. He was serious in a way I'd never seen him before. He'd always been so casual at the track, and that weekend, he was not kidding around anymore. He had a different step to him. He acted like he was on a mission. Sure enough he was, it was the best he ever performed. He beat Beadle and Ron Colson (who I think crossed the centerline and got disqualified). Then, McEwen got a bye run, so during the single, he was able to shut it off at half-track and didn't hurt any parts. So, there we were: me and Mongoose racing in the final. He threw everything he had, and he just flat-ass beat us. He just f——ing beat us in the final round.

People have asked if I let him win or maybe spun the tires on purpose, and I can say that would never happen. I wanted to win that race. We messed up, and maybe we were cocky, thinking he would be easy to beat. Normally, we would have taken the clutch out of the car and reset it, but we didn't do it that round because we felt that it would be okay. Well, it wasn't okay, and it smoked the tires. He ran really well—a killer run. And he left ahead of me. It was just his day to win.

At the end of the track, I was still in the car in the shutoff area, and I was not happy to have lost. When somebody beat me, I would shut off the car, get the hell out of there, and go back to the pits so that I didn't have talk to anybody. But when Tom beat us, I thought, "Don, you need to go over there and congratulate Tom. You need to do that." He was still sitting in his car, just had the body up, and I went under the body and said, "Man, you did it. You smoked our ass." He said, "What happened to you?" And I said, "Spun the tires, but you ran good. Jamie would have been proud of you." And his eyes were full of tears.

When he got out of his car, he wasn't really celebrating the win like I thought he would. His crew was going crazy, but he wasn't really celebrating like that. He wasn't ribbing our guys, there was no, "I told you we could beat your ass" or anything like that. He was quieter. To me, it seemed like that moment was the end of his racing career. He was fulfilled. Even though he raced a little after that, I never felt like he was really in it that same way.

"That was the only race I was ever okay with losing."

That race changed a lot about our relationship because I gained a lot of respect for him. Before that, I loved him, but I didn't respect him as a driver or as a racer because he didn't try hard enough. I'd really try to beat him because I didn't feel as though he deserved to win since he didn't work as hard at it. He didn't sacrifice and do what it took. After he beat us at Indy, I saw him differently. I saw what he could do. That was the only race I was ever okay with losing. Mostly.

Eventually, You Lose

We went on winning for four consecutive years. It was getting tougher and tougher every year, and in 1979, the *Blue Max* Funny Car driven by Raymond Beadle finally knocked us off our perch. We didn't leave anything on the table, but the table itself was changing. Racing became more stressful as time went on. It got more serious as more money started coming into the sport.

The Gene Snows, the Ed McCullochs, and the Tom Hoovers were out

MEMORIES FROM PAT GALVIN

I grew up working on a neighbor's Funny Car, and from time to time, we would race Prudhomme. We were all in the Valley. I think the first time that I ever really truly had a conversation with Don was when my boss, Bob Pickett, got the Mickey Thompson U.S. Marines Funny Car deal in 1975, and we started seeing Don all over the country because we ran the same races. We got along with him, and being local Southern California racers, we were accustomed to him kicking our ass because he was that good. He was a couple notches above us, as he was for just about everyone. It made everyone work harder to try and compete with him.

He was always very nice to us. He was really friendly, which is not the character he's known for, but he would always talk to us in the staging lanes and have something funny to say. Maybe he took pity on us. There wasn't a huge divide between teams back then. There would be times when a race would get rained out or there'd be a lack of hotel rooms and our two crews would sleep in one room in some little dumpy hotel with people on the mattresses, floors, bedspreads, and in the bathtubs.

I worked for Snake in 1976, and it was everything you could imagine. He won everything; he dominated everything. He was the best tuner, the best driver, the best everything, and there was never a moment that he wasn't completely switched on. He and Brandt were a dream team. Everything was very intense at all times because Snake had gotten himself to that level where the only direction he had to go would be down

because he won everything. I think that fear was a great motivator for him—a fear of losing what he worked so hard for—so he worked really, really hard to stay on top. Every little detail, everything he looked at or touched, he would study. He would stand behind you with his hand on his chin, watching you work, and he would question how you did things, why you did things, just always looking at every aspect of success.

What set him apart from everyone else is that he was able to focus on a level that was at least two steps above everyone else. He could be in a crowd of people and hear a pin drop if that's what he was listening for. He wouldn't even know the crowd was there. At that time in my life, I couldn't understand the focus and the grind that made him do it. I do now, but I didn't then.

No one had ever really dominated like that in drag racing prior to him. So, I think there were people who resented him. The vast majority of people in life, but especially in racing, end up resenting the people who do so much to have such greatness. They resent their drive. I respected what he was doing. Cool wasn't even the word for him. His stuff was just always a step ahead.

The thing about Snake that the average person probably doesn't know, and many other racers who competed against him didn't really know, is that there really is no greater friend in the world. When you have a problem, he's there for you. He's the guy who calls you every day. He's the guy who goes to the hospital and visits you, and nobody knows how he even knew that you were sick.

Raymond Beadle in the **Blue Max** *was one of my toughest competitors, and yet for some reason I never was mad at him for beating me the way that I was at Garlits or Bernstein. He was one of the only guys who I liked hanging out with after a match race or event, even if he beat us. Of course, I liked it better if I had beat him. (Photo Courtesy National Hot Rod Association/NHRA National Dragster)*

there. Gordie "240 Gordie" Bonin and Gary Burgin were guys who were always nipping at our heels the whole time. There's a lot of names and a lot of guys who were real strong runners. But for a few years, we were running just a little bit better. I know that didn't make us a whole lot of friends, although it was rare that it went beyond the racetrack.

Double It

There are many important moments in racing that you only recognize as important later, after the bugs are worked out and the records are being broken. I remember being at Orange County, for a test day I think, not a race, and Raymond Beadle was there in the *Blue Max* Funny Car. They were testing a set of dual-plug heads they'd got from Pro Stock racer Butch Leal.

Dale Emery was Beadle's crew chief, and he was a smart guy. He had the heads on and a set of dual magnetos to power them. That was the first time I'd seen 16 plugs on a nitro car and the f——ing thing sounded like two Fuel engines hooked together. Beadle was only supposed to make a half pass, but he wasn't the kind of guy to let off when on a run. He just couldn't take his foot out, so the thing blew up big time. Dale Emery was so pissed off, he loaded the car in the trailer, pulled out what was left of the 16–spark plug engine, pushed it over in the corner of their shop, and let it sit there.

It wasn't until later in the 1980s that other guys started making aluminum heads with dual plugs specifically for nitro cars. Man, I can still picture my first glimpse of that thing with all those wires going every which way, spark plug wires and tubes, plugs in each hole. It was a huge change for drag racing when they finally figured it out. The NHRA should have outlawed them right there; it would have saved us all a lot of trouble.

Raymond Beadle's crew chief Dale Emery was the first guy I saw experiment with twin-plug heads and two magnetos. We didn't do it on our car until much later (in the 1980s). You can see all the spark plug wires in this shot of the Skoal car from 1987 (left). In this 2018 photo of a Mopar nitro engine (above), you can clearly see the big twin magnetos. They managed to get the wires a little more neatly packed as we kept working with the technology. (Photo Courtesy National Hot Rod Association/NHRA National Dragster)

5

THE 1980s

From left to right: Billy Bevel, trophy girl, me, another trophy girl, Terry How-land, and Joe Contie. I feel bad for never knowing the girls' names. Other than Linda Vaughn and her crew, the trophy girls didn't usually stick around for very long.

Everything is more. Bigger fuel pumps, 16 spark plugs, and it's so loud—like all you can hear. The bodies are sleek and aerodynamic. Compared to this, the early cars were little baby cars. You're tucked away in the center. There are more bars and more gear. When you get the thing to half-track, it will start wanting to carry the left front wheel, just push you back in the seat and hike the left front wheel up. When it does that, you know that this son of a bitch is on a run, it's locked up and moving. This is a Funny Car in the 1980s.

At Least We Tried

Dale Emery wasn't the only crew chief experimenting as drag racing moved into the 1980s. We were all looking for a way to go faster, and when you start really messing around with a Top Fuel or a Funny Car, they tend to bite back.

I think it was 1980 in the Dodge Omni and still with the Army, before the Pepsi sponsorship. We were at Orange County, and it was during a big race, a 64 Funny Car race or something like that. We were running a set of heads we received from Dick Landy. Landy was a serious Dodge guy, and he knew a

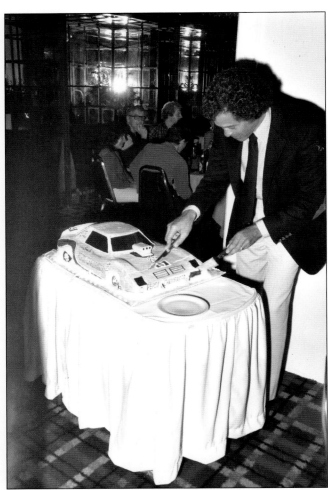

For my 40th birthday, someone made me a Funny Car cake.

lot about the Hemis. He was also a Pro Stock guy, and the Pro Stock racers had taken the head work and engine building to a whole different level from us nitro guys. They would cut the heads apart, port them, epoxy them back together, and rework the manifolds. It was crazy.

They were smart guys, and we wanted to see how it would work on our engine, so I asked Landy to make me a set, only we didn't really think it through. The Pro Stock cars were naturally aspirated, so they weren't seeing the pressure that the nitro engines saw. The Omni was really hustling, but then down in the lights, it blew a chunk of the epoxy out of the cylinder head. The engine blew up and caught on fire. It was probably one of the biggest crashes I ever had.

When it finally stopped, I wasn't on fire, but I was hot. They had to hose me down. I wasn't really hurt. I mean, it hurt my feelings, but it was kind of a rough year anyway. It was actually the beginning of a rough decade, although we still had a few good races ahead of us.

Soda

When the U.S. Army sponsorship ended, I had help from two folks in particular: Jim Davey and Eric Dahlquist.

Davey was the local Pepsi bottler in Los Angeles. He'd helped out on the Army car too, and if you look at some photos, you can see a little Pepsi logo alongside the Army one. So, I had Pepsi on board.

I met Dahlquist back when he worked for *Hot Rod* magazine and Petersen. He had sort of taken me under his wing. He lived in the Valley and worked for General Motors. He got me hooked up with Pontiac, and we decided to run the new Trans-Am car with a real slick front end. They were just coming out with that. We built a body: the Trans-Am body. It was really ahead of its time. That yellow and white car was really popular. It was one of my favorites.

Turning Corners

Even though I had my moments of looking over at the road racers, I pretty much gave up the idea of doing that professionally after Gurney gave me his little "you'll figure out how" pep talk back in the 1960s. All the same, every so often, the chance to get behind the wheel of something with a turning radius would come up, and that was always a fun thing to say yes to.

Toyota started doing the celebrity race in the early 1980s. It paired actors, such as Clint Eastwood and James Brolin, in cars with what they called "pro drivers." That could be Parnelli Jones, Dan Gurney, and guys who drove cars for a living. McEwen and I were invited to participate, and I was all excited about it.

I was totally wrapped up in it and tried hard. We used to go to Willow Springs way out in the desert and practice. One of the guys crashed really bad. Pretty Boy Fabian? He was out there, and Bill Simpson was riding with him. Anyhow, they ended up crashing and flipped the car, the whole thing, and got hurt pretty good. I thought, "Jesus, this s——'s dangerous too." So,

After the Italy trip, I got more into road racing and did a few years of the Toyota celebrity races. We practiced at Willow Springs. One afternoon, Paul Newman was up there with his own car. You can see my Ferrari in the background.

Jim Brolin and I are talking with Linda Thompson at the Long Beach Grand Prix. She used to date Elvis, and then was Bruce Jenner's first wife.

I'd try to hang it out a little, but mostly I had fun doing it. I never took it really seriously because I had drag racing to do, and I was just more cut out for drag racing.

The joke was that on the straightaways I was pretty badass, but in the turns it was a whole different ball game. I was lucky because Dan Gurney was in that first Long Beach race and showed me some stuff that helped when I did a couple of later races. I did win one in Michigan, so I wasn't a complete failure at it. The thing is, you need to recognize your skills.

In one of the later races, we were at Watkins Glen. I thought I was really hauling ass, you know, really hanging it out there. Then, David Pearson just drifts by me in the corner with his arm hanging out the window. I don't know if he was smoking a cigarette, but he could have been. I thought, "That's it. I'm done. I'm not cut out to do this." I mean, here you got it hung out and the guy drives around the right side of you, off in the dirt and passes like it's nothing.

Jim Brolin and I met Clint Eastwood off Ventura Boulevard, and we went out to Riverside Raceway to test Toyotas for the Grand Prix. We met at a donut shop, and Eastwood was driving a Ferrari Daytona Coupe. We caravanned out there, and Jim and I were looking at Clint in that Ferrari the whole time.

Clint Eastwood looks like he's about to punch me, and McEwen doesn't look like he's going to take my side.

Just showing Dan Gurney the line around the Long Beach Grand Prix course.

Tech Changes

The 1980s was a time of fast changes in drag racing. It had already started in the 1970s, but you could still be competitive with a smaller team if you were smarter and more innovative than the other guys. In the 1980s, we moved into technology changes that required bigger teams and more specialized tuning. It was just a really different experience.

In the Hot Wheels days and even beyond that, we all ran a pretty standard engine. You could buy a complete engine from Keith Black or from Ed Pink then ship it to England or wherever and put it in your Funny Car and race it. We were messing with the chassis and starting to figure out the bodies, but the engines weren't that different from one another. Then, when the 16-plug heads came along, that changed things in a major way.

You could light off more fuel, so you needed a bigger fuel pump. Then, Sid Waterman got involved. Then, Enderle, Hilborn, and all these manufacturers started coming up with different types. And then these bigger superchargers came. When you're able to put more fuel in it and more spark in it, you can have more air too, so we went up to 14-71 superchargers from 6-71 blowers. Everyone started going faster, and the cost of racing started going up. I can remember thinking, "Uh-oh. This is getting expensive."

It's all connected though. It's not just a new piece of tech and suddenly you have smart crew chiefs like Dale Emery and Dale Armstrong in the mix. You have the new tech because you have the smart crew chiefs, and their job is to seek out and understand the tech. Once those guys got ahold of these engines, the sky was the limit. Just whatever you could come up with. Run what you brung into the track. You could do anything you wanted to do with a supercharger. That changed the sport a whole lot.

At the time, everyone was so excited about going faster, seeing these new parts, and trying to beat the other guy to the new tricks that we weren't looking to slow things down. We didn't really understand how escalating costs could take some of the fun out it.

One time, Kenny Bernstein, tried three f——ing magnetos on the car, and they made a set of heads where they drilled into the side of the combustion chamber and put another spark plug in there. Three of them. That's the truth. Dale Armstrong came up with that. And I thought, "Holy s——." I think they ran it at Indy, they tested at Indy, and I don't know exactly what happened. I do think it blew up, but it was likely just a matter of putting more fuel on it and they would have probably been successful. But I think everybody, including Armstrong, thought, "Hey, this is getting carried away." It took longer to take the spark plugs out of the thing than it did to change the supercharger.

Finally, the NHRA put some rules on us. Okay, you're only allowed 16 spark plugs and two magnetos. In today's world, if you're going to change something like that, you have to present a plan to the NHRA and lay out what you're thinking of doing to see if it's going to fit into their program. You can't just make a bigger supercharger now and run three spark plugs. That's why the cars are so close nowadays.

Back when we used to run the *Blue Max*, Beadle and I used to have a tenth on the field. If a guy beat you off the start line, you wouldn't give a s——, you'd run past him at the other end. In today's world, they're just a hundredth of a second apart. I think it's better for the teams now, but it was a thrill to innovate back then, especially if you were smart. It wasn't much fun innovating if you were stupid. You could lose a lot of races while you were figuring s—— out.

"You can't just make a bigger supercharger now and run three spark plugs."

MEMORIES FROM DONNA PRUDHOMME

I've been asked my whole life, "What's it like to have Don Prudhomme as your father?" My answer has always been, "I don't know any different." I was very young when I realized Dad was famous, and honestly, it was hard for me because I was shy and wanted to blend in and not be showy, and here's my race car driver dad dropping me off at school in a Ferrari. I used to make him drop me off down the street.

Because my mom and dad weren't close with their parents, I've always felt that their racing friends are more my family than my actual relatives. Tom McCourry, Tom McEwen, and Roland Leong, they're all second fathers to me. Pat Galvin and Waterbed Fred, I've grown up with their families. Racing just seemed normal to me.

We'd get these great loaner cars from the sponsors. Oh my God, it was totally cool. I'd have a big, lopey Camaro and then six months later I had one of those really fast pickups, a Typhoon. So, all of that was badass, although it hardly helped me blend in. It might have been easier to just have a little white Mustang or a Jetta like everyone else.

Dad taught me to drive when I was 12 or 13, and I remember one time my mom and dad had a problem getting a sitter for me, so they left me on my own. I said I would drive myself to school. Well, I locked the car door with the engine running and had to call them at the hotel. Dad yelled at me for not thinking, but I told him he shouldn't have left me home alone. So, we were even.

I sort of fell into helping my parents with racing, but I never even considered driving. Maybe if it was a little later, like the Force girls, I might have tried it, but when Dad was racing, you had to bleed to do it. It wasn't something you'd try out just for fun. I'd been helping Mom and Dad since I was in elementary school in some way or another. For example, my spring breaks were going to sell T-shirts. In hindsight, it would have been nice to be a veterinarian or something, but I don't have any regrets. I'm glad that I went to college, and I'm glad I came back to help with the shop.

I think my dad gets a bad rap for being tough, but he's a lot softer inside than people know. He's not a total dick. I don't know how else to say that. There were so many years where he got so much grief. I worked with the team back in Indy, and he was tough, but everybody sucked. It was a hard time for everybody. I think he was hard on people because of how much he loved the sport and his teams, and he wanted it all to work and it was not easy.

I'm so glad we're not racing anymore. That was the best thing that happened for all of us because now we have a family relationship again.

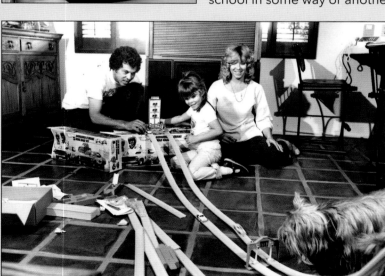

I didn't have kids when I had the Hot Wheels sponsorship, but we still had the toys once Donna was old enough to play with them. – Don

NASCAR

Even when he was beating us, I always liked Raymond Beadle. He was into everything. Beadle was the kind of guy who would lose interest in one thing really quickly and get into something else. By the 1980s, he was losing interest in drag racing. He discovered a much bigger fish to fry, and that was NASCAR.

Drag racing was one thing, but NASCAR was huge. He was a Texan, he was a "How y'all doing?" kind of guy, so he fit right into NASCAR. He went down to Charlotte, started up a NASCAR team, hired this young driver, Rusty Wallace, and ended up winning the f——ing championship with a Pontiac. I thought it was pretty damn cool. He just came out of nowhere and won the championship a couple of times. Beadle and I stayed friends until he died, and I'm still friends with Rusty to this day.

School Daze

Racing was hard on my family. Like most guys who were racing, I was gone a lot. I wasn't home to spend a lot of time with Donna while she was growing up. I'm lucky because my relationship with Donna now is much closer than it was when she was a kid. I was on the road, and once your kid is in school, you can't just drag them off to the races like you could when they were little. I missed a lot of the early days, and when I was at home, I wasn't in the best of moods.

Lynn was great about keeping me involved, even though it was hard on her too. So, when Donna started having trouble in school, we were ready for that because it was something I was very worried she would have inherited from me. Lynn found a special school that understood dyslexia, and it brought Donna right up to speed. That was just so incredible for me because I had struggled, and here my kid was able to read and ended up going to university. That was a big deal, and I'm proud of her.

That was the look. That was the look. I told them to take this photo out, but Donna overruled me.

That was a custom truck that General Motors built for me. It was part of the sponsorship: the truck and the support van. Back in the Hot Wheels days, we had to buy the trucks ourselves. Plymouth helped us find it, and it wasn't expensive, but they didn't give them to us. They were more into the Pro Stock factory guys. Landy and Sox & Martin, those guys got trucks for free. By 1982, we were getting trucks, vans, tech support, everything.

Part of the deal with General Motors was wind-tunnel time for developing the Trans-Am. Before that, we really didn't do that kind of development, but afterward everyone did. That car set an ET record and was the first over 250 mph.

Filming a commercial for GMC trucks.

I think this is in the Pepsi Challenger. Compared to today's Funny Cars, there's not much around me in terms of safety, but at the time, it was top-of-the-line safety gear.

250 MPH

The speeds we hit in the 1980s were incredible. I remember when it was a big deal to run 150 mph. To be the first one to run 250 mph in a Funny Car, that was a milestone. It was at the 1982 Cajun Nationals in Louisiana. We ran 249 and then came back with 250 mph. After that, everyone was doing it.

I think anytime you set a record, it gives people a rabbit to chase. It's like Bonneville: if someone sets a new top speed, then all of a sudden, someone comes behind them with a better widget on their car or something and figures it out and runs faster. Whatever record is set, someone will come after and go faster. That's just the nature of the sport. Even so, it's always nice to say that you were the first one to do it.

The Pepsi Challenger Pontiac was one of my favorite Funny Cars. It just looked so good, and it was so streamlined.

All Eyes on Me

One thing that happens (I think it happens in all forms of racing) is that if you do unusually well, everyone else will look at your car to see what you have done. In a dragster or a Funny Car, you can't really hide much. The competition is going to be standing right next to you at the line looking over at you while your guys look at them. If you ran well, at the next race, everyone is going to have whatever new part gave you the advantage.

The big technical change we made in the early 1980s was the fuel pump. Everyone was running the same kind of fuel pump, and we switched to a vein-style pump. We first ran it at an AHRA race, and it was obvious that it was going to shake things up—at least when we figured out how to keep everything together for the whole run. Anyway, we set a track record at the AHRA event, and Indy was the next week.

After that first run, back at the hotel, McEwen was giving me and Brandt a hard time. He was saying the clocks were phony and that the time was off. I told him it was so solid that I'd spot him, give him a head start, and run around him. That's how confident I was in what Brandt had figured out. But we knew that once we repeated a top speed and quick time, everyone would scour the car until they figured out what we had done, so we decided to throw them off track.

We had a nitrous bottle (at the time, folks were experimenting with nitrous on the Fuel cars), but for Indy, we just plumbed the empty bottle right into the fuel pump. Brandt did the whole performance, reaching down to turn it on, and even turning it off at the finish. In reality, it was plugged in the line, a total dummy. We threw everyone off, and it was magnificent.

A couple of guys tried it at the next race and froze their fuel pumps solid. People were blowing up stuff left and right. Soon after that, the NHRA outlawed nitrous in the Fuel classes. They didn't want to see that much damage and all the cost and cleanup. We raised hell, of course, but it didn't really matter to us because we weren't running it anyway.

It didn't take long for the other teams to catch up on the fuel pump tricks. Then came the computer age, and boy, that changed the whole world for me.

I don't know why guys grow mustaches. I can't remember why I decided to grow one. I guess it was the style, and I wanted to try it out. Never been much for it.

MEMORIES FROM KENNY BERNSTEIN

I grew up in Texas, and of course, we read all about the California dudes out having a lot of fun drag racing. Prudhomme's name was right in there with Beebe & Mulligan, Tom "the Mongoose" McEwen, and all those guys. I used to read about them all the time and just wish I could do what they were doing. I was working on a team in Dallas called the Anderson Brothers Top Fuel dragster. They decided to go to Bakersfield, California, in 1964, and I went with them. That was the Fuel and Gas Championships. There must have been a hundred dragsters there. It was the most phenomenal thing. I still remember it today.

We were in line getting ready to run, working on the car. That's the way you did it in those days. You stayed in the line, just kept moving forward, and worked on your car as you waited. I walked down to see Prudhomme and Roland and watch them work on the *Hawaiian*. They had just made the quickest run of the day. Prudhomme had just got out of the car. He still had his fire suit on. He looked at Roland, and he said, "I thought it was a lot better than that. That's pretty disappointing." That was the attitude I saw from him. I never saw that change through all the years we raced against each other. That's how devoted he was, how strong he believed in what he was doing, how much he wanted to be successful. He just was never satisfied. Like I said, that was the quickest run of the day at that time.

I don't remember when I first really talked to Don, but it had to be much later, probably in the early 1980s when I came back to racing. I took a hiatus from 1970 to 1979, went off to grow up and go to work and make a living instead of trying to race. That was all great, but my first love was always racing. I was fortunate enough to get with Budweiser and get off and going in that direction. I was so lucky to be paired with Dale Armstrong, but at the same time, Don Prudhomme and his boys didn't sit still either.

I remember one time we were in Montreal running and it got late, and there were no lights there at all. We were in the finals against Prudhomme. We were running well, and he was too, but it was dark. I mean dark. Steve Gibbs, a gentleman from the NHRA who was running the events, came to me and Prudhomme and our crew chiefs and asked if we wanted to load up. We said, "Man, we don't want to go back tomorrow. Let's just run these things. Put some cars out there and shine some lights on that drag strip. We'll get down there some way."

It was like how they did it back in the 1950s, only it was the 1980s by then. We both left the starting line well. I went to 100 feet or so, and it shook the tires and broke the rear end. He won the race. I was kind of glad it broke the rear end, to be honest, so I didn't have to see the top end in the dark at speed.

We used to take motorcycle rides together. Sometimes we had five or six people, and sometimes it was just our wives and us. One time, we rode from Denver, Colorado, to Sonoma, California. Then, we rode up to Seattle and raced. Then we rode across Seattle and over to Sturgis. One time, Don and Lynn and Cheryl and I were running through the redwoods. It's really beautiful up there, but it's a real windy road. I was leading the pack, and I went around a corner, and the back end of my bike kind of slipped a little bit and I went, "Wow, what the hell was that?" A couple of seconds later, I heard a crash. Cheryl was sitting right behind me, and said, "They went down. Don and Lynn went down." He had hit that same spot, but he didn't get lucky, and it got out from under him and slid right into the side of a cliff. It was a bad wreck. It threw Lynn off the bike, and Don hit his head pretty good—split the helmet open. The ambulance came, and the tow truck came for the bike. One thing about it really sums up Don's personality. Once he knew that Lynn was okay, he went over to look at the bike. He was standing there with his pants about torn off of him from the wreck. He looked like he had been through a war, and he wondered aloud if he could fix it so we could keep going.

Later in our racing, it got a little testy. There's no question about it. Although, I never totally understood why. Joe Amato and I were vicious rivals on the racetrack, but we loved each other off the racetrack. Don and I, maybe we're too much alike. We both wanted to win. We didn't want to get beat by anybody else, and we certainly didn't want to get beat by the other beer car. It got brutal. Man, we didn't have much to say to each other for quite some time.

He's a competitor who stayed in that competitive mode all the time. When it wasn't necessary to be in that competitive mode, he would still be in it. People took it wrong, like he was tough to deal with, but when he could get out of that space, he was such enjoyable company. If people could see him away from the track they'd say, "This is Don? This is the Snake? I don't believe it." When you're an A-type personality, you want to win, and you got all the load on your shoulders, you're paying the bills, and you're not having success, it's very difficult to be nice all the time. The good thing is we're big, grown men, and we worked it out as time progressed. We got back to that other side of the street, and that's a lot more fun.

Little Wiggly Marks

When the computer-savvy crew chiefs came into the picture, I think it was beyond what Brandt and I were doing. Drag racing was changing a lot, and Raymond Beadle and Dale Emery were really the first guys in that new era of drag racing. One was the crew chief and the other just the driver, and they had people who had specific jobs on the car. For example, someone was just the clutch guy.

In my situation, it was Bob Brandt and myself tuning the car. We both tuned it, but I made the final decisions. Bob may argue that, but we would both be in the shop or the pits, looking at the clutch going, "Instead of three half nuts, let's put two half nuts on it." I don't think Beadle or Kenny Bernstein were doing that, and it was an advantage to them, being able to specialize to focus on just one part of the process.

That's when Kenny really started being badass. In 1982, he got Dale Armstrong as a crew chief. They were a hell of a team. That's when things started getting really difficult for the rest of us. The computers first started coming in too, and Dale Armstrong was a guy who was really on top of the computers from the beginning. Me, I tried to get the computers thrown out because I knew that they were the beginning of the end for guys like me.

The first in-car computers were nothing compared to what they have now. They would take data from the car, such as driveshaft speed, when the clutch would lock up, and fuel pressure. It wasn't real difficult stuff, but it was stuff that you'd previously have done just by the feel of it. That's what I had always been so good at, so the computers gave people an advantage that maybe only a few drivers previously had.

The modern teams would laugh at that technology now. They had this long tape. You'd plug it in, and this roll of s—— would come out with all these wiggly marks on it. I said, "F—— that. I don't want any part of all of those wiggly marks." Everybody would gather around the tapes and try to figure out why the clutch wasn't locking up or whatever it was telling us. A new era was arriving, and you had to adjust to it. You had to do it; otherwise, you'd get left behind.

Trying to Stop the Computer Age

That said, I pulled a bit of a Don Garlits move. I tried to keep things from changing. We went head-to-head with the NHRA guys a lot, sometimes every weekend over some little thing. The sport was growing faster than they could really keep a handle on. There was so much innovation going on, so many new manifolds and blocks and heads and aero. It was just hard to keep up with it.

You would show up at a track, a guy would have a new manifold, and it wouldn't be illegal because nobody had ever thought of it before, so nobody thought to make a rule against it. You could run almost anything in those days. The computers were the same thing. We had meetings about it because it was the talk in racing. Dale Armstrong and Kenny Bernstein weren't just the best at understanding them, they owned the company (Bernstein owned the company). So, you can see why it took some time for the rest of us to catch up. I did catch onto it after a while, but it was a rough learning curve.

Racing Kenny at Pomona. I hate photos where the other guy is ahead of me at the launch. I think he was ahead of us at the finish too, which I hate even more. He and Dale Armstrong were hard to beat.

The Super Slump

If you read or watch any interviews with me from 1983 to 1985 or so, they tend to start off with some line like, "Don Prudhomme, going into his third winless year . . ." I can tell you, I wasn't too happy about that. It was just a dry spell. I learned to accept it because it happens in every sport; whether it's football, baseball, or basketball, you get into these slumps.

So, the first year I didn't worry too much. I didn't expect for it to go for two, three years, but it did. We just had to work our way out of it. It was all that transition to the crew chief–run tuning structure. I was still heavily involved with tuning the car, and I don't think I was doing such a good job. I knew that I needed someone in there working on the engine, and I'd play a different role. I'd just be the driver.

But that was really hard for me to accept, and it was hard to do because once you are one of the cooks in the kitchen, it's hard to let someone else make the meal. You still have your opinion about how it should be run. So those were years I just struggled, and it was rough to see Bernstein doing so well. It got to where I couldn't stand the color red. I have a hard time drinking a Budweiser to this day. When I order a beer, that's the last one on the line that I'll drink. And actually, it tastes pretty damn good, but I never wanted to admit that before.

Wendy's Woes

I was disappointed that we weren't running better, but it wasn't all bad. We had some good times with Pepsi and Pontiac. Eventually, I called Jim Davey about Pontiac doing more with me and he hooked me up with Wendy's. Wendy's was serving Pepsi products, so it was both names on the car. I

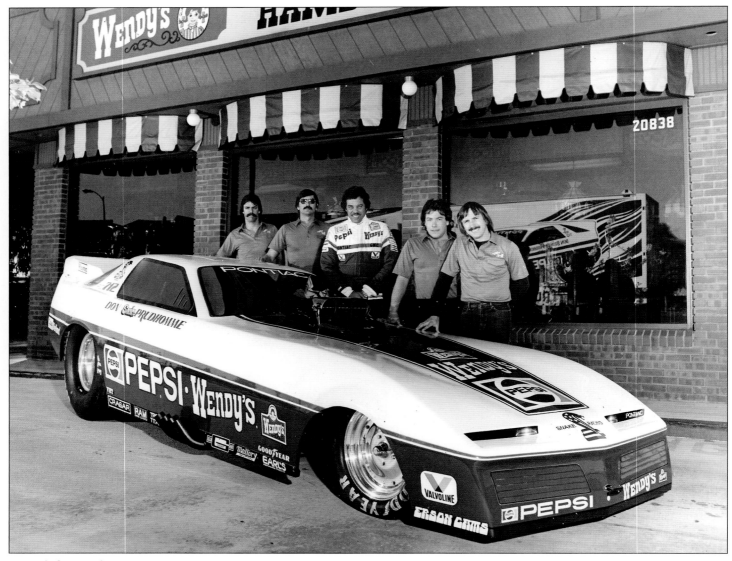

From left to right: Big Scotty, Steve Dragus, me, Kent Capasso, and Bob Brandt with the new Pepsi-Wendy's Challenger in front of a Wendy's restaurant. Some teams had show cars for display, but we used our actual race car for display.

don't really blame anyone, but the Wendy's folks were not into racing. They just didn't really care about it, although they still wanted us to win.

I used to have to go to these Wendy's stores and sign autographs, and I can still remember this time I was at a Wendy's restaurant in the evening and there wasn't anybody there. There was a little girl in there signing autographs with me who was probably, I don't know, 10 years old and had little freckles on her nose and this red wig on. I looked at her and I thought, "Is this the way Mario Andretti got started? Does A. J. Foyt sit next to a little freckled redhead in an empty fast food store to sign autographs?" It was kind of not what I expected.

Burnout, Not the Good Kind

I think we were just burned out by the 1980s. We'd been competing so hard through the 1970s and winning so much, but it takes a toll. I was getting frustrated trying to keep the sponsors happy and keep money coming in. The price of racing just kept going up, and it happened quickly. I just didn't have that step anymore. You just don't have that extra little something that it takes to stay ahead. It affected everything.

Because I was so unhappy, not winning, not running well, and trying to find the money, it caused a lot of tension between Lynn and myself and even Donna. Poor Donna. She was just a kid, and it wasn't a great experience for her. I

One time I went down to Mexico with the painter Bill Carter and McCourry's brother-in-law Barney Green. We ran into this local cowboy trying to chase down a horse, but he was drunk and had fallen off his donkey. We helped him catch the horse, and then we all got drunk and took turns falling off the donkey. I like this photo, it was during a stressful time, and it was a rare break.

look back, and I was kind of a s——ty guy to be around. Maybe a little nasty too.

I didn't know where the whole sport was going, and that made me tense and worried. I didn't know exactly where I was going. We had won all those championships, and I think during that time I was figuring I could kind of relax after that and take it easy. But things got even more difficult. Brandt and I were pissing each other off; we were like a marriage that went sour. I needed my space from him, and I think he needed it from me.

If any of you reading were around in the 1980s, you'll know that there were other issues in sports at that time too. There were drug and alcohol problems in racing just like elsewhere, and that only added to everyone's short fuses and money issues.

Being the Opposite

All my life, I'd tried to base my behavior on being the opposite of my own parents: I wanted my marriage to be a partnership and not a battlefield, I wanted Donna to feel safe and supported by me, and I wanted to make sure that alcohol never took over my life. I dreaded becoming my own father. Things were really bad with him by that point. He was just a full-blown alcoholic, you know?

One time, he came by the shop drunk and wanting money. He was shouting, waving a hammer, and saying he was going to hit me with the hammer. Brandt and I took him to the bus station in downtown L.A. and figured we'd send him to his brother in Arizona. They wouldn't let him on the bus because he was too drunk. How f——ing drunk do you have to be that you can't ride a Greyhound bus? I didn't know what to do, so we took him over to the General Hospital and put him in a wheelchair and pushed him inside. We were thinking that they'd put him in bed and dry him out, but he beat us back to the shop! To this day, I don't know how.

A Bad Place

Not long after that, my folks were divorced (well, I don't think they ever got a divorce, but they split), and my sisters kicked my dad out of my mom's apartment. The last time I remember seeing my dad was in Tucson, living in a little trailer behind my uncle Wade's place. I tried to talk with him and

"I didn't want to do any of it anymore, and that's not a recipe for success."

thought I could offer him some help, but he wasn't interested. He spent every day drinking, and he was just as happy as a lark. So, I just left him alone. I went back to the track and never talked to him again. I found out that he passed when I got a call from the hospital.

I'm telling you so you'll understand when I say that by the mid-1980s, I was in a bad place. I didn't like my dad when I was growing up, and suddenly I realized I was drinking a lot and I was almost turning into him. I was being mean around the house and not nice to Lynn and Donna. It made me not like myself.

I still had to race. I still had to get sponsors (otherwise we wouldn't make a living), but I didn't want to do any of it anymore, and that's not a recipe for success. Something had to change, either racing or family, and I never even once considered ditching my family. I mean, I wasn't a great guy to be around, so I was kind of concerned about Lynn ditching me! The part that I had to get rid of was the racing—the way I was attacking it, the way I was doing it. So, I quit at the end of 1985. I just shut the shop down.

Gone Fishing

I couldn't have imagined spending a whole year not racing, but boy, was that ever the right choice. It got my marriage back together. It was such a good time that I didn't even think about racing. We had some money saved up when I took the year off, and while $100,000 would not go very far on a race car, it went a long way as far as living on it. If I'd been racing that year, I'd have pissed that money away in no time at all. That's just a couple of superchargers and a few cylinder blocks.

I didn't even want to talk about the future and didn't want to talk about anything related to drag racing. We ended up going up to Paso Robles in California a lot. I had made some friends at the Long Beach Grand Prix, the actors Jim and Jane Brolin. They lived in Paso Robles. They had this ranch, and I use the word loosely. It wasn't a fancy ranch, but they had acreage. Jim talked me into buying some land too. So, we bought 40 acres, which didn't cost a lot of money back in those days up there. In 1986, we put a little trailer on the property, and I used to go fishing and relax up there almost every weekend.

Wally Parks had a place up there in town. Wally would come out to the property, and we would have a campfire at night and sit around, catch bass

> "Something had to change, either racing or family."

Taking the year off in 1986 was the best move I made. I stayed up in Paso Robles catching bass and not worrying about anything.

The year off was great for everyone. I think Lynn caught bigger fish than I did.

Tom McCourry and I were still getting into trouble in the 1980s. Tom passed away in May 2006. I was with him in the hospital the night before, and when I called his wife, Linda, to check on him, he was gone. We were friends for our whole lives. We would have dinner with him and Linda almost every night when I wasn't on the road. We were like family.

in the lake during the day, and cook them that night. I was enjoying life for the first time. It was like how normal people live, or how people should live. I hadn't been able to do that for so many years, maybe ever. I always had a good relationship with Wally, but that year we got even closer. With him, I could talk about racing and what was going on. He was concerned about me. I thought maybe he would be mad that I wasn't racing, but he could see the strain that I was under, and he gave me some good advice. He said, "You need to relax and collect your thoughts."

Second-Guessing

No sponsor, no racing, just park everything. We were done, no employees. It was just Lynn and me. As the year went on, I started really missing racing for the first time in a long time. I was hearing a lot about Bernstein. He

Everyone in motorsports owes a lot to the late, great Bill Simpson. He was instrumental in developing protective clothing and improving helmets and in-car safety gear. So many of us wouldn't have made it without him.

It's not quite the launch of the Hot Wheels car, but look at those wheels up. The Skoal sponsorship came in and got me back into racing.

was doing this and that, and he was the Budweiser King and all corporate. He used to wear a suit around and take pictures of his car—with a suit on.

I'd peek at the television, and he was out there winning races and looking so professional with Budweiser. It was a far cry from signing autographs at a Wendy's with a freckled redhead. The way he was running his operation, the professionalism of his team, pretty car, great budget. I'm thinking, "Man, I really f——ed up here. That could've been me, I should . . ." But to be that guy, I'd have to change my attitude. I would have to change a lot if I'm going to get back in this game. I better change. I better really think about how to do this in a different way than how I was doing it before.

I started thinking about getting back into it. I ended up going to the Indianapolis 500 that year, and A. J. Foyt was at the speedway. I was in his garage, and he had Copenhagen on his race car. He introduced me to his right-hand guy, who worked for Copenhagen Skoal, and he suggested I meet the chairman of the board for U.S. Tobacco, Lou Bantle. They introduced me to him, and he didn't blow me off exactly, but he didn't seem very interested in what I had to say. I didn't give up though. I said I wanted to talk to them about sponsoring a drag race car, and he finally introduced me to Johnny Hayes, who ran motorsports for U.S. Tobacco, Skoal, and Copenhagen.

Hayes and I started talking, and we put a deal together. That's how it all happened, from nothing to a deal. Hayes was a real character. I introduced him to the NHRA guys, and he loved it. He loved the whole idea. He wouldn't tell me that he loved it, but he loved it. You know, he was that kind of guy. We worked out that they were going to sponsor me, and they put a fellow in charge by the name of Jay Wells.

Jay Wells was my guy, and it was a perfect marriage between U.S. Tobacco and me. I was this older "legends" guy in the sport by then, and I matched up well with their other sponsored drivers like A. J. Foyt and Harry Gant. The wildest thing was that they didn't pressure me to win. In our first meeting with the NHRA guys, someone said, "Well, now you have to go out and win." Johnny Hayes turned right to him and said, "No, no, no. We would like for him to win, but he doesn't *have to*. He doesn't have to." I thought, "Holy s——, I like hearing that." I mean, that was like a big relief. Of course, I still wanted to win.

Even in the 1980s, I was hands-on with the car. I'm holding a hydrometer, which we used to measure the mixture of nitro and alcohol. There weren't any rules at that point saying that we couldn't run 100 percent, which is what we did back in 1969. But the later engines were higher compression, and they ran best at 85 to 90 percent.

I won a bike in 1987. That was the first race I won when I came off of the year out of racing. I was so happy I wanted to ride that Suzuki back to California. I think that's Gary Smith from U.S. Tobacco. It was quite common back in the early days to win a vehicle when you won a race, but that Suzuki was kind of the last time I remember them doing that. When I was racing with Roland, we would sell the things back when we won them; we couldn't afford to keep them. We needed the cash. I kept that Suzuki though; it was a nice bike.

Matchless

When I talk about the changing pressures of racing, it's helpful to look at the schedule to explain. During the Army car championship run, there were 8 national events. In 1988, there were 18. Imagine the increase in travel, money, crew, and time. Now, it's not like we just ran 8 races back in the 1970s and stayed home the rest of the year. We had all of those match races—the actual way to make money. But match racing was almost a team effort. I liked to win all the matches, but I would get paid either way. It was more about being there and running.

Once the championship came into play, there was no more match racing. The sponsors didn't care about match racing, they just cared about running national events and getting newspaper and television coverage. That felt different in terms of team pressure, but also it affected how the racers interacted with each other. I wouldn't describe myself as friendly in any era, but when we were on the road for the match races, if it was against somebody I liked, we'd race, then we'd hang out.

I always enjoyed being on the road with Raymond Beadle. In our match race days, we'd hang out in a hotel together, we'd go out to the track, we talked to each other, and so on. It was just a few guys, not a big team. There was no pressure. I wanted to win the races. I've always wanted to win, but that was internal pressure. The national events were more outside pressure. With sponsors like investors, racing became a business. The cars became so expensive to run with the crew and all, that you couldn't really make money match racing. The last time I can remember running a match race was against Shirley Muldowney up in Canada when I had my rear-engine dragster. I think she beat us.

Crew Chiefs

It wouldn't be totally unreasonable to say that the stars of drag racing in the 1980s weren't the drivers as much as the tuners. It was the battle of the

Racing John Force at Indy in 1989. I beat him like a drum. Could I still? I'd like to think so. (Photo Courtesy Ron Lewis)

crew chiefs: Dale Armstrong, Leonard Hughes, and Austin Coil. I was at the point where I was kind of maxed out as far as my tuning ability because when I would think that we need more weight on the clutch, the computer would say, "No, we don't," and it was hard for me to accept that and leave it up to the computer. I was still involved, but I knew a smart team owner was one who was looking for a smart crew chief.

The thing is, it wasn't enough to just find a smart crew chief. The driver and the crew chief had to be on the same wavelength all the time. It was very important, and it was a real problem for me all the way up until I retired. The crew chief would give directions like, "Shut it off here, don't do it there." I would shut it off when I was damn good and ready to shut it off.

The new crop of drivers (and as much as I love John Force, I am including him here), they weren't ever engine guys, and in some ways, it was easier for them to trust someone else to make the tuning decisions. Force trusted Austin Coil, and Bernstein relied on Dale Armstrong. It used to piss me off to have a crew chief make the calls.

I didn't like the computers because I could tune the car by the seat of my pants, and I didn't need a computer to tell me that the car needed more gear in it. I could tell you that without a computer, or at least I thought I could. But here's Bernstein beating me, and he didn't even know how to shift the car. They had to put an automatic shifter in it when he first started driving it. He turned into a hell of a driver, winning several championships, but in the beginning he had to have someone waving at him down track where he was supposed to shift. And yet, he could beat me because Armstrong was so good and gave him the right instructions, and they had the time and the energy to try new things and learn the new technology.

I couldn't run the team, drive, tune, and be innovative all at the same time. I knew that if I wanted to stay in the sport and compete, I had to do the same thing. I needed a crew chief to make the calls on the engine and the car itself. I never did quite get used to that.

We won the U.S. Nationals and the Bud Shootout in 1989. It's still one of my proudest wins. (Photo Courtesy Ron Lewis)

Social Life

I think that people imagine my life during this time as pretty wild. You know, I was back in racing, there was big money in the scene, and there were major changes to the cars and big teams, but really I spent a lot of time in the 1980s with the guys who worked on the cars and at home with Lynn and Donna. I think most of the guys would tell you that I was pretty much a loner. I was into the race cars and not the social scene. I didn't spend all my evenings going to parties and things like that. Mainly because I wasn't invited to any.

The good thing about running the national events was that you could have a bit of a life after that. Instead of spending every weekend on the road going to match races, once you had a big sponsor, they didn't care how you spent your time off. You could spend it at home, or you could join them on golf or fishing trips. Skoal liked to have the sponsored drivers and their families join them at functions. I think the execs thought it made them look cool, or maybe they liked us. I don't know, but it was all part of the new attitude around racing.

It was all very high-end, not like signing autographs in a fast food joint. Skoal had places in Connecticut and in Palm Beach, Florida. They'd invite us down, and we'd play golf. There I am—this poor kid, who used to get teased about being Black or not being Black and being poor—playing golf with the chairman of the board of U.S. Tobacco, just golfing with the bigwigs.

By this time, I very rarely thought about my race. Maybe it was because of the hair—everybody had big fuzzy hair in the 1980s and tans, but I think for the most part I just kind of blended in. I really don't know. Johnny Hayes used to run things for Skoal, and every once in a while, he'd say something in a joking kind of way, but I almost didn't notice. I was so busy, and I didn't think much about it.

"There I am—this poor kid, who used to get teased about being Black or not being Black and being poor—playing golf with the chairman of the board of U.S. Tobacco, just golfing with the bigwigs."

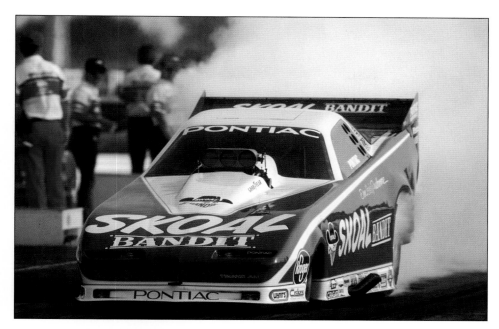

We did well with the Skoal Funny Cars in 1988 and 1989: we set a Funny Car record and won Indy. It was a respectable ending to a Funny Car career. (Photo Courtesy Ron Lewis)

We won the U.S. Nationals seven times, and each time was a thrill.

The Bud Shootout

I've said that losses always stuck with me longer than wins, but there are a couple of big wins that still make me proud. The Bud Shootout in 1989 was one of those. Everybody wanted to win that because they paid $50,000 to win, and you had to qualify to run. You'd run the Bud Shootout on Sunday, and then the big race was on Monday. Well, to win both of them was really something. We won both Sunday and Monday. That was one of the greatest weekends of my career.

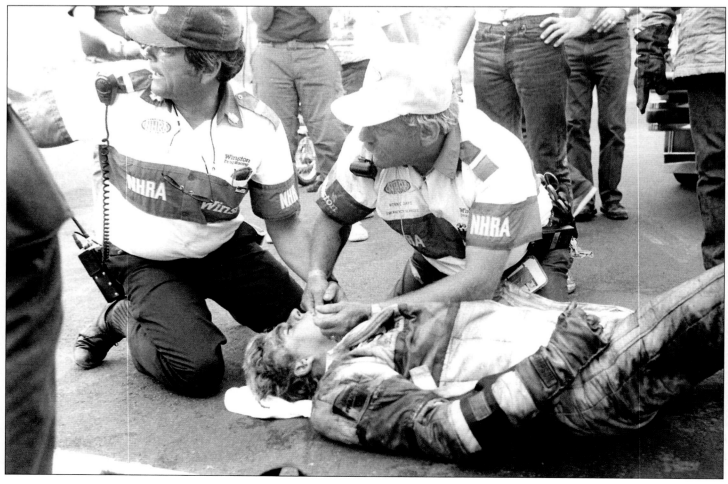

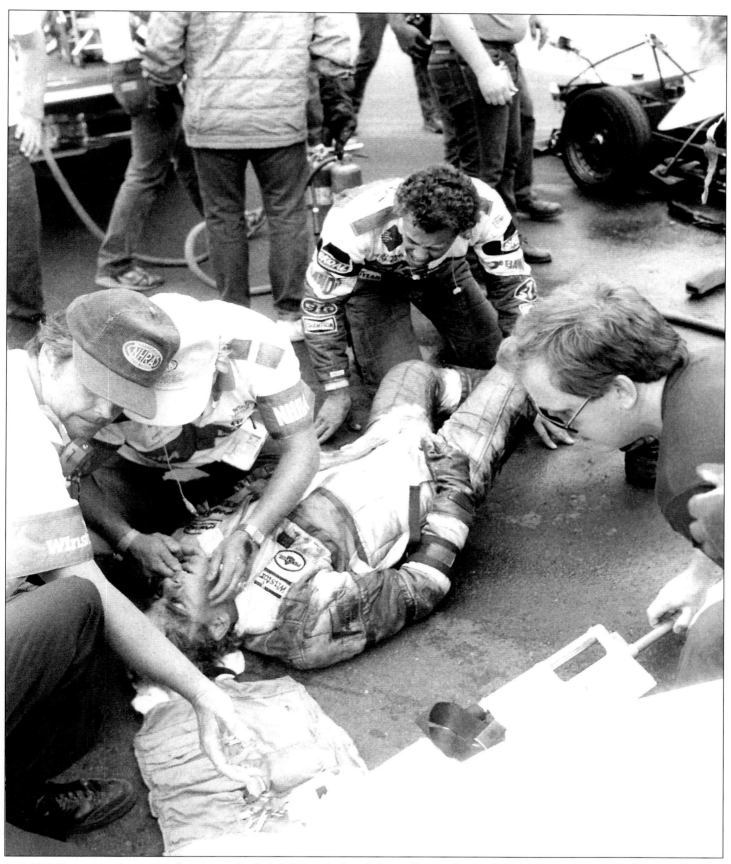

In 1989, Don Gay Jr. crashed right at the finish line. I helped the Safety Safari pull him out of the car, and I'll never forget the sight of him all burned and black. He recovered, but that crash really made me think about switching to a rear-engine dragster.

One of the things that made it so special is that Wally Parks was there at the end of the track when I pulled up after the win. I remember seeing him through the windshield with a smile on his face. And when I got out of my car, he hugged me. He'd worked really hard to encourage me to come back into racing, to readjust my thoughts and be ready to win again. To see him there at the finish line, it was like having your dad be proud of you. I never had that kind of relationship with my real dad.

The Indy weekend is almost the only thing that I remember from that year, and I don't know if this is what McEwen felt after his win there, but even as I was having this great year, I could feel my career as a driver coming to an end. For some stupid-ass reason, I thought I should be in a dragster to end my career. I started in a dragster, and even through all the success in a Funny Car, as far as I was concerned, dragsters were the kings of the sport.

Now, Bernstein was running really great too. We had the best two cars. It was him, me, and John Force. Force was coming up, and he was getting to be really strong. I don't know if Bernstein and I were both just getting tired of Funny Car racing or what, but I wanted to drive a dragster again, and so did he. We had such a great run in Funny Car that I felt that we could put it in a dragster and haul ass, not only dominate Funny Car but also dominate in Top Fuel.

> "For some stupid-ass reason, I thought I should be in a dragster to end my career."

Another Fire

Drag racing was dangerous. Even by 1989, people still were injured and even killed on track. If you were on a run and you saw your opponent wreck, that stayed with you. I saw some terrible crashes during my career, and one that really scared me was Don Gay's fire at Bandimere in Denver, Colorado.

I was racing him on a qualifying run. We left the start line together. Those were in the days where we had tremendous tire-shake problems. The car would go into a violent shake, and you had to shut it off. If not, you were going to crash or hurt yourself—physically hurt yourself, it shook so bad. In Denver's high altitude, it's really hard to tune the engine, so we were all struggling with tire shake. I was racing him, I shook, and he had the same problem. I looked over at him, and he was still there, but I think what happened is that he had such bad tire shake that it knocked him out. Then, his car went over and slammed the guardrail on the left side and bent the headers back into the body.

When I got out of my car at the top end, his car came pulling up to me, and it was on fire. It was completely engulfed in fire, and I thought, "What? Where's he at?" I couldn't believe that he was still in the car. But he was knocked out; he couldn't do anything, and the car was all fire. I was still wearing my fire gloves, face mask, helmet, and fire suit, so I was able to do more than the Safety Safari could at that particular time. I dove in there to get his seat belts undone and help drag him out of the car. Then, the Safety Safari got him on the ground and got him breathing because at first he wasn't breathing. It was a scary situation. We could have lost the kid.

I knew him and his dad. I felt terrible for him, but looking back on it, I think that fire helped me make up my mind that I need to get into a Top Fuel dragster with the engine behind me. It wasn't just his fire. It was other fires that we were having. Cars were made out of fiberglass instead of carbon fiber, and the things would burn up like a f——ing match. From then on, I thought, "I need to have the engine behind me in a dragster."

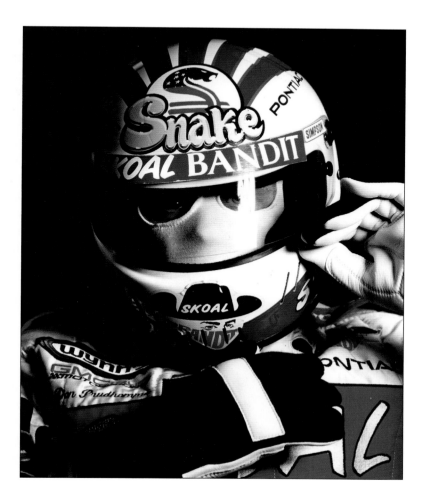

The only thing in front of you are the front wheels and the racetrack. The engine is behind you, making a noise that seems far away. Now you're the nosecone on a missile going 300 mph, and it's just you choosing the path. If you make a mistake, it's up and over. It's surgical, focused, and modern. This is a Top Fuel dragster in the 1990s.

Back to a Dragster

In 1990, Kenny Bernstein and I went back to dragsters. It was the biggest mistake I ever made. I wanted to do something different from the Funny Cars, get a new challenge, and boy, did I ever. The first thing I did was go out testing the car, and I immediately turned it over backward at Bakersfield. It was just horrible.

Here's this brand-new dragster, we're warming it up, and I'm sitting in it, like, "Holy s——, this is reality now." I went up to the start line, made the very first pass, and it broke a front wing strut. The front wing collapsed on the car when I was at about half-track, and the car went straight up in the air and turned over backward. I remember looking at the sky thinking, "What the f—— am I doing in this thing?"

I first met the Greek, Chris Karamesines, around 1960. Here, we are racing each other around 1990. He's still a handsome bastard.

I never had a blow-over until then, and I don't recommend them as an activity. I was just looking up at the sky going, "What the f—— did I do?" This was a huge mistake, and then it was *crash, boom, skid,* down to the end of the track. It destroyed the car. We had just put it together. The car was beautiful, all painted, all nice. So, we got her back to the shop and built a new car.

To be honest with you, I was kind of spooked after that. I didn't really like the car; I didn't like the idea of sitting up in front, even though I'd done it before with the *Yellow Feather* and the Wedge. I'd gotten used to the Funny Car. It took me a long time to get halfway comfortable in that dragster again because it was not only my car blowing over, it happened to other cars. Eddie Hill had a blow-over, and so did other guys. The whole dragster thing was crazy. Bernstein was going through a terrible year too, and we looked at each other like, "Why did we do this?"

Blow-Over No. 2

Later that year, we took the car to the wind tunnel up in Canada and learned some things about it. We figured that we were on the right track. We went to Montreal for the nationals there. The car left the starting line, the clutch hit wrong, and the whole thing jumped up in the air. The front end came up and I didn't get out of it in time. It went and turned over backward, crashed, and went over the guard rail at the other end of the course.

As I was going up, looking up at the sky again, it was the same refrain, "What the f—— am I doing in this thing?" It was too late to put the Funny Car back together again, so I just kind of had to lick my wounds and go through the rest of the year in the dragster.

Looking back, I know that the mistake was in the setup. A dragster is entirely different from a Funny Car, and we wouldn't let ourselves believe that it was really that different. Finally, Mike Kloeber, who was crew chief at the time, quit or got fired, depending on which of us you ask, and John Medlen came in. He had been racing with Bernstein as Armstrong's right-hand guy. Somehow or another, we got hooked up, and he came to work for me. He really helped straighten out the car, and I started liking dragsters again.

Why Aren't You Winning?

By the time Medlen came on board, I was just a driver, not a tuner. I was just driving the car, and Medlen was doing the engine work. He was great, but something that happens when you move from being the owner/driver/tuner to having a hired tuner is that you start tearing up more parts. Right? They are hired to make the car go fast, but they aren't paying for the parts. Their priorities are different than if you own it and work on it.

We were tearing up a lot of stuff in those years. I was in the middle between the sponsors and the crew. One side was wanting to know why we were spending so much, the other was wanting to know why we weren't spending more, and both were thinking it was my fault. Eventually, Medlen got tired of me yelling at him, and we parted ways. We were working on the car out in Indy, and I decided that he had to go (he knew it was coming). We went to lunch, and I said, "We can't do this anymore. One of these days you're going to be a hell of a crew chief, but right now I just can't afford you. I can't afford to send you to school while you learn." It wasn't the first time I'd had this happen, but man, it's really hard to fire someone when you like them.

The Final Strike

Even though Funny Cars made my career, I always loved the dragsters best. I started my career in dragsters and I wanted to end my career in dragsters; why, I can't really tell you now. I guess it had a kind of symmetry that appealed to me, or maybe I just didn't want to finish up without having been in the fastest, quickest, most powerful car on the track.

I was thinking about retiring, not well-formed thoughts, but I had an awareness that I wasn't enjoying what I was doing. Racing was way past the point where I was setting up the car, and it was exhausting having different tuners working for me. I wasn't very good at directing all those people. Maybe I wasn't doing such a good job driving either. I'm not sure. I guess we were still winning.

By that time, Wes Cerny was working with me, and we were doing well. I just wasn't having a very good time. I could tell that things weren't perfect with Skoal either. I don't know if they just didn't want me to represent them anymore or maybe they thought I was too old? When you're not winning, people think you're too old. You have a hard time explaining, "Well, it isn't me, it's the f——ing engine, it's the clutch, or it's the crew chief." Losing always reflects on the driver. If you're not winning, it's the driver who's screwing up. I didn't think it was all the driver. I knew it was crew chief too,

"One side was wanting to know why we were spending so much, the other was wanting to know why we weren't spending more, and both were thinking it was my fault."

It's a pretty nice setup, if you go back and compare it to the Army car days. We had an awning and flooring instead of just working on the ground. The guy looking up is Tracey Laird. I don't know who's on the left, looking away from us. It could be John Medlen, he was crew chief at the time. Jay Wells is the guy in the background.

but then I was responsible for him as well. So, in the back of my mind, I was ready for something to change, and I wasn't surprised when it did.

An Offer Too Good to Refuse

Lynn and I were at this party, something Skoal put on at a place called Watch Hills in Connecticut. It was a big home that they used for entertaining. You know, tobacco companies weren't exactly poor. Watch Hills was where Skoal had its annual meetings, and the company would bring out the racers it sponsored. There would be these big parties with the other Skoal guys, such as Harry Gant and A. J. Foyt. We'd all go up there, hang out with our wives, drink, and eat, and that part of being a big-shot racer with a big-shot sponsor was great.

It was at one of these parties, where we were all hanging out and the execs were having their meetings, when Johnny Hayes came out into the dining room and called me to go join them. I got in there, and they said, "Hey, here's the deal, we want you to retire." Richard Petty had just retired and done a last year called the Fan Appreciation Tour and everyone loved it. They wanted me to do the same thing, one last season, and they wanted to call it "The Final Strike."

They said that I didn't have to retire, but they made me an offer that—how's that saying go?—yeah, I couldn't refuse. They said they'd do the final year and then keep me on salary for five years and I wouldn't even have to do anything, just occasional appearances. It was a good salary too. Before I said yes, I went out and talked to Lynn. She said, "Take it. Don't even look back, take it." Because we weren't making as much while racing as they were offering me to stop racing. We made a lot more on the surface, but it all went back into the team. Racing was very expensive.

Stressless

When Lynn said take it, I felt relief. I realized that I had been dreading waking up every Sunday morning knowing that I had to cut a light and that my whole f——ing future or my whole driving career counted on me cutting the light. At that point, I felt like the starting line was my only contribution

> "They wanted me to do one last season, and they wanted to call it 'The Final Strike.'"

Bill "Willy" Wolter worked for us for 25 years, all the way through my retirement. He drove the truck for us when we were racing, and he was instrumental in helping me restore the Hot Wheels trucks when I did that in 2009.

Look at the wheels up on that car. Pretty badass. That's Pomona qualifying during the last World Finals I raced. (Photo Courtesy Ron Lewis)

to the car, and it wasn't satisfying.

I wasn't making sure that the engine ran well and all the stuff that I used to enjoy, the mechanical side of it. It sounds weird that I was more stressed with less to do, but without all that to think about, the pressure of waking up and cutting a light really started to get to me. When I had more to do with the car, there were more ways of feeling satisfied with the day. It was way more fun when I was involved with the mechanical side of the engine. And that is probably why I had so much trouble with my crew chiefs. I knew too much about their side of it. At least I used to think I did, and they didn't think I did. It was difficult for me to just jump in the car and drive instead of having helped prepare it.

The thing was, you just couldn't do all the jobs anymore and still be competitive. I mean, maybe Garlits tried, but he was a different cat than any of the rest of us. From the very beginning, I wanted to race like him, but I didn't want to be like him. He'd be at the track with a dirty T-shirt on, and I wanted a nice clean uniform. Garlits was never the kind of guy who would get invited to go golfing with the Skoal CEO, and I wanted to get those sponsors.

I couldn't have been like him, had his attitude, and made it in racing. I needed sponsorship, and I had to know how to talk to the sponsors and be

That was my last time in a drag car. This was the last pass. The only time I have set foot in a drag car since is when I did some burnouts in the restored Shelby car for The Rodder's Journal. *(Photo Courtesy Ron Lewis)*

My retirement party was at the Playboy Mansion, and it was arranged by Susie Arnold, who worked for NHRA public relations. Everyone was there, including Rusty Wallace, John Force, all the Winston team, Barbara and Wally Parks, Waterbed Fred, and Tom McCourry. It was a spectacular party; it lived up to all my expectations of what it should be.

with the sponsors. And he was the opposite. We started out almost the same. He started with nothing. We both came up in the paint shops, but he didn't like to see the sport grow. He didn't like the guys with tractor-trailer rigs and nice uniforms and stuff. He wanted it to be a little trailer and his pickup truck and have one guy working for him. And that was kind of his format. He wasn't in on the corporate world. I don't know, looking back at it, maybe he was right.

Larry Dixon

Larry Dixon had been on the crew for my dragster. I was really close with him, and I knew that he wanted to drive someday. I helped him take the classes, and I got his license for him. I let him license in my car, and he just did great. He was really good, and everything just clicked. I knew we could do something together.

After watching him test the car, I got really excited. It wasn't like I watched him drive the car and thought, "S——, I can do a better job than that. Let me in the car." I didn't feel that way at all, and I didn't know how I was going to feel, but I was just thrilled for him. I thought, "Man, we've got a future here." I could turn this into something bigger than it was. It was our last year with U.S. Tobacco, and that's when I called Rusty Wallace and said, "Hey, Rusty, we've got this kid. I need Miller."

Miller Time

I met Rusty Wallace when Raymond Beadle hired him to drive for NASCAR in 1986. Rusty and I got along from day one, and when I heard Miller wanted to get involved with drag racing, I thought that maybe I'd have an in with Rusty because by then he had a Miller sponsorship with NASCAR. Lynn bought Larry a suit, and in the morning when we had our meeting, I went over to his room and he didn't know how to tie his tie. So, I tied his tie for him, and I looked at him and thought, "Look at this handsome kid. We've got a deal here, how could they say no?"

We met with Steve Lauletta and Mike Welsh, two guys who we ended up being best of friends with down the road. Lauletta told me after the meeting was over, "I used to play with your Hot Wheels cars," and I thought, "We've

Dixon did really well in the dragster. It never stopped being exciting to see my team cars win. (Photo Courtesy Ron Lewis)

That's the Genuine Draft car. In the first year of that car, we ended up in the winner's circle in Phoenix. I was proud as hell. It was a thrill to stand behind the car and watch it win. It was better than driving it. (Photo Courtesy Ron Lewis)

got this." I sent him a Hot Wheels set after the meeting. Larry got the job, Cerny tuned the car, and we had a hell of a year. He won rookie of the year; he did really great.

Stepping Back

It was a thrill. Oh, yeah, it was a thrill. I was just so excited because it was a new chapter in my life, you know? Normally, when you get out of the cars, you're done. You walk away. I didn't see any other people making this transition from driver to team owner. I thought once I got out of the seat, that would be it. I didn't realize that my name was strong enough that I could carry on in racing and have someone drive for me.

The things I thought would be a problem about getting out of the driver's seat didn't end up being the problem at all. It was stuff I never expected that caused trouble down the road. At the start, I wouldn't have guessed that I would enjoy being an owner. I thought I'd have trouble watching other people in the car and not getting the wins myself, but once it happened, I never even thought much about it. I was focused on being a business owner. I wanted to grow and take care of it.

Once I quit driving, I never wanted to get back in the car again. I felt just as good standing on the podium as a car owner as

I did as a driver. It was a big achievement to go from car painter to race car driver to race car owner and still be winning races.

Leaving Northridge

For my whole career, my whole life, I'd always been in the San Fernando Valley, just outside Los Angeles. It never even occurred to me to leave, but like everything else, the Valley was changing with time. It was getting built up (more suburban, more crowded), and it started to be a problem with the race shop. When we first bought the building, it was just like the other small industrial shops around it, but when developers started to build in the area, eventually it got so that we couldn't even pull our tractor trailer in behind the shop because the alley was too narrow. We needed to move, but there weren't a lot of areas in the Valley that would work any better.

Wes Cerny, who was our crew chief at the time, was the deciding factor on moving to Vista, down by San Diego. He lived near Temecula, more than 100 miles south of the shop, so it was a bad commute for him to come up to the Valley. He had a friend who was a realtor, and they found this piece of land in Vista. I just fell in love with the area and so did Lynn. We bought it and started building the shop. It's the same shop that I still own today.

The thing is, after selling the Valley shop and our house, we pretty much spent most of the money on the new shop, and we still needed to buy a house down there. We found a good deal up in the hills in an area called Rancho Santa Fe. It was a ritzy neighborhood, but I didn't realize that at the time. I was just interested in the house because it was pretty rundown and overgrown, and I figured that we could just barely afford it. We were in the process of buying it, and me, Lynn, Donna, and the dogs were living in a hotel room down in Vista.

One evening, we were watching TV and the news came on about this cult where all the people committed suicide. Heaven's Gate, they were called. They wanted their souls to board a spacecraft that they thought was following the Hale–Bopp comet. McCourry called and said, "Hey, isn't that the house you just bought?" It wasn't our house, but it was just up the street. They would have been our neighbors.

Make That Money

Moving out of the Valley into a big new house and a big new shop was a good feeling. But it definitely made me aware of our finances and how much we needed to make to pay for things—not that I ever forgot.

I always tried to be generous with money, help my family, and pay people fairly, but I never liked talking about it. It always felt like it could go away in an instant, and I knew what it was like to have nothing. I wasn't the only one to feel like that.

After I met Jim and Jane Brolin at the Long Beach Grand Prix, we stayed friends. The Brolins were friends with Clint Eastwood. Sometimes we'd all get dinner, and I was always shocked to see Eastwood wearing these old shoes, all broken down and dirty, and a dirty T-shirt. He didn't dress like a rich movie star. I asked Jane about it and she said, "He's always worried about being broke." Here he was a millionaire, but he came up the hard way and always worried about money.

Well, I was the same way. Even when I was making money, I was always

> "Even when I was making money, I was always worried about losing it."

worried about losing it. I think pretty much anybody who came up with nothing feels the same way. You never really feel like you've got it made. Even riding around in a Lear jet or something, you know it could all go away if just one bad thing happens. It's always in the back of your mind. Even now, I just don't like getting into the money thing. Because it could go away as fast as you make it.

Last Battle of the Tire Wars

When you look at milestones in racing, in any kind of racing, it's not just that someone finally got smart enough or brave enough to go faster. There's always a link between the different technologies, and on a car or motorcycle, the tire tech was often the limiting factor in going faster. If you can't get the power to the ground, or can't keep it there safely for a run, you're not going to set a record. So, while the driver and the crew chief are important parts to making a record-setting car, there are also components totally outside the team's control that can change racing history.

Drag tires always had a hard time keeping up with the engines. M&H and Goodyear were truly at war. They were trying new tires at such a pace that the newest version could be outdated by the next weekend. It was expensive and dangerous, and both companies were about ready to stop making Top Fuel and Funny Car tires. What ended up happening is that the NHRA and Goodyear made a deal that Goodyear would be the sole tire supplier for the top classes. M&H was pretty much okay with that because they were able to build tires for different classes. The exclusivity meant that Goodyear could put money into developing a tire without worrying that they were going to have to redo it the next week.

A lot of people don't know this, but drag racing almost came to a big screeching halt. If Goodyear would have pulled out, I don't know where the sport would be today. Leo Mehl, who used to run Goodyear worldwide, told me that the hardest tire they ever had to develop was a Goodyear slick to hold up and go over 300 mph. They develop a lot of different tires, Formula 1, IndyCar, you name it, but drag racing, it was a very difficult tire for them to build, and if they hadn't stuck with it, the story would have ended here.

Ron Capps and Roland

Larry Dixon was driving the dragster and we were doing pretty well. We had Miller as the sponsor, and that was great. I stayed in touch with U.S. Tobacco folks, even after the Final Strike tour. I think it was the first or second year of the sponsorship with Miller when I saw this young guy come over to Larry in the pits, and he caught my eye. They were buddies, and when I asked Dixon about him, he said, "Oh, that's Ron Capps. He drives an alcohol car, he can drive a Funny Car too."

Later, I met Ron, and he had this unbelievable personality. I just really liked him, and I wanted him on my team. I went to U.S. Tobacco and talked to them, and they met Ron and they felt the same way. He was just that charming. I often tell people, "Hey, if you want to learn how to be a drag racer and how to treat sponsors, call Ron Capps. He's the guy."

He was a real natural, and he had experience with the drag strip and so on. He had a good idea of a car and I didn't really have to show him anything. He was right on top of it. And we formed a really good relationship.

"The hardest tire they ever had to develop was a Goodyear slick to hold up and go over 300 mph."

MEMORIES FROM RON CAPPS

I knew about Prudhomme as far back as I can remember because I played with Hot Wheel cars as a kid, and my dad drag raced. We lived on the central coast near Santa Maria Dragstrip, and it wasn't Orange County or Irwindale famous, but a lot of big-name guys would go up there. So, from a very young age, I was indoctrinated into drag racing, right off the bat. It was always drag racing, never NASCAR, football, or other sports. I built the models of all the Funny Cars and dragsters. I built Don Prudhomme's Funny Car in every configuration. My brother and I bought all the Hot Wheels sets and combined them and made longer tracks, and the Snake and the Mongoose were bigger than life for me.

We used to go to the Bakersfield race. At night, everybody took their rigs to the hotels, and you could walk around the parking lot and stand 2 feet away from Don Prudhomme building an engine in the trailer. They would back their rigs up to the hotel rooms and he'd be washing parts in the bathtub and the sink of the hotels. I'll never forget when I went up to get his autograph one time and he growled at me. I was 6 years old, and I remember walking up to a table while he was eating breakfast, and he just growled. But he signed it! It was just so intimidating, and I brought that up to Lynn and Don when I started driving for him.

Snake Brought My Name Up?!

That happened because Larry Dixon called me—this was once I was grown up and racing myself. Dixon said, "Hey, man. I'm just letting you know, we were at a dinner meeting with another sponsor and Snake brought

From left to right: Ron Capps, "Waterbed" Fred Miller, and me. Fred didn't work for me, he just joined us in the winner's circle. I first met him when he worked for Billy Meyer, and we became great friends when he was working for Raymond Beadle on the Blue Max car. The coolest thing about being in the winner's circle was sharing it with people. It was really common to have a friend or even a fan join us and hold the trophy for a photo, which is why I don't know who some people are in the photos! (Photo Courtesy Ron Lewis)

your name up out of the blue. I'm just kind of letting you know." And I was like, "Oh my God." Come to find out that he had started to talk with the Copenhagen guys about sponsoring a Funny Car.

A few months later, I received a phone call, and I hung up on him first because I didn't believe it was him. Lynn called me back and said, "I know you and Don got cut off. This is Lynn Prudhomme. Can you hold for Don Prudhomme?" I never did tell him that I hung up on him. He said, "Would you be interested in driving a Funny Car? I know you're a dragster guy." I said, "I would drive your tour bus." He said, "Can you fly out?" I had to tell him that I didn't even have the money to get a sport coat, let alone a ticket. He and Lynn had to get me the ticket and loan me money for a suit.

We had the meeting, and three days later he called and said, "Hey, man, they loved you. I'll get you more information. Can you fly to the Indy race? We'll announce everything there, and I'll be in touch with you. Lynn's going to put you on the payroll if you're cool with that, but we don't want you to worry about money." He threw a number out, which was more money than I made in a year and it was just crazy rock star stuff to me.

Rock Star

Everything he did blew my mind. Once we were at Maple Grove for a race and the Andrettis were about an hour and a half away from the track. We went to visit Mario Andretti on Friday morning. We pulled up, and there was this older Italian guy on a lawnmower. I thought it was the gardener. It was Mario Andretti's dad! We spent the day there just hanging out and barely made it back in time to qualify. As I was getting in the car, it hit me, "I just hung out with Don Prudhomme and Mario Andretti."

It was just normal to him. Mötley Crüe would come by, and they thought I was cool because I drove for the Snake, and everybody loved the Snake. We landed the jet one time in Indy, and as we were getting off, another jet taxied up. It was Aerosmith. The whole band got off, they recognized Snake, came over to him, and invited him to the show that night. He's like, "Nah, not for me, but Capps might want to go." Anytime we would go do something, there was not a better thing happening on the planet than what we were doing.

To this day, I will do something, and my wife or my brother will go, "Oh, that was a Snake-ism." I learned so much from him, and not just about racing. I learned how to dress and how to pack for trips. Without ever telling you you're dumb, he would manage to give you advice. Like, "Hey, man, next time . . ." He used to tell me, "Medium starch on your shirts. Tell the dry cleaner." Still to this day, I do that. He taught me the importance of a good pair of shoes. It sounds stupid, but he was so right about it.

Snake knows a lot about a lot of different things, and people don't always get it. It's not that he acts dumb, but if he knows something really well that somebody is talking about, he doesn't let on about it. He doesn't let them know that he's hip on what they're saying. He just lets people talk because he may get a little more information than he would've had if he had said, "Oh yeah, yeah, I know all about that," and gone on and interrupted them. That's another thing that I try to do because of him. That's smart. He's a smart guy.

What Did You Call Me?

I was so busy with racing that I didn't think much about race, not like when I was a kid. I think deep down I suspected that certain folks were talking about me, but it didn't happen very often where somebody would say anything to my face. There's only one moment that I really remember. There was a Funny Car driver named Al Hoffman, a Southern racer, and the guy who tuned his car was Tom Anderson. He was a good tuner, and they ran well. We got their old car for Capps; it was the first of the Skoal Funny Cars. Tom Anderson came with the car. He quit working for Hoffman, and I guess Hoffman was pretty mad about it.

I don't know if it was the very next race, but soon after that, I was in the staging lanes and Al Hoffman walked by. He didn't like me. We never had a falling out, but he was a rough, tough, old-school, dirty-shirt racer. He wasn't my kind of guy, and apparently, I wasn't his kind either because he comes by the car and says, "I'm so surprised that Tom [Anderson] went to work for you. He said he would never work for a n——." I didn't know what to do. It took my breath away. I mean, I could have hauled off and hit this guy—and believe me, I wanted to. But he was younger and tougher than me. I didn't think it was a good idea to have a fight in the staging lanes and then have to explain it later and have everybody know what he called me.

I just got on my little motor scooter, took off, sat in the trailer, and shook it off. But I still remember it, and it still has a sting to it. There weren't that many times where someone said a slur to my face as a purposeful insult. Usually it was more of a joke. One of McEwen's friends back in the Greer, Black, Prudhomme days used to make little monkey motions at me, and I never really understood it at the time, although I knew he was making fun of me. When Ed Pink called me a "schwartze," which means black in Yiddish, was he trying to insult me? I don't think so, but I didn't like it.

I didn't like feeling like people knew something about me that I didn't know or believe. The thing is, when someone does that, they kind of have you over a barrel because if you respond to it they win. They got your goat. So, I always just ignored it, tried to pretend I didn't get it or that it didn't apply to me.

New Crew, Old Friends

I never again really had the closeness with a crew chief that I had with Brandt once I became just the driver, and certainly not once I was team owner. Wes Cerny did a real nice job, but our personalities just didn't match, and the way we worked on the car was different. Cerny, as good as he was, had a lot of other interests, and one was being at home.

I was the type of guy where if the car didn't run today I wanted to stay after the next day and test. Well, he used to carry this briefcase and it used to make me furious when I would hear the latch click on it after a bad day because it meant he was going home. I'm going, "Hey, you need to stay and work some more. We need to do this and that. You need to go to Indy." But he was what they call a fly-in crew chief: he didn't spend all his time in the shop. He'd fly in, give instructions, and leave it up to somebody else.

I wanted more attention on the car. You can see where this is going. We ended up parting ways. Roland Leong came on the Funny Car with Capps. That was a really good marriage because Roland came on before Cerny left and those two got along well. Cerny helped Roland with a few things on the Funny Car, some stuff that he learned in the dragster, which was a retarder situation—a way to retard and advance the timing while it's running down the course.

It was all about that tire shake. Austin Coil, who worked for Force, showed Cerny about an advance-and-retard deal on his magnetos, a little timer. Cerny did that on our dragster, and we just flew after that. The thing was hard to beat. It was trick: a pneumatic air trigger would physically move the magnetos and drop the spark and then advance it again. When it dropped the spark, it was just like a traction control on the car. Roland did a magnificent job on the car with Capps. It was really set up for his liking, and he was able to finesse it. He was famous for putting different thickness of head gaskets on it to really fine-tune things. He was a pretty clever kid. He did a good job. Things went along well for a few years, but as the team grew, so did my complications.

> "He was younger and tougher than me. I didn't think it was a good idea to have a fight in the staging lanes and then have to explain it later and have everybody know what he called me."

From left to right: Donnie Bender, Bill Walter, and Dick LaHaie with Larry Dixon in the car. (Photo Courtesy Ron Lewis)

No More Run Whatcha Brung

Dale Armstrong left Bernstein and came on the dragster with Dixon to replace Cerny. When Armstrong came to me, he was basically burned out. He was an innovator, and once they started putting rules on the cars, he didn't enjoy the game as much. Armstrong had come up with this engine package that had to do with the overdrive on the supercharger and the compression ratio in the engine. He came up with a nice combination where you could run the car and not hurt it.

We took it out in Dallas, ran it, and didn't hurt a part. The thing ran really well. I mean, real competitive. But the rest of the racers didn't go for it, and Dale just threw his hands up and said, "The hell with it." So, I think he was pretty well done after that. And then Dick LaHaie came on board with a very different approach.

Armstrong never liked a stock part. I remember this injector he and Bob Brooks built. It had a massive scoop on top of the engine that sucked in more air than you could match with fuel, and it was violent. It would work brilliantly or it would blow everything up and smoke the tires. No in-between.

LaHaie did things differently. He liked a stock injector and ran the engine and clutch a lot different. He didn't tear up parts. LaHaie, and I say this with all due respect to all the other crew chiefs I've ever known, knew more about burning a gallon of nitro than any of them. As far as taking nitro and putting it through the engine, making a magnificent run, and coming back with all the parts looking brand new, that was Dick LaHaie. Armstrong was an innovator. He invented things. LaHaie was a fine-tuner.

The Trouble with Crew Chiefs

"It would work brilliantly or it would blow everything up and smoke the tires. No in-between."

If I had known how hard managing teams was going to be, I might have been more like Garlits, trying to keep drag racing small. If you look at the turnover, it's exhausting. First, I had Wes Cerny on the dragster and Tom Anderson on the Funny Car. That didn't work out because Anderson had another job, and he just didn't have time to do both. They flew into the races. They worked on the car. When the race was over, they went home. During the week, it was on the phone, talking about how they're going to fix the car. So, I was looking for someone to work on the car full-time.

The people who were good had other jobs. It took a long time for salaries to get good in drag racing, so I wasn't paying Anderson enough to work for me full-time. He had a second job that kept him busy and distracted. Another problem was that Cerny didn't like Anderson. These f——ing crew chiefs. I'm telling you, they didn't like each other. They hated each other, f——ing hated each other, and in a lot of cases, they hated me, or at least hated having to work for me. I got a lot of guys toward the end of their careers, and they were burned out, maybe not as excited about the new technology as they needed to be and certainly not willing to help each other out.

Cerny made it hard to work with Anderson, and Anderson had other things he wanted to do, but Cerny liked Roland Leong, so Leong came over to Capps's team. Now that was great with me because I loved Roland. Cerny would work with Roland, would help him solve problems and vice versa. He wouldn't help Tom Anderson. He wouldn't touch a Funny Car while Anderson was there.

"Ace" in the Place

Leong and Capps got along great, but what happened, as I recall (Roland might say different), was that the performance of the car started stumbling, falling off. How can I say this about my best buddy? First off, he wasn't a full-time guy either. He was a fly-in, fly-out guy just like Cerny was a fly-in, fly-out guy. I wanted someone who would spend more time with the car, and so that's when we hired Ed "the Ace" McCulloch.

I knew that if Roland stayed, we wouldn't stay friends. It isn't good to be that close and try to work together because you can't just go up to your buddy and shout, "What the f——'s wrong with the car?" I didn't want to get on his ass and he didn't want to get on my ass. We're best friends today, so hopefully Roland agrees that it was worth more than staying on the team.

"I knew that if Roland stayed, we wouldn't stay friends."

The Manager

I think I've established that I didn't have the best managerial skills. The people I worked with either got me or they didn't, and if they got me, we worked together quite happily. Skip Allum is a good example. He started as a public relations guy. He was originally working for Miller doing beach volleyball or something like that, and they moved him over to the drag racing program—poor guy.

We hired him away from Miller because he was so good at what he did. He was my right-hand man, and he took care of business. This kind of work, heck, maybe any kind of work, it's all about surrounding yourself with people who have your back. Roland was like that. Skip was like that. If there was something coming down, one of the guys complaining, it was never one of these deals where they could hide it and say, "Don't tell Snake." Everyone knew that if they told Skip about a problem, he was going to tell me. That was good because it meant that everyone trusted each other. All problems went to him, and if he couldn't solve them, he'd tell me. We worked really well together.

He also did public relations and sponsor participation, proposals, talking to the main people and keeping them happy. That's all the stuff I hated doing! Much later, when I shut down the team at the end of 2009, he stayed on for at least another five years because I just didn't want him to go! We used to sit around in the office and say, "Well what are we going to do today?" and neither one of us really had a job, but we liked each other's company.

My right-hand guy, Skip Allum. You're only ever as good as the people around you, and Skip was great.

THE 2000s

Tommy Johnson Jr. on a run. I always loved the way the blue Skoal car looked. I liked the design of the multicar team. We had a blue car, a red car, and a green car, and those were all the Skoal colors. I was always involved with the design of the cars. I liked the teams to match. (Photo Courtesy Ron Lewis)

I could never understand how guys could spend all this money to go racing and stand on the start line and watch the car, because to me, the thrill of it all was driving. Then, you're behind that son of a bitch, watching it disappear and leave the starting line, shaking the ground. Inside the car, you can't feel the ground. Outside, the shock waves go up your body and out the top of your head. To this day, I've never been around anything that was more exciting than standing behind a Funny Car when it leaves the starting line or a Top Fuel dragster at launch. To me, that's the ultimate.

Tommy Johnson Jr.

Capps was doing well in the Funny Car, but we saw Force kicking ass with his two-car team. They were learning from each other. I thought, "Geez, what a good idea. We put another Funny Car on, we get twice as much information and so on." Little did I realize that it was twice as much headache.

Skoal agreed to try a two-car team, but it didn't really work out for us. I learned that I might be a good driver and a good business owner, but I wasn't so hot at managing a bunch of hard-headed crew chiefs. That was a f——ing nightmare. And unfortunately, Tommy Johnson Jr., who was a really good driver, got caught up in the middle of it all, and he didn't really get the recognition for how talented he was.

In 2005, Hot Wheels had a big anniversary event at the NHRA Museum. From left to right: me, Art Chrisman, Tom McEwen, and John Force.

No Two Cars Alike

When you have multiple cars, you might think that it's just a matter of doing the same thing to both of them and then they should run the same, but the reality is that none of the parts are exactly the same, and certainly none of the people involved are. Your clutch disks are different. The tubing the chassis are made of is different. The way it's welded, the way it flexes—everything's different. It might look the same, but they don't act the same. Each blower is different, the next set of heads might be different. Each car is going to have its own little pet peeve that you have to figure out. Even if the data for both is sitting there on the computer screen, it's very hard to make them both the same on track, and of course the drivers are different, and that affects things too.

I'll Help You and You Help Me

Nowadays, the teams do a much better job with this, but I had another problem when I was running multiple teams: the crew chiefs didn't like each other, and for the most part, they didn't like me either. A guy like Ed McCulloch, he was working for me, but he used to race against me. He's not just going to settle in and do what I tell him. Even if I was signing the checks, I was still the last guy he wanted to cut a break to. It's just the way we came up. We didn't help each other. You were trying to beat the other guy.

I guess, to be accurate, we'd help each other occasionally, but like when Garlits helped us back in 1969, he was already out of competition. I think he was there to learn what we were doing as much as he was there to be a pal. There was a method to his madness. In general, we didn't really share parts that much. If you only had two blowers, you weren't likely to loan one out. It's hard to share parts you don't have. So, if you were out, maybe you'd help a buddy who was still in it, but it wasn't teamwork the way they do it now.

One time, Raymond Beadle blew the roof off his car, and Bernstein was out, so they cut the roof off of their car and patched it on Raymond's car so they could make another run, but that was rare. So, you can imagine that the guys who raced in the 1970s as single-car teams against each other might

"The crew chiefs didn't like each other, and for the most part, they didn't like me either."

have trouble getting rid of that mentality to run in multicar teams. That was Ed when he came to work for us; it was still all about him winning the race.

Nobody Likes Anybody

So, there were problems with me, Ed McCulloch, and Mike Green. They really didn't like each other, which is funny because Mike Green is just the nicest guy, gets along with everyone . . . except McCulloch. Then over on the dragster side, Dick LaHaie didn't like the Funny Cars. If the Funny Car was on fire, he wouldn't piss on it to put it out. I'm serious. He hated the Funny Cars. One time, I asked LaHaie for help. I said, "Hey, man, we're really struggling with this Funny Car. Is there any way you could stay after on Monday or so and help us tune it?" And he said, "I'll do it this one time, but don't ever ask me again." He worked for me, but I was like, "Yes, sir. Okay, but please do it this one time." What could I do? He had me by the balls.

I think my crew chief troubles can be summed up with this story. We were racing in Seattle, Washington, in the early 2000s, and Tommy Johnson and Ron Capps were in the cars. They're both Skoal cars, so same sponsor, same everything. Mike Green's car is throwing the rods out every run: *boom, boom.* We must have gone through two or three engines. I wasn't at the track because Lynn was in the hospital. She had a serious operation, and I was with her in San Diego. I never missed a race, so this was a big deal, and I was out in the hallway on the phone trying to run the team from the hospital. Mike Green told me that the car was throwing the rods out again and he thought it might be the camshaft. I said, "Well, put another cam in it. We got lots of cams."

He answered, "No, we don't. Ed's got the cams. I don't have the cams." He wouldn't ask Ed because he figured Ed would tell him no. So I called up Ed and said, "Hey, man, Mike Green and them over there, they need a camshaft." You know what he told me? He said, "Do you realize that we have to race those guys tomorrow, and they got lane choice?" That's what he f——ing told me. I about s——.

From left to right: Bob Brooks, Larry Dixon, me, and Dale Armstrong. Brooks was the assistant crew chief on the car working for Armstrong. Those were happy times racing with Armstrong. We remained good friends after that, which wasn't always the case with guys who worked for me. (Photo Courtesy Ron Lewis)

> "I was out in the hallway on the phone trying to run the team from the hospital."

They didn't want to think about the big picture. If you have a team and even one of the cars gets in the winner's circle, it's good for you. If one of the Skoal cars wins, that's great for the other Skoal car. It's great for the team, the company. Just get one of them in the winner's circle. But they didn't think that way. For the old-school guys it was, "I've got to win the f——ing race, and if we don't win, I don't want the other car to win." True story.

Lynn was lying there in a hospital bed, and I was dealing with these two men who couldn't work together, and I thought, "I'm over this." I didn't want to deal with the crew chiefs anymore.

Raising Champions

Despite all my complaints about the crew chiefs, the early 2000s were great years. Dixon and Capps were doing really well. Dixon won two championships, and Capps came second in the Funny Car points. Between the three drivers and me, we racked up 100 wins by 2005. There were 49 with me as the driver, and 51 from Capps, TJ, and Dixon. Not too shabby! Yet, when I think of my career, I tend to think about all the bad s—— that happened during those years. I don't know why that is. Well, I do know.

There was a tremendous amount of pressure. When you start winning, it's just more pressure to keep winning. And the folks at U.S. Tobacco, Skoal, and Miller, they wanted the cars to win, constantly win. That was something that we just couldn't deliver all the time. That was another bit of a headache, especially when we brought on the second Funny Car. It was like, "Why did we give you two cars now? Why aren't you winning?" Every Monday morning, I had to answer that. "Hey, how come we didn't win? What happened?" "Well, we smoked the tires." "Why did they smoke the tires?" How do I explain that?

They were under a lot of pressure too. Alcohol and tobacco weren't hip anymore, and they were dealing with internal rumblings about pulling out of sponsorship altogether.

Hats Off to Ron Capps

From the very beginning of my drag racing experience, I had to get used to the idea that it's not a solo operation. The bigger the team, the more personalities are involved, and the less control you have over who does what and when. I really liked having Ron Capps driving for me, and I think he liked working with me, but he had to watch out for his own career too. Toward the end of the Skoal sponsorship, we had two cars, and Skoal wanted to cut back. We were having problems with the crew and cars and weren't doing very well at the races. Tobacco was also taking a big hit in the press, so it wasn't cool to have tobacco products on your car or be associated with them.

Capps, with his personality and his driving skills, had other teams who wanted him, and he got offered a deal from Schumacher (the Brut Faberge team), and he took the deal. I was unhappy at the time. I wanted him to stay with us, but I understood why tobacco wasn't the best look for his career. We had Tommy Johnson, so it wasn't that I didn't have a good driver when he left, it was more that I was losing a good friend. I missed having him to talk to.

Ron Capps liked to celebrate by standing on the back of the car. Thank God he wasn't a heavy-set guy; otherwise, he would have caved it in. (Photo Courtesy Ron Lewis)

MEMORIES FROM LARRY DIXON

I knew Snake from when my dad raced. We were in the Valley, and Snake was in the Valley. My dad retired from racing in 1979. I was still bit by the bug but not old enough to drive to the event. So, I would literally ride my bicycle to Snake's shop and beg a ride to that weekend's event, whether it was Bakersfield, Orange County, or wherever.

In 1988 when I was a few years out of high school, they were looking for crew help. Snake gave me a call. He actually called the house. My buddy answered the phone and said "Hey, it's for you." I'm like, "Who is it?" And he says, "It's Don Prudhomme." I'm like, "You're full of s—, he isn't going to call me." And then I get on the phone, and it was Snake.

From left to right: Wes Cerny, Larry Dixon, and me in the winner's circle in Phoenix, celebrating Larry's first win. (Photo Courtesy Ron Lewis)

Short-Term Gig

I went to work for him. I figured that it would be a short-term gig but stayed there for 20 years. I crewed on his Funny Car for two years, and then about four or five years on the dragster. The Funny Car was more, I don't know, probably more "fun" (if I had to pick a word) than the Top Fuel car. He did a ton of match racing with it, so we were bouncing around the country. There was one stretch where we raced 14 weeks in a row. But servicing the car between runs was way, way less back then than it is now. If you did a match race, Snake would throw you a couple hundred bucks side cash for doing it, and it was cool.

When I started there, Snake had maybe won one race in a five-year span. But two or three races into my time there, they got on a good tune-up with the clutch and the fuel system, and all of a sudden, it was like, win a race, set the national record, run it at another one, win another race. All of a sudden, it was really fun. I think he won every year for the rest of his career driving-wise, so it was neat to be a part of that.

What he did was hard. That first year of the Top Fuel car, we finished second in the points with the Funny Car, and then he hopped into the dragster. It wasn't like you could buy a turnkey car, just put your setup in it and go run. They were still refining those cars, and no one really had a handle on things. There were a bunch of different manufacturers and different wings, and it was just kind of a free-for-all back then. And you're trying to ramp all of this up to be able to get to the level of what you're used to competing at in Funny Car. That was rough on everyone.

Back then, the team was three crew and one crew chief. That's all. Snake had a genuine interest in what we wanted to do. He would ask us, and if he could help us make it happen, he would. When he came to me, I said, "I want to drive," and he said, "Really? Well, how are you going to get there?" I saw other guys moving their way up from alcohol dragsters, so I left Prudhomme for most of the 1993 season to go drive the alcohol car.

Alcohol Dragsters

I didn't set the world on fire, but I didn't wreck anything, and I didn't set myself on fire either. So that all worked well, but I wasn't getting paid anything, and I still had to pay rent. I ran my savings down, and ran the credit cards up, and then it was like, I needed to go back and get a job. I went back to Snake and asked him if I could work for him again, and he didn't really want to hire me, but I think Roland convinced him to let me come back. For Snake, when you quit, that meant you were over it and you're done fighting his fight.

Wes Cerny wanted to go testing, but Snake had an appearance he had to do. He couldn't test, and he couldn't find anyone to drive the car. Finally, Snake pointed at me (I was building short-blocks at the time) and said, "Get that f—ing kid his license, and that way you guys can f—ing test any time you want." That's how it started.

Championships

Snake was cool because he didn't care that my driving style was different. I didn't have to act like him to drive his car, which I dug. We got two championships together. In the end, when the money was running out and Miller left, it wasn't the same. I knew that Snake's team wasn't where my future was going to be.

I didn't want to go anywhere. I still felt like we had the best team at the time. I didn't want to disrupt his team, but I knew when I said I wanted to leave how he had been with Roland, or Ace, or gosh, even Tommy Ivo. I knew he wasn't a "shake hands and part ways" kind of guy. It was going to be a messy divorce, and it was. When you're fighting his fight, you're one of the soldiers, and when you're not fighting his fight, you're an enemy army. I understand it, and that's how he is. That's what I liked about working for him for 20 years because I loved his kill-or-be-killed approach to winning.

I've been to the winner's circle in Indy five times—four of them were with me driving and one was with Snake driving. That weekend with him driving the car, being part of the winning team like that, it ranks up there with any win that I've ever had.

Nitro haze and heat. Dixon in the Miller Lite dragster. I don't miss the stress, but I sometimes miss the rest of it. (Photo Courtesy Ron Lewis)

Lynn and I always tried to be careful financially. Even once we were doing well, we didn't forget what it was like to have nothing. It was her idea to buy a jet. She knew how much I hated traveling to the races. You'd go, you'd do poorly, you'd be stuck there until your flight out. I was pretty burnt out on the travel. Connie Kalitta owned airplanes, and he mentioned he had a jet that would solve my problem. It re-sparked my interest in the races because I could go when I wanted to go and leave when I wanted to leave. It had a lot to do with me even staying in the sport because of the convenience and also the time it gave me to talk with the drivers. Dixon lived in Indianapolis, but Capps used to fly with us a lot out of California, and I always looked forward to the times that we could fly together. It was Skip Allum, Capps, and me, and the three of us had some of the greatest times ever in that plane. Eventually, it was too expensive. I never wanted it to affect what I was spending on the race cars, so we sold it after about eight years. I still miss it.

Bad Breakups

I've often thought about my relationship with Larry Dixon and racked my brain about how it got so bad. I still do not know. I think a lot of it had to do with success. In a smaller sport like drag racing, it's easy to think that you're a bigger deal than you are. I learned that way back when Keith Black told me that drivers are like spark plugs and when Roland went on to win without me in the *Hawaiian*. I think that fame is what drove a big wedge between us.

One time, Garlits told me, "Snake, you and I think we're probably a pretty big deal, but if you go beyond these fences and out from this racetrack, there isn't anybody out there who knows who the hell we are. If you don't believe me, walk down the street in New York City and see if anybody says, 'Hey Don Prudhomme, I'd like to have your autograph.'" Maybe John Force can do that now and get recognized, but back when Garlits and I were drag racing, the fame was only around the track. You get a whole different perspective at the moment when you're putting your helmet on at the racetrack. The racetrack is bigger than anything, but the racetrack compared to the world? It isn't so big.

When we built the race shop in Brownsburg, Indiana, Dixon moved to Indianapolis, and our relationship just started going sour. In a small place like Brownsburg, where racing was a major part of people's lives, he was a big deal. He could walk into a Bob Evans and people would recognize him. He was on Miller billboards. There were cardboard cutouts of him in stores next to the beer displays. The beer wars against Budweiser was one of the biggest stories at the track, and it got a lot of media attention. He did a good job in the race car, but I think a lot of it went to his head. I think he didn't really realize the value of what he was doing and the type of money he was making.

You can guess where this is going. He told me that he needed more money, he couldn't make it on what he was being paid. His wife didn't like me, and I think we just grew apart. Eventually, he told me that he wanted out. The thing is, it wasn't just Dixon, it was everyone. It was the teams and the crew chiefs. Nobody liked anybody else, and it was a struggle. It wasn't an immediate disaster, but looking back, I can see the threads of what became a problem. People used to think I was the asshole on the team. I was an asshole, but I wasn't the only one.

Spencer Massey

When Spencer Massey got in the dragster, he was magnificent. He was one of the best talents that I'd ever seen come along. I remember he got in the car at the shop in Indy to get all fitted up, and he pulled his leg up and tied his shoelaces while he was still in the seat. Holy s——, this guy's a gift, you know? It's a tight fit in a dragster cockpit. He was just marvelous. I couldn't say enough good about him.

It's too bad that we didn't get to go the distance together. He did one hell of a job for us in the short amount of time that he drove for us. What happened that screwed everybody in 2008–2009 was that the stock market crashed, and no one could find a sponsor. There were practically bread lines of racers lined up around the few remaining companies that seemed solvent. People expect you to wave a wand, go out there, and find a sponsor. However, if the money isn't there, it doesn't matter how good the team or the driver is.

Blow Up

In racing, things can change in a second. The car can crash. The engine can blow up. The sponsor can leave. After 50 years of racing, you figure that you won't be caught off guard, but in the end of 2009, U.S. Tobacco was sold to Altria (the parent company of Phillip Morris) and that just surprised the s—— out of us.

We were in the midst of our contract, and the Altria people assured us that they still wanted to race, so it was business as usual for a while. We had our contract all set up to renew and two days later they called back and said, "Oh, by the way, we can't do it. The higher-ups don't want to do it. They're getting out of racing." We lost our sponsorship and there wasn't enough time between September and January to put a new deal together.

The economy went right down the toilet; nobody had any money. I remember going to the SEMA show, and you could shoot a cannon through the halls; it was just empty. Well, that's the way it was when we started looking for a new sponsor.

While Skip and I were making calls, Spencer was getting calls from other teams trying to hire him. I kept telling him, "Hey, just hang on a little bit. We're working on a deal, we're working on a deal." But you can only ask a guy to stick around with no job for so long. He was getting nervous, and for good reason.

One of the sponsors we were working on was Monster. Monster had been in the sport with Bernstein, and that fizzled out. It wasn't such a good match because Powerade was big in the NHRA, and the companies weren't as excited about advertising competition between two of the same type of product as they were during the beer wars. I knew the people at Monster pretty well and went out to see them in a last-ditch effort, real eleventh-hour stuff to try to put the deal together.

It's Over!

I was driving Lynn's Porsche Cayenne, and I went down the street from the Monster offices to put gas in it. I was so stressed and distracted that I took off from the gas station with the hose still attached. Took the handle right off the pump. *Boom!*

"If the money isn't there, it doesn't matter how good the team or the driver is."

It's a shame that we never got to see what Spencer Massey could do. He impressed me in the short time we had together. Unfortunately, we all got caught up in the economic crash, and that was the end of racing for me. No big parties for that retirement. We just went home to lick our wounds. (Photo Courtesy Ron Lewis)

I stopped and called Skip and said, "Call the shop, and tell the guys that it's over. We're closing up." And that was the last time. I just couldn't deal with trying to find money that wasn't out there to find anyhow. And my mind was so f——ed up that I'm filling the car up and I pulled the pump right out? I said, I just don't need this anymore.

Not hiring me was the best thing that Monster could ever have done, and getting out of the sport was the best thing that I ever did. I never questioned it. Once I made a decision like that, I felt good. I mean, I didn't really like having to go to the press tower at the Nationals and make the announcement that we weren't going to continue, but we had so much overhead and we weren't going to find it. The best thing for me to do was get out, retire, and quit. I don't regret that at all.

I'm not saying that it saved my life, but it saved my health and my family. Once the deal closed up, really closed, I knew I was going to be all right. It turns out that there's a pretty big world out there. A lot more going on besides drag racing, although it wasn't immediately obvious to me.

Retirement

The first day of retirement was horrible. It took me months and months to get over it. I really was heartbroken because it wasn't that I wanted to retire, but I just couldn't do it anymore. I had to let go of all these employees and people. I had a shop in Indy and had to shut it all down. The economy just took a big dive, and we got caught up in it. We had Spencer Massey and people on payroll, and they needed a job, but I didn't have a job for them, so it was tough.

It was sad because we built all this up—CNC equipment and engines and chassis—and to see it all being auctioned off felt pretty lousy. We had pallets stacked up at the shops and people would go through and pick and choose parts like they were at a garage sale. I couldn't even be there. I didn't even go to the shop. I had one of the other guys, I think it was Donnie Bender, selling the parts. It was like birds coming in and picking the meat off the bones.

People bought Funny Car bodies, chassis, heads, and crankshafts. We had all kinds of parts and pieces. It's not like I could sell the business. It isn't like a McDonald's or a 7-Eleven store. A race team doesn't really have any backbone to it; it's just parts and pieces. It's not like you could sell Don Prudhomme Racing to somebody who's going to come in and buy the whole thing. The company isn't any good without a sponsor, and you couldn't get a sponsor. So, what you end up with is like 50 cents on the dollar, 30 cents on the dollar. Your ego is crushed, and you're crushed that you're out of racing. It's an embarrassment. I just wanted to stick my head in the sand. But, as things worked out, it ended up being wonderful.

I like to encourage other people with that. Sometimes when you think this is the worst thing in the world that can happen to you, it's the best thing in the world that could happen to you. You just don't realize it at the time.

Nostalgia

Just when I was shutting everything down, my buddy Chip Ganassi called and asked if he could rent part of the Indianapolis shop for his IndyCar team. That was perfect because it helped financially. While we were setting it up, he suggested I go to the IndyCar races with him. Honestly, that got me through some really, really tough times: being buddies with him, going to NASCAR and IndyCar races, and getting to be a part of racing but not having to watch the NHRA go on without me. He saved me more than he'll ever know.

Another thing that happened right when I needed it was a revival of nostalgia racing. I owned a bunch of my old cars, and when people started getting into the history with the magazine articles dedicated to older cars and the cacklefests, that gave me a way to relive some of those early years and get back to my roots.

I tracked down the original ramp trucks and began restoring them. That had a lot to do with getting my head straight too. I hired two fellows, including Willie Wolter, who worked for us before on the race cars. We put a spray booth outside and did all the work ourselves. That restoration took the better part of a couple of years by the time everything was done. It brought me back to the beginning, putting primer on, block sanding, and spraying the base coat and clear coat. I was glad that I had those skills. It's important to do something with your hands when your mind is going in circles.

At the same time, I started reconnecting with some of the guys from the early years. Most of them had retired long before me. So, while I was

"It's important to do something with your hands when your mind is going in circles."

After retirement, I got into restoring the Hot Wheels ramp trucks. Once they were done, I didn't have any desire to hold on to them, so we sold them at the Barrett-Jackson auction in 2014.

Before I sold the Hot Wheels trucks, they were used in a movie about me and McEwen called Snake and Mongoose. *This is a shot from the set with me and Roland next to the actors who played us. Jesse Williams played me, and Leonardo Nam played Roland.*

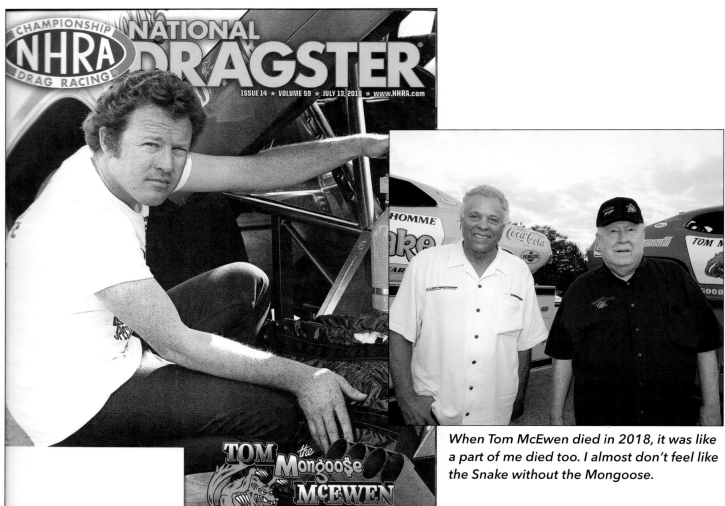

When Tom McEwen died in 2018, it was like a part of me died too. I almost don't feel like the Snake without the Mongoose.

busy racing, stressing out looking for sponsors, and dealing with crew chiefs and drivers, McEwen, Prock, and all those guys were going to lunch and talking about how f——ed up I was. When I finally got out of it, I could go to lunch too, and talk about how f——ed up I was. McEwen and I became close again, after all those years apart.

Learning Louisiana

I mentioned in the very beginning that I only did DNA testing and met my Creole relatives after my career was over. When I found out that I was Black, or mixed-race, or Creole, or however you think I should describe my family, it was a relief of sorts. All my life, I'd been getting those little hints that other people saw me differently than I saw myself, whether it was Ivo's jokes back in the 1950s or some jerk using the N-word around me.

It's a strange deal to feel like you don't know yourself. Since meeting my family in Louisiana and learning more about Creole culture, I've asked myself—and been asked—if I think my life would have been different if I had known that I was Black from the get-go. Well, how do you answer a question like that? I think it would have been harder. I mean, I know it would have been because I saw how tough it was for Willy T. Ribbs, Wendell Scott, and the few African-American people in motorsports.

Let's face it, Black people in general had it rough. It wasn't just drag racing. I don't regret not being the first African-American racing champion or anything like that, but I do regret not getting to know my family. When I met the Louisiana cousins, they told me that their folks told them never to introduce themselves to me at the track as relatives. They didn't want to blow my cover, make it so I wasn't passing. It was like when my mom wouldn't let my grandparents visit anymore because she didn't want the neighbors to guess we were Black.

Sometimes, when people were asking for photos and autographs at the track, I would get nervous when African-American fans asked me about race. They weren't being rude—I think they wanted to connect—but it would make me uncomfortable because I never knew how to answer. In the 1970s, a guy would say, "Hey, man, you a brother?" and I'd answer, "I'm everyone's brother," which in a way was true, but it was sort of a cop-out because I didn't want to let anybody down, but I really didn't know what to say. I didn't know what I was!

I wish I could undo that. It would have been nice to have known and been comfortable talking to anyone who asked. When Jeanette started looking into our family, I met cousins, aunts, and uncles. We went to Louisiana and learned about the culture and family history. It's been wonderful. I'm only sorry that I didn't meet everyone sooner.

After Racing

I know I was a hard-nosed racer, but I wouldn't have changed anything about that. That's the way I had to do it, and I won't make any excuses for it, but it sure has been nice to be away from it and get to be a little more easygoing. When I was racing, I didn't realize there were so many things you could do that weren't drag racing!

From left to right: Chip Ganassi, Linda Vaughn, and me in 2019, when she was inducted into the International Motorsports Hall of Fame in Daytona. Linda was a part of the racing scene my whole life. She was one of my favorite people to see at the track and all the awards shows.

MEMORIES FROM JEANETTE PRUDHOMME GRAVES

Our childhood wasn't all bad. We would go to church together Sunday mornings, and my mom was a great cook. We would always have a big Sunday meal. Even after Donnie and Monette got married, they would still come home on holidays. I was the youngest, and I was always so happy for them to arrive so we could all be together. If we really focus on those bad memories, they can erase the nice ones. I think the best thing out of all of it is that we kids were close then, and we've all stayed close.

Don left our home as a teenager because he had amazing opportunities with racing to go out and be somebody. And from what we were brought up in, I'm glad he did leave when he did because he got such a huge jump on the scene. He followed his heart and did what he needed to do. I was so proud that everybody knew who he was and so proud that he was my brother. I didn't get the opportunity to go to the races much in the early days because I was so young, but I did go more later on. I always thought it was cool because my brother or Lynn would get us passes and make us feel special.

Don and I look a lot alike; we both have dark curly hair and darker skin. Growing up, there were times that people would ask me, "What nationality are you? Are you sure you're not Black?" This was during the 1970s. People were talking more about race and being proud of their heritage. Even as a kid, I figured that we had some Black family, but when I asked my mom questions, she would get hostile. She would really get mad and change the subject. That made me think that there's something more there.

When I was a kid, our parents would fight at night, and my dad would bring up Cane River. I remembered that name. I knew we had some connection there. After my mom died, my daughter and I went to Cane River, and we met a cousin there. That's how we learned we were Creole. It's been a journey because this is all new to all of us, but the family in Louisiana, they understand why our parents moved to Los Angeles and passed themselves off as being White. They say they did it to make it easier for us. They told us stories of how our dad was one of five brothers, and they would be on a bus and the darker brothers would have to sit in the back of the bus and the lighter ones could sit in the

Aunt Jeanette - Ida - Gloria - Aunt Judy - Dad - Aunt Joyce
Monette

The property this house stands on is still owned and farmed by Monette's. Your dad had an emotional time as he remembers visiting this house as a very small boy. Down the road our cousin Ida saw the house she was born in and spent early childhood. Ida is my mothers brothers daughter.

The journey to Louisiana with my sisters answered a lot of questions we'd all been wondering about our whole lives. This is the house where my mom was born and raised. I hadn't been there since I was maybe 6 years old.

front. And then I've also heard that a lot of the White people outside of the Cane River didn't accept them and neither did the Black people, so I think that's why our parents and so many from there moved to Los Angeles.

I think with our parents both being alcoholics and our childhood being kind of rough, it was very freeing for us to go back there and see that we've got a very interesting heritage. I'm very proud of the whole scene, and I love getting to share that with my brother and sisters too. It was a weight lifted to know the truth. I'm really proud of my brother for doing this and bringing this all up because I'm sure that he is helping other people by talking about it. During the 1940s and 1950s there were a lot of people from Louisiana and the South who moved to California and passed as White, and it's the kids who really had to suffer, who were being lied to. So, now they can see this and say, "Wow, that's us. We're not alone."

I had a movie made about my life. I found IndyCar racing. I found off-road racing. I bought a BMW road bike, and I started taking trips down into Mexico. I even entered the Mexican 1000 again, and this time I finished it! I went to France and saw the 24 Hours of Le Mans in person. It would have been cool to have done that back in 1969, but at least I can say I have been there now.

I reconnected with so many of the people I came up with, and it's been a real gift to be able to spend time with friends and family, especially when I think about all the folks who didn't make it this far. Racing is a dangerous game, and many of the guys didn't make it out alive. It took a lot of focus, sacrifice, and luck. I always wished the fans could have known me from being at home instead of at the racetrack. I was a different guy. I mean, I was a nice dude at home, but at the track, I needed to be the Snake.

MEMORIES FROM ANTRON BROWN

My grandpop was from Pensacola, Florida. His whole family was, and my great grandpop, he was Creole. Now, Creole people can be French mixed with Indian or can be Black and Indian. Creole sometimes will be Black and French or African-American. So, the thing for me growing up and looking at Snake, he reminded me so much of all of my family. He had the same type of hair, and he had the olive complexion skin with the hazel eyes. When I finally met him, I said, "Don's a brother." And I used to always hit him up and tease him about it.

It's not strange to me that he wouldn't have known, or that his parents wouldn't have wanted him to know. I hear stories from my grandpop and my great grandpop about how the world was different back then, and Snake, he was racing down in the South. It could have been brutal. Not just brutal. Not just people just being demoralizing with words, but I mean he could've been in fear for his life. And Don, he wouldn't just have been a Black man racing, he was winning everything. He was dominating. That's a whole other thing.

When you look up the word *cool* in the dictionary, there's a picture of Snake. He always seems laid back; he never gets up on the chip. I think he always knows how to navigate and make choices and not get emotional about things. That said, I think that's really cool for him to finally dig in and really find out where he's from. People always want to know their heritage, where they're from and what it's all about. I'd like for him to find the puzzle pieces that he's been missing.

The coolest part is that his story can actually be told now and reach so many others. It can help other people rise, to understand some of the stuff that he overcame and what he went through. That's what it's all about at the end of the day. It can be that little ray of hope for a kid to look up to. He was my ray of hope. When you look on the side of a Mount Rushmore in drag racing, you'll see Prudhomme as being one the faces of the sport.

In 2018, I went back to the Mexican 1000, which is now a rally put on by the National Off-Road Racing Association (NORRA). I had so much fun that I did it again in 2019, with codriver Jagger Jones (Parnelli Jones's grandson).

These days, my crew is even hairier than they were in the 1970s. From left to right: JJ, Jesse, Shelley, and Jack.

This is what I'm driving these days. Our old dogs were all named after Formula 1 drivers: Niki, Alex (for Zanardi), and Senna.

Doing this book has given me a chance to look back at everything I've done. There was more good than bad, and I'm lucky and grateful for everyone who helped me through.

Additional books that may interest you...

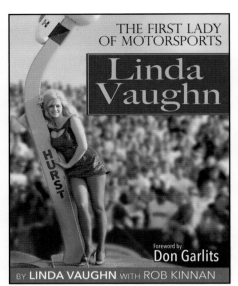
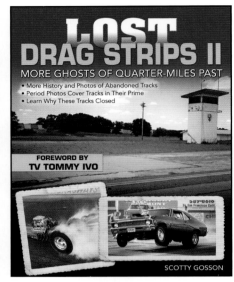

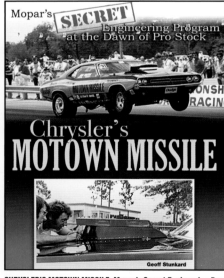